Training in Virtual Environments
A Safe, Cost-Effective, and Engaging Approach to Training

Training in Virtual Environments

A Safe, Cost-Effective, and Engaging
Approach to Training

Satyandra K. Gupta
Davinder K. Anand
John E. Brough
Maxim Schwartz
Robert A. Kavetsky

CECD/ETC Series

University of Maryland, College Park, Maryland

Book cover by Anna Kavetsky

Library of Congress Control Number: 2008923494

Direct all inquiries to:

CECD
3120 Glenn L. Martin Hall
University of Maryland
College Park, MD 20742
Ph.: (301) 405-5294
http://www.cecd.umd.edu

International Standard Book Number: 978-0-9777295-2-4

Printed in the United States of America   1 2 3 4 5 6 7 8 9 0

Printed in Southern Maryland

Preface

Training of scientists, engineers, and technicians has been a very significant activity in manufacturing, health care, military equipment installation and maintenance, disposal of hazardous substances, and aviation. This activity can be very expensive. Often training is cut short in many applications because of cost overruns or to save time. In many cases the old training methods are not well documented, have changed with new designs, or have been lost in the corporate memory because of aging and retirement of the workforce. These reasons have placed heavy demands on finding newer, cheaper, reliable and flexible methods to train the future workforce.

The use of simulation tools to mimic real environments has been well developed for training pilots. This technology has existed for decades and is routinely used in the aviation industry. However, virtual environments that provide a fully immersive environment with voice and natural action-based interfaces are relatively new tools available to train the future workforce.

Assembly and disassembly operations are a crucial part of service, maintenance, and manufacturing operations. The advent of low cost personal virtual environments (PVEs) is presenting new opportunities for improving the training process associated with assembly and disassembly operations. These operations are spatial manipulation tasks. In order to successfully perform spatial manipulation tasks, the operator has to learn (1) how to recognize specific parts from a given set of parts, (2) how to correctly orient and position parts in space, and (3) the optimal spatial manipulation sequences for performing a given task. Examples of such training scenarios include maintenance of complex equipment (e.g., aircraft, power generation equipment, military equipment, etc.), manufacturing of explosive or energetic devices, and "rendering safe" or disarming explosive devices. In these training scenarios, a mistake made during the actual task can lead to catastrophic failure, resulting in personal injury and/or property damage. Therefore, one must master the task before actually performing it. Furthermore, a single person typically performs a variety of different and unrelated tasks and often does not get an opportunity to perform the same task on a frequent basis. In these situations, certain details of the process may be forgotten over time, and one must go through periodic re-training to refresh the memory of the already-learned tasks. Additionally, some tasks are not repetitive, and one must be prepared to adjust to slightly different situations. These characteristics make training a challenging problem for this class of tasks.

This book provides an overview of different components of virtual environments. The technologies covered in this book include displays, tracking systems, and user interaction devices. This book also provides an overview of the basic modeling framework for creating objects in the virtual environment and manipulating them. This material is expected to help the reader understand different technology choices in constructing virtual environments and their advantages and disadvantages in training applications.

The advent of low cost PVEs is presenting new opportunities for improving training. The authors have assembled a PVE in their laboratory with a budget of less than USD 50,000 from off-the-shelf components. This PVE consists of a head mounted stereo display with head tracking and a wand for user interaction. This PVE gives the user a complete 3D immersive experience. The book describes in detail various components of the Virtual Training Studio, a PVE-based training environment. We conducted detailed user studies involving 30 subjects and two tutorials to assess the performance of the VTS system. During the first study, involving a rocket motor, 94.4% steps were performed correctly by the users during the physical demonstration after completing the training. During the second study, involving a model airplane engine, 97.3% steps were performed correctly by the users during the physical demonstration after completing the training.

Our system also enables the rapid creation of training instructions without the need for specialized coding. This reduces the time and the cost of building new training instructions. Demonstrations in the virtual environment also make the system user-friendly and allow the process expert, who is most likely a mechanical or manufacturing engineer, to directly control how the instructions for device assembly are generated without relying on programmers. Another benefit of our system is the consistency of the generated instructions. Hard-coding the data for each instruction set may often lead to inconsistent instructions with slight differences in either the look and feel or the behavior of features. Generating training instructions automatically from virtual demonstrations also ensures that the instructor can visually verify that the training instructions being generated are complete and no step is missing in the sequence.

The work reported in this book was a collaborative effort. Chester Clark, Ralph Pettersen, and Lisa Davie supported this work from NSWC Indian Head, where a laboratory similar to the one at the University of Maryland was created. Cindy Yeager and Darrin Krivitsky gave feedback on the training needs of NSWC Indian Head and helped us in defining the program requirements. The work of two students and a software engineer merits special recognition. Zafer Tuncali and Jeb Brough both wrote Master's theses in the Department of Mechanical Engineering at the University of Maryland, College Park. Maxim Schwartz developed a significant amount of software to drive the PVE. Ronald Kostoff assisted with some literature review pertinent to chapter five. Sanyukta Purwar drew the figures and Ania Picard prepared the manuscript into a book format. Finally, Lise Crittenden edited the book and assisted in the initial stages of the book development and Anna Kavetsky designed the book cover. To all of them our sincere thanks.

Currently, the Center for Energetic Concepts Development at the University Maryland, College Park and the Energetics Technology Center in La Plata, Maryland are working on developing methodologies for training in virtual environments. This book reports on this work and provides background information. We hope that this book will generate interest in not only learning more about training in virtual environments, but also in using the virtual environment as a routine tool for design and simulation.

College Park
Maryland

Author Biographies

Satyandra K. Gupta is Professor of Mechanical Engineering and Systems Research at the University of Maryland. He received a Bachelor of Engineering (B.E.) degree in Mechanical Engineering from the University of Roorkee (presently known as the Indian Institute of Technology, Roorkee) in 1988. He received a Master of Technology (M. Tech.) in Production Engineering from the Indian Institute of Technology, Delhi in 1989. He received a Ph.D. in Mechanical Engineering from the University of Maryland at College Park in 1994. He has authored or co-authored more than one hundred and fifty articles in journals, conference proceedings, and book chapters. Dr. Gupta is a fellow of the American Society of Mechanical Engineers (ASME), a senior member of the Society of Manufacturing Engineers (SME), and a member of the Society of Automotive Engineers (SAE).

Dr. Gupta has won many honors and awards for his research contributions to computer-aided design and manufacturing area. He received many Best Paper Awards from ASME. He received the Young Investigator Award from the Office of Naval Research in 2000, the Robert W. Galvin Outstanding Young Manufacturing Engineer Award from the Society of Manufacturing Engineers in 2001, a CAREER Award from the National Science Foundation in 2001, the Outstanding Systems Engineering Faculty Award from the Institute for Systems Research in 2001, and the Presidential Early Career Award for Scientists and Engineers (PECASE) in 2001. He also holds a US Patent titled "Apparatus and Method for Multi-Purpose Setup Planning for Sheet Metal Bending Operations".

Davinder K. Anand is Professor Emeritus of Mechanical Engineering and Director of the Center for Energetic Concepts Development, both at the University of Maryland, College Park. He received his Ph.D. from George Washington University in 1965, and from 1991-2002 chaired the Department of Mechanical Engineering at College Park. He has served as a Director of the Mechanical Systems Program at the National Science Foundation, and his research has been supported by NIH, NASA, DOE, DOD, and industry. He has lectured internationally, founded two high technology research companies (most recently Iktara and Associates, LLC), published three books and over one hundred and seventy papers, and has one patent. He is a Distinguished Alumnus of George Washington University, and was awarded the Outstanding and Superior Performance Award by the National Science Foundation. Dr. Anand is a Fellow of ASME and is listed in Who's Who in Engineering.

John E. Brough is a Branch Manager in the Chemicals and Extrusion Technology Division at the Naval Surface Warfare Center. He received a BS in 2000 and an MS in 2006 in mechanical engineering from the University of Maryland. He helped design, develop, and test the Virtual Training Studio. He conducted his master's thesis research on the cognitive aspects of learning complex device assembly in a virtual environment. He has seven years of experience with government research and development programs and two years of international experience working on a Defense Threat Reduction Agency Program to eliminate weapons of mass destruction in the former Soviet Union.

Maxim Schwartz is a software engineer at ETC, Inc., La Plata, MD. Previously, he was a software engineer at the University of Maryland's Center for Energetic Concepts Development and a core member of the Iktara & Associates technology development team. His main expertise is in development of geometric algorithms for virtual environments. His current work involves building a virtual environment-based training system to enhance learning of device assembly, disassembly, and maintenance processes. His experience includes 3D visualization development, as well as web-based and database application development. He received a Bachelor of Science degree in Computer Science at the University of Maryland, College Park in 2003.

Robert A. Kavetsky is CEO of ETC, Inc., in La Plata, MD. He was the founder of the N-STAR initiative at the Office of Naval Research, a Navy-wide effort aimed at reinvigorating the S&T community within the Navy's Warfare Centers. He received a BSME in 1975, an MSME in 1977, and an MEA in 1978, all from Catholic University. He was head of the Explosion Damage Branch, Program Manager for the Undersea Warheads Program, and Program Manager for Undersea Weapons at the Naval Surface Warfare Center. At OPNAV in 1999-2000, he helped develop S&T programs for organic mine countermeasures and expeditionary logistics, and then at NSWC Indian Head created

"Workforce 2010," a government, industry, and academic consortium focused on developing Indian Head's next generation workforce. He has authored a number of technical and S&T workforce-related policy and program publications for ASEE, ASME, AIAA, and other forums, and he was the lead author of the book *From Science To Seapower: A Roadmap for S&T Revitalization.*

Acronyms

2D	Two Dimensional
3D	Three Dimensional
3DOF	Three Degrees of Freedom
6DOF	Six Degrees of Freedom
AABB	Axis Aligned Bounding Boxes
AC	Alternating Current
AMLCD	Active Matrix Liquid-Crystal Display
ANOVA	Analysis of Variance (statistics)
AR	Augmented Reality
ASCII	American Standard Code for Information Interchange
B-REP	Boundary Representation
CAD	Computer-Aided Design
CAVE	CAVE Automatic Virtual Environment
CRT	Cathode-Ray Tube (display)
CSG	Constructive Solid Geometry
CTAT	Cognitive Tutor Authoring Tool
DC	Direct Current
DLP	Digital Light Processing
DMD	Digital Micro-Mirror Device
DSP	Digital Signal Processing
DVD	Digital Video Disc
EVL	Electronic Visualization Laboratory (University of Illinois at Chicago)
FCU	Force Control Unit
FFWD	Fast Forward
FLCOS	Ferroelectric Liquid Crystal on Silicon SAT
FMD	Face Mounted Display
FOV	Field of View
GUI	Graphical User Interface
HMD	Head Mounted Display

IBRM	Image-Based Rendering Method
IOs	Instrumented Objects
IPD	Interpupillary Distance
IR	Infrared
LCD	Liquid-Crystal Display
LCOS	Liquid Crystal on Silicon (display)
LED	Light Emitting Diode
MBRM	Model-Based Rendering Method
NTSC	National Television Standards Committee
OBB	Oriented Bounding Boxes
OLED	Organic Light Emitting Diodes
PC	Personal Computer (usually Intel-compatible)
RF	Radio Frequency
PPT	Precision Position Tracker
PVE	Personal Virtual Environment
RMS	Root Mean Square
RS-232	Recommended Standard 232 (computer serial port)
RWD	Rewind
SAT	Separating Axes Test
SOP	Standard Operating Procedure
STE	Special Type Equipment
STL	Stereolithography
SVGA	Super Video Graphics Array
SXGA	Super eXtended Graphics Array
TV	Television
USB	Universal Serial Bus
UVAVU	Unbelievable Vehicle for Assembling Virtual Units
VATS	Visual Assembly Tree Structure
VE	Virtual Environment
VEGAS	Virtual Environment for General Assembly
VGA	Video Graphics Array
VIRIP	Virtual Interactive Panel
VPS	Voxmap Point Shell
VTS	Virtual Training Studio
VR	Virtual Reality
VRML	Virtual Reality Modeling Language
XML	Extensible Markup Language

Contents

List of Figures

Color Insert

List of Tables

Chapter 1

Introduction

The advent of virtual environments is presenting new ways of training tomorrow's workforce. Virtual environments offer numerous benefits in training applications. First, virtual environments allow extensive user interactions in a very convenient and natural manner. This interaction is greatly beneficial for increasing the user's retention of spatial information compared to text-based or video-based instructions that are non-interactive in nature. Second, virtual environments provide users with a 3D immersive experience. This feature helps users gain a better understanding of spatial relationships compared to 2D displays. Third, virtual environments support multi-media instructions. One can watch standard videos, view 3D animations, view text instructions, listen to audio instructions, and interact with 3D objects in the scene. This chapter presents the basic terminology associated with virtual environments and their role in training applications.

1.1 Definitions

1.1.1 *What is a Virtual Environment?*

A virtual environment (VE) can be defined as a computer-generated environment used to simulate the real world. Many different types of virtual environments are possible. On the one hand, these environments can be as simple as a semi-immersive computer-based environment. On the other hand, these environments can be completely immersive, hardware-based, three-dimensional interactive experiences utilizing sound and force feedback to simulate, as accurately as possible, a real environment [Ong and Nee, 2004]. Virtual environments can be created that are completely photorealistic, called the image-based rendering method (IBRM), or they can be created from 3D solid models, called the model-based rendering method (MBRM) [Huang et al., 1998]. Typically, IBRM virtual environments are less interactive. They typically only allow movement through the scene and no manipulation of objects, because they are image-based textures applied to the environment. On the other hand, MBRM virtual environments contain less visual realism because the scenes and objects are computer-generated, but they allow for manipulation of the environment. One method is not necessarily better than the other. They each have their role depending upon user objectives and the applications needs. In general, IBRM are used in game applications and MBRM are used in technical applications. The type of virtual environment that this book will focus on is of the MBRM type as shown in Figure 1.1.

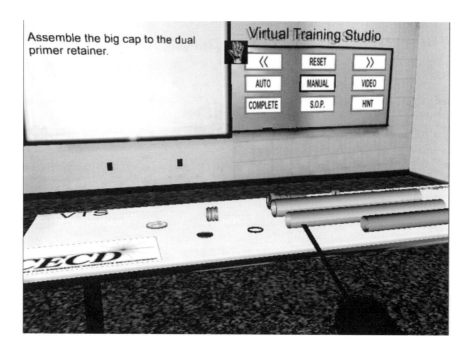

Figure 1.1: A screenshot of the Virtual Training Studio, an MBRM virtual environment

1.1.2   *What is Virtual Reality?*

Virtual reality (VR) is a more specific form of a virtual environment which provides the user with a feeling of presence. Presence is the feeling the user experiences of "being there" [Nichols et al., 2000].

Presence can be thought of as the user's feeling of engrossment in the virtual environment. Immersion offers the conditions which promote the feeling of presence [O'Neil and Perez, 2006]. Immersion can be produced by feeding the user a continuous stream of realistic visual, audio, and touch stimuli and by enabling the user to naturally interact with virtual objects in the environment. It is not necessary to stimulate all three senses for immersion. Often the right combination of stereoscopic images and good user tracking can produce a sufficient level of immersion and a feeling of presence.

1.1.3   *What is Virtual Environment-Based Training?*

Virtual environment-based training allows trainees to step into a virtual environment, which simulates a real environment, in order to learn how to perform a task.   Additionally, the user can be semi-immersed in the VE by using a two-dimensional (2D) interface or fully immersed in the VE by using a three-dimensional (3D) interface. Virtual environment training can be used as a stand alone training method or as part of a more integrated approach where it is combined with other forms of training.

1.2   Brief History of Virtual Environments

The concept of virtual environments has been around for some time. One of the first attempts at creating virtual environments was made in 1956 when cinematographer Morton Heilig began creating a multi-sensory virtual experience using a machine called Sensorama. Sensorama, resembling an arcade machine, as shown in Figure 1.2, used projected film, vibrations, odors, wind, and audio to make the viewer feel as if he were actually in the film. For twenty-five cents, the user could sit in a chair and view a two-minute 3D full color film in a one-person theater. The viewer could watch a video of a bicycle ride, a ride in a dune buggy, a motorcycle ride through New York, a helicopter ride, or a belly dancer. The entire experience was prerecorded and played back to the user, so no interaction was supported. In 1962, Heilig also applied for a patent to what can be considered one of the first head mounted displays (HMDs). The invention involved the use of wide field of view optics to view 3D photographic slides. The proposed HMD also supported stereo sound and an "odor generator."

In 1961, the first actual HMD was designed and built by Charles Comeau and James Bryan, employees of the Philco Corporation. Their HMD, called Headsight, contained a single cathode ray tube (CRT) element and used a magnetic tracking system to ascertain the direction of the head. Headsight was designed for remotely viewing dangerous situations with the aid of a remote controlled closed circuit video system.

Figure 1.2: Morton Heilig's Sensorama (one of the earliest attempts at virtual environments)

During the 1960s and 1970s, major advancements were made in the field of virtual reality. Important contributions were made at MIT by Ivan Sutherland and Lawrence Roberts. One of the contributions was the research that allowed CRTs to become affordable devices for display of computer-generated images. An important component of this research was integration of HMDs with a tracking system in order to allow users to interact with the generated virtual environment. In 1965, Sutherland's work led to the creation of a head mounted display called Ultimate Display. Not only did it support stereoscopic display using two CRT elements, but it also had a mechanical tracking system.

Roberts made a significant contribution in computer graphics in 1963 when he wrote the first algorithm to eliminate obscured surfaces from a perspective picture. Work at the University of Utah further advanced the field of computer graphics, which is an important component of virtual environments. Two significant contributions made at Utah were an area search method by John Warnock (1969) and a scan-line algorithm by Garry Watkins (1970). In 1971, Henri Gouraud made further important advancements in computer graphics by developing a simple scheme for continuous shading. This scheme used interpolation between points on a surface to describe continuous shading, leading to a closer approximation of reality.

In the early 1990s work at the Electronic Visualization Laboratory (EVL) at the University of Illinois, Chicago, led to the emergence of a projector-based display system called CAVE. The CAVE resembled a room with walls, ceiling, and floor represented by projection screens. Images were sequentially rear-projected onto each wall by several projectors (one for each screen). The users wore shutter glasses synchronized with the projectors, allowing them to view alternating images for each eye in order to perceive a stereo effect while standing inside the room. This development, along with major advances made in the processing speeds of computers, made projection-based CAVE technology a popular and successful alternative to HMDs, which up to that point dominated the market of immersive virtual environments.

1.3   Components of Virtual Environments

1.3.1   *Stereoscopic Vision*

One of the most consistent components of virtual environments is the stereo display of objects in the virtual environment, which aids the user in the feeling of immersion. There are generally two methods for obtaining stereo display. One of them is the use of head mounted displays. The other method is based on projection of images onto a surface.

Head mounted displays are visualization devices which make use of either liquid-crystal displays (LCDs) or miniature cathode-ray tubes (CRTs). The user wears the device on top of the head and receives two streams of slightly different images of a scene through the two eyepieces. One set of images is slightly offset laterally from the other, simulating the interpupillary distance between the two eyes. Due to the power requirements of the LCDs, the HMD is usually tethered to a power source as opposed to carrying portable batteries. Current HMD technologies allow viewing resolution of up to 1280 X 1024 pixels, generally at about 50 degree field of view. By eliminating all outside light sources, HMDs are highly effective at presenting a wearer with a completely virtual environment without occluding the view with any real objects that may be present in the vicinity.

Projection-based displays employ a similar set of two-image streams projected onto a surface by multiple projectors. Users normally wear lightweight LCD shutter glasses that filter out projected images for a particular eye. This way, one projection can only be seen by the right eye while another projection can only be seen by the left eye. The shutter glasses are normally synchronized with the projectors to block and unblock vision for each eye at a high rate. Although multiple users may observe the same 3D scene with a projection-based display method, only one user receives the most accurate stereoscopic view – the user being tracked by the system. With a projection-based display method, real objects present in the environment may somewhat lessen the immersive feel.

1.3.2   *User Tracking*

Another very common component of virtual environments is the tracking system used to monitor the movements of the user in order to properly update the virtual environment. Tracking systems generally fall in one of the following categories: magnetic, inertial, optical, acoustic, and mechanical. Magnetic tracking systems use magnetic fields to determine the user's position as a set of x, y, z coordinates and the user's orientation as yaw, pitch, and roll. This is called six degrees of freedom (6DOF) tracking because the user is free to move in all six of these directions with the system tracking every one of these movements. Magnetic trackers generally involve a remote transmitter and a set of receivers worn on the user's body. Optical tracking systems generally involve the use of at least two cameras to track light emitting diodes (LEDs) worn by the user. The optical tracking systems use triangulation to determine the user's x, y, z position. Inertial trackers are devices worn by the user which generally use a set of gyroscopes, accelerometers, and magnetometers to keep track of all six degrees of freedom. Such devices are often subject to accumulating errors, called drift, over long periods of time. Acoustic trackers operate in a way similar to magnetic trackers in that there is a transmitter and a receiver. Acoustic systems use the speed of sound to measure distance to each of the receivers from the transmitter. Triangulation is then used to obtain the user's location. Finally, mechanical tracking systems use the information about the kinematic structure of the tracking device and sensors, on several joints, to measure the position of a tracked object that is attached to the tracking device. Such systems have the highest measurement speed, but often heavily restrict the user's movements.

1.3.3   *Haptics*

Haptic feedback is another common component of a virtual environment. The word haptic comes from a Greek word for touch. Haptic feedback can promote the feeling of immersion and presence by stimulating the user's sense of touch or by providing realistic force feedback to convey forces simulated inside the virtual environment. One of the most common methods of providing haptic feedback is via vibration that is activated in the device held by the user or within the glove worn by the user. If a glove is being used, vibrations can be generated for each finger to indicate contact between a virtual hand and some object in the virtual environment. Another common method of giving the user haptic feedback is through force exerted on the user's hands. Forces on the user can be exerted with simple inexpensive devices like joysticks and with more advanced devices like gloves, which are capable of exerting forces or providing resistance to individual fingers. Some gloves are even capable of regulating the temperature transmitted to each finger in order to convey to the user thermal characteristics of virtual objects.

1.3.4   *3D Sound*

Three-dimensional sound is another possible component of a virtual environment. Unlike stereo sound, which feels like the sound is originating inside the user's head and moves with the user when used with headphones, devices which produce real 3D sound using headphones make it seem like the sound is coming from an external source and stays in the same place as the user rotates his or her head. Generating realistic 3D sound is a challenging problem. This is due to the fact that there are many sound cues that are used by the human brain to interpret the position of the sound source and some of the cues are dependent upon the anatomical structure of the individual listener. For example, one type of auditory cue relies on the amplification or attenuation of sound (depending on the frequency) that occurs when some of the sound reaches an ear directly and some of it reaches the inner ear indirectly by first bouncing off the outer ear or the pinna [Burdea and Coiffet, 2003]. The attenuation or amplification is due to the interference between the direct sound and reflected sound. In addition to the outer ear, the user's face and shoulders also cause such attenuation or amplification. The human brain is sensitive to this type of variation between sound arriving directly and sound that is reflected into the inner ear by parts of the human body. The device synthesizing the 3D sound must also take into account sound reflection from walls, the difference in intensity of the sound coming from a single source into each of the ears, depending on how the user's head is turned, and the small delay between the time sound reaches one ear and the time it reaches the other ear, depending on the position of the source and how the head is turned.

The most effective method for generating 3D sound is by using headphones with devices called convolvotrons. Three-dimensional sound devices which employ convolvotrons use the position and orientation of the user's head reported by the tracking system to perform computations and synthesize sound for each of the two headphones. By using headphones, the convolvotron-based devices isolate sound for each ear, ensuring a high 3D sound fidelity. Unfortunately, such sophisticated devices can be very expensive. A less expensive approach is to use multiple loudspeakers. However, when using loudspeakers, the sound system cannot isolate sound for each ear, and the sound always appears to come from the speakers and not the environment. Hence, speaker-based 3D sound systems generally do not offer the realism of the headphone-based sound systems using convolvotrons.

Due to the challenges presented by highly realistic 3D sound and often limited usefulness, this virtual environment component is not used as commonly as the previously mentioned components. For this reason, this book will not go into the details of 3D sound devices.

1.4   Next Generation Training Needs

Currently, most people train for performing service, maintenance, and manufacturing operations by first studying the text-based manuals and then practicing the acquired skills under the supervision of an experienced trainer, engineer, or technician. After adequately learning the required skills, the trainees take certification tests. This training model has been effectively used in the past and has produced well-trained professionals. However, the costs associated with this training model are usually very high, due to the amount of resources it requires. As we move towards a society with a richer variety of specialized equipment, a highly mobile workforce, demands for instant service, maintenance, and production, and mounting cost pressures, companies need to explore ways to significantly improve training for performing service, maintenance, and manufacturing operations. Furthermore, due to the rapid influx of new and changing technologies and their associated complexities, accelerated training is becoming a necessity in order to promote and maintain an advanced and educated workforce.

In this book we will mainly focus on those training scenarios where workers need to learn a variety of tasks to execute a procedure and require certification in each task before actually performing the procedure. Examples of such learning scenarios include maintenance of complex equipment (e.g., aircraft, power generation equipment, military equipment, etc.), assembly of devices containing energetic material, as well as "rendering safe" or disarming explosive devices. In these learning scenarios, a mistake made during the actual task can lead to catastrophic failure, resulting in personal injury and/or property damage. Therefore, one must master the task before actually performing it. Furthermore, a single person typically performs a variety of different and unrelated tasks and often does not get an opportunity to perform the same task on a frequent basis. In these situations, certain details of the process may be forgotten over time, and one must go through periodic re-training to refresh the memory of the already-learned tasks. Additionally, some tasks are not repetitive, and one must be prepared to adjust to slightly different situations. These characteristics make training a challenging problem for this class of tasks and require exploring modern digital technologies for improving the training process.

1.5   Role of Virtual Environments in Training

Virtual environment-based training systems are useful tools that can be used to educate and train individuals in an environment that is non-threatening, relaxed, and allows for users to make and learn from their mistakes without consequence. The following is a partial list of advantages to training in a virtual environment:

- It can occur at any time without the need for the physical components or other workers' assistance.
- It does not involve the real components, so cost savings can be realized if practicing the assembly is destructive or detrimental to the components. The need and the associated costs for physical mock-ups are also eliminated.
- It is safe and isolated from industrial and environmental hazards.
- It can be repeated multiple times.
- Individual steps can be repeated, giving the trainee an opportunity to analyze the process from different perspectives and views.

Although VEs are useful training tools, they are not without shortcomings. The following list describes several disadvantages to training in a virtual environment:

- There can be a disconnect between the real world and the virtual world. Users may not be able to transfer 100 percent of what has been learned in the VE to activities in the real world.

- Some users of VE can experience motion sickness, which makes using the system physically impossible.
- The initial buy-in for the equipment is high.
- Special software must be developed.
- Tutorials are time-consuming to create.

The advantages and disadvantages depend on the implementation and the quality of the components selected.

1.6   Structure of the Book

The first half of this book presents hardware technologies and modeling techniques needed to implement virtual environments. Chapter 2 contains an overview of display technologies and hardware. Chapter 3 presents various hardware technologies which add interactivity to virtual environments. Chapter 4 discusses modeling techniques that can be used in the implementation of virtual environments. Chapter 5 presents an overview of different systems that have been developed for virtual environment-based training. While the first half of the book presents virtual environments in general, the second half presents a very specific example of a virtual environment-based application developed by the authors. This system is called Virtual Training Studio (VTS). Chapter 6 gives an overview of the VTS and introduces the three main components of the Virtual Training Studio: Virtual Workspace, Virtual Author, and Virtual Mentor. Chapter 7 discusses the important features of the Virtual Author in more detail. Virtual Mentor is then presented in more detail in Chapter 8. Chapter 9 discusses the user testing and case studies which were performed with VTS in order to assess its training effectiveness. In Chapter 10, we conclude with discussion of some emerging technologies.

Chapter 2

Overview of Display Technologies

This chapter presents a brief history of the various display devices and techniques that have been used to convey three-dimensional (3D) information. It also explains the basic principle of stereo vision, which allows the human brain to interpret depth and to mimic reality using devices which produce only two-dimensional (2D) images. This chapter also brings the reader up-to-date on the current state-of-the-art of stereo display technologies as of this writing.

Section 2.1 dicusses benefits of depth perception in training. Section 2.2 explains the visual cues the human brain uses to judge depth. Many of these visual cues must be generated by the hardware devices in order to trick the human brain into perceiving depth. Section 2.3 presents one of the earliest methods of simulating stereo vision-head mounted displays (HMDs). Section 2.4 presents various projection-based displays including large scale visualization using walls, workbench displays, and a successful projection technology called the CAVE.

2.1 Benefits of Depth Perception in Training

The ability to perceive depth information can aid in the understanding of a task or a concept by allowing the viewer to visualize the presented data more effectively. We live in a three-dimensional environment and have grown accustomed over many years to absorbing and processing three-dimensional information. When a certain task must be carried out in a 3D environment with 3D objects, it may be more difficult to visualize and learn that task when receiving only 2D data.

There are many examples of training people to perform spatial tasks. Virtual reality (VR) and 3D visualization have many applications in the field of medicine. Stereoscopic viewing allows simulation of the human body for educational purposes. Visualization of 3D relationships can be beneficial in simulating plastic and reconstructive surgery, in pathology studies for surgeons, education in anatomy, and endoscopic training. Another important application of 3D viewing is flight simulation, both for military and commercial purposes. Simulating proper depth perception is important in mimicking, as closely as possible, realistic flying conditions and sensations which pilots in training will experience in a real flight. Manufacturing-related training is another application where trainees can greatly benefit from depth perception. Manufacturing training applications often involve assembly, disassembly, and maintenance of 3D devices, where it is important to clearly convey to the user how each component of an assembly is put together. Stereoscopic viewing may also help trainees to recognize certain important features of the assembly and recognize the differences between very similar parts. Other areas of application where 3D visualization can be very useful include architecture, weather simulation, chemistry, and scientific visualization of volumetric data.

2.2   Principles of Stereo Vision

Humans have much better depth perception than most other animal species. Unlike the eyes of large four-legged animals like horses, donkeys, and cows, human eyes are positioned side-by-side in front of the head. This positioning creates a lot of overlap between the images received by the left eye and the images received by the right eye. Each eye receives a view of the same environment from a slightly different perspective. At the same time, each eye receives a certain amount of unique information that the other eyes does not. The human brain combines the two overlapped images and produces a fused binocular mental picture. Differences in the two images is one of the cues used by the brain to judge depth. The word *stereo* originates from the Greek word *stereos*, meaning solid or firm. Stereo vision allows us to see an object as a solid and mentally estimate all three of its dimensions – width, height, and depth. Stereo vision also allows us to more accurately estimate the location of an object relative to the position of the head. The sharp, clear vision that humans have aids in the perception of depth. If the vision in one or both eyes is too blurry, some of the depth perception is reduced.

There are a number of visual cues that are used by the human brain to perceive and estimate depth. The cues can be broken up into two categories: physiological and psychological. For some cues both eyes need to be open. Such cues are binocular. For other cues, only one eye needs to be open. These are called monocular cues. The human visual system uses all available cues to assess depth. The physiological and psychological cues are:

- Binocular parallax
- Convergence
- Monocular movement parallax
- Linear perspective
- Accommodation
- Retinal image size
- Texture gradient
- Overlapping
- Aerial perspective
- Shades and shadows

Binocular parallax is the difference in the images received by the eyes as a result of the eyes being in slightly different positions. The human brain is very sensitive to such differences. Figure 2.1 shows how binocular parallax works. When viewed from the left eye, the dark brick appears further to the right of the wall than when viewed from the right eye. Binocular parallax is affected by the interpupillary distance (IPD). IPD is the distance between the pupil of the left eye and the pupil of the right eye. Binocular parallax is the most important depth cue. *Convergence* occurs when the eyes point inward as a person looks at a near object. The brain detects the muscle tension and uses that information as a factor in determining depth. Both binocular parallax and convergence are examples of binocular cues. The rest of the cues are monocular. *Monocular movement parallax* is a depth cue that is seen when the viewer is moving laterally. Objects that are near have a greater change in position than objects that are further away. An example of the *linear perspective* cue is the viewer looking down a road and seeing the two sides of the road converge on the horizon. *Accommodation* is the change in tension of the muscle that controls the focal length of the eye lens when a person views nearby objects. This is not a major depth cue and requires the objects to be very close. *Retinal image size* is a cue the human brain uses when the actual size of an object is known from experience. The brain compares the image coming into the eyes to the knowledge about the true size of that object to estimate depth. The *Texture gradient* depth cue is based on the fact that when the viewer is close to an object, more details about its texture can be seen, while a distant object will often look like it has a smooth texture. *Overlapping* is the cue used by the brain when one object blocks or partially obscures another. The viewer knows from experience that the blocked object is further away than the blocking one. *Aerial perspective* is a depth cue that is used when looking at a very distant entity like the mountains. The entity may appear bluish or hazy due to the fact that there are water particles and dust in the air between the entity and the viewer. The final depth cue is called *shades and shadows*. It refers to the fact that objects that are closer to a light source will cast shadows on objects that are farther from the light source. By knowing the location of the light source, the viewer is able to get a better idea of the location of the two objects in space. The cue also refers to the fact that objects that are closer often appear slightly brighter than those that are farther away.

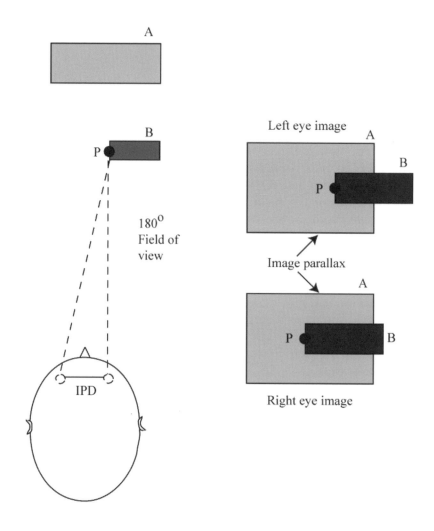

Figure 2.1: Binocular parallax

In order to effectively convey depth to the viewer, stereo display devices and the software that feeds them the 2D images must make use of the above described depth cues. The section that follows presents one of the earliest stereo display technologies – head mounted displays (HMDs).

2.3   Head Mounted Displays

Head mounted displays are display devices that are worn on the user's head. Generally, HMDs have some form of liquid crystal display (LCD) for each eye and a lens assembly for each LCD. In addition to LCD, some of the other technologies that have been used as image panels are: cathode ray tube (CRT), liquid crystal on silicon (LCOS), or organic light emitting diodes (OLED). HMDs take advantage of the binocular parallax visual cue by sending a different set of 2D images of the same scene to each eye. The images differ by a small horizontal shift that is calculated based on the IPD. HMDs make use of special optics which are placed between the eyes and the small image panels. The optics allow the eyes to focus at very short distances without becoming tired too quickly. The second purpose of the lens assemblies is to magnify the images displayed by the small LCD screens. The magnification determines the viewer's field of view (FOV). Figure 2.2 presents a simplified design of a typical HMD.

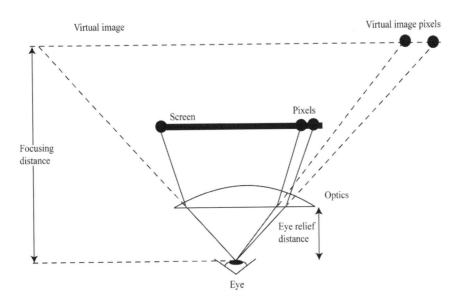

Figure 2.2: Simplified design of a typical HMD

One undesirable side effect of the magnification is that the distance between the LCD screen pixels gets amplified on the virtual image, reducing the overall visual resolution. With HMDs, there is often a trade-off between FOV and resolution. Certain techniques may be used to improve the resolution after the magnification. Those include increasing the number of pixels on the LCD display, improving the apparent resolution by dithering the image, and tiling subimages of normal resolution into a bigger image with higher resolution. Such techniques will often have negative side effects of their own, however, in the form of increase in size, complexity, and cost of the HMD or reduction in frame rate.

The first LCD-based HMD, which was available in the early 1990s, was called the VPL Eyephone [Burdea and Coiffet, 2003]. It had a resolution of 360 X 240 pixels, a weight of about 2 kilograms, a horizontal FOV of 100 degrees and a vertical FOV of 60 degrees. One of the biggest drawbacks of the Eyephone was its large weight which induced wearer fatigue. In the late 1990s, Olympus came out with its own LCD-based HMD called the Eye-Trek. This was designed to be an affordable monoscopic HMD to be used for watching movies with video and DVD players or playing PC games. Unlike the Eyephone, the Eye-Trek weighed only 100 grams. Due to the small size of this HMD and its resemblance to eye glasses, it was referred to as a face mounted display (FMD). The Eye-Trek incorporated active matrix LCD (AMLCD) display panels that were positioned above the optics. A variable curvature free form lens was used to compensate for the image distortions caused by the optics assembly. The Eye-Trek displayed a virtual image that was equivalent to watching a 52-inch screen from 2 meters away. One of the later versions of the Eye-Trek, which was being produced until around 2001, was the model 700. The Eye-Trek 700 had a resolution of 533 X 450. This high resolution, for a consumer HMD of that time, was achieved by using double polarization and double refraction effects. Olympus called these techniques optical super resolution.

At about the same time, Daeyang was producing a similar FMD called the Cy-Visor. The Cy-Visor used the LCOS display technology. The liquid crystal layer was mounted directly on a silicon chip. The silicon chip was used as a control circuitry. The advantages of this type of LCOS LCD display were a reduction in power consumption, reduction in volume, reduction in production costs, and a higher resolution compared to AMLCD technology used by the Eye-Trek, where transmissive panels allowed light to pass through the liquid crystal substrate into the wearer's eyes. The disadvantage of the LCOS technology was the lack of backlighting. This meant that LCOS reflective displays needed external light to display the image. The new technology allowed the Cy-Visor to produce images with a resolution of 800 X 600 pixels and a field of view of 60 degrees horizontally and 43 degrees vertically. The Cy-Visor, at 160 grams, was only slightly heavier than the Eye-Trek, but produced a better resolution. While Olympus is no longer producing the Eye-Trek, as of 2007, Daeyang is still producing a product similar to the Cy-Visor called the i-visor. The i-visor uses two SVGA OLED panels. It weighs 120 grams, produces a diagonal FOV of 42 degrees, and supports stereoscopic display. The stereoscopic input must be field sequential and generated by a 3D-enabled graphics card.

Field sequential stereo takes advantage of the interlaced video format used by CRT displays like common NTSC TV sets. In this format, each video frame consists of either a set of odd-numbered scan lines or a set of even numbered scan lines. The two sets of scan lines are called fields. A CRT display renders the two fields sequentially. Due to the high refresh rate, the afterglow of the phosphor of CRT tubes, and the brief retention of images by the retina of the human eye, the sequence of fields is perceived as a smooth stream of images. Interlaced format has been historically used to reduce the required bandwidth of the display and hence reduce cost of the hardware. Field sequential stereo takes advantage of the NTSC interlaced format used by common standard definition TVs by displaying images for one eye on odd-numbered scan lines and images for the other eye on even numbered scan lines. Active shutters positioned in front of each eye can then be synchronized with the display of each frame to make sure each eye sees only the frames that are assigned to it. FMDs which employ field sequential stereo generally have the capability to not only provide stereo viewing, but also enable 2D "big-screen" viewing of DVD/video tape movies as a result of their compatibility with the NTSC format.

Modern, professional-grade HMDs offer major improvements in terms of resolution and field of view. One example of such an HMD is the nVis nVisor SX [NVIS, 2006]. The nVisor was designed for advanced virtual reality applications and costs about USD 24,000. Its LCOS reflective image panels offer a crisp resolution of 1280 X 1024 pixels for each eye and a diagonal FOV of 60 degrees. The nVisor weighs about 1 kilogram and provides some convenient mount points for tracking devices. Image data is fed into the nVisor by a control box, which receives dual input from a dual output graphics card of a PC, one image stream for each eye. Video input to the control box may be in analog or DVI format. The nVisor is very well-balanced on the wearer's head, reducing fatigue. A common problem with many large HMDs is that they tend to be front-heavy, causing the wearer's neck muscles to grow tired over time.

Another example of a modern high-end HMD is the Virtual Research VR1280. Like the nVisor, the VR1280 supports advanced virtual reality applications by receiving video input through a control box from a dual output graphics card, where one video stream is for the left eye and the other for the right eye. Also like the nVisor, the VR1280 offers dual SXGA 1280 X 1024 resolution, by using two reflective FLCOS displays, and a 60 degree diagonal field of view. By building a large percentage of the components in-house instead of purchasing from third parties, the Virtual Research team has been able to offer lower prices. The VR1280 costs about USD 16,000.

2.4   Projection-Based Stereo Displays

Some displays create stereo images by employing projectors. Use of projectors has both advantages and disadvantages when compared to HMDs. One advantage is that the stereoscopic viewing is available to multiple viewers as opposed to just one with the HMD. Another advantage is that often viewing projection-based images is less tiring for the eyes and is less likely to cause motion sickness. A disadvantage of the projection-based displays is that they usually do not provide the same feeling of immersion as an HMD, which surrounds the viewer with a virtual environment and blocks out all or most of the external light. This reduced immersion of the projection-based displays may be a possible reason for the reduced chance of motion sickness.

Projection-based display technologies have historically used CRT projectors. Three tubes are used by a CRT projector for red, green, and blue colors to produce images with a high resolution of 1280 X 1024 pixels at a frequency of 120 Hz. CRT projectors suffer from an inability to project bright images. Digital projectors on the other hand are able to produce images with an order of magnitude higher luminance.

The stereo effect can be achieved by two methods of projection: active stereo projection and passive stereo projection. Passive stereo projection is conceptually the simpler of the two. In a passive stereo projection, two projectors are used to project two video streams on the same area of a projector screen. The light coming from each projector is passed through a polarization filter mounted on the front of the projector. The filters can be arranged in such a way that light produced by each of the two projectors is polarized. By wearing polarized glasses, the viewer is able to see one video stream in the right eye and the other video stream in the left eye. When employing a passive stereo display system, a special silver matte screen must be used to preserve polarization and prevent each eye from seeing both video streams.

The need for polarization can be avoided entirely with the use of an active stereo display technology. The viewer wears special glasses consisting of two IR-controlled LCD light shutters working in synchronization with the projector. A single projector operates in a frame sequential stereo mode. It splits the number of scan lines in two, and the user, wearing active stereo glasses, sees a stereo image that is refreshed at half the frequency of the projector. The projector alternates the display of images for the left eye and for the right eye rapidly enough for the viewer to not perceive a flicker. Since the projector is synchronized with the active stereo glasses, when an image for the left eye is produced, the active glasses shutter for the right eye closes. When using a CRT projector, the higher refresh rate of the incoming signal requires the use of a 'fast green' coating for the phosphor in the CRT tube to reduce its visual persistence.

2.4.1   *3D Wall Displays*

A 3D wall display is a type of stereo projection that allows a large group of viewers to observe stereo images on a large projector screen. The screen may have a flat or a curved surface. Large wall and dome displays often use a series of projectors to create a single tiled, high resolution image. This is due to the fact that in order for a single projector to cover a large image surface, it needs to be moved far from the screen. The greater the distance between a projector and the screen, the greater is the reduction in image brightness. Furthermore, the larger the screen is, the lower the ratio of pixels per square inch of the surface area, which means increased image granularity.

The projector array is often positioned behind the screen, as shown in Figure 2.3. To preserve the quality of the compound image, steps must be taken to maintain a uniform color and brightness across the entire screen. Tiled images are often blended by first overlapping adjacent images. Areas of overlap will then be brighter than the rest of the image. To compensate for this added brightness, the image coming from the graphics computer is usually pre-processed. Pixel intensities in the overlapped areas are dimmed appropriately before being sent to the projectors. A matrix blending approach may be used to regulate pixel intensities in a tiled projection containing varying degrees of overlap throughout the displayed image. This approach employs a two-dimensional look-up table to adjust the intensities of each projected pixel. Each projector may need a custom-look up table since projectors may have different display characteristics. Multiple pairs of polarized projectors can be used to create a tiled 3D image. This allows the use of inexpensive polarized glasses by large audiences.

The PanoWall X Series by Panoram Technologies is one example of a flat, planar 3D wall. PanoWalls are large scale, rear-projected image walls that use high brightness, digital light processing (DLP) stereographic and non-stereographic projectors. The projectors are mounted on optically alignable projector assemblies featuring high grade front-surface mirrors and alignment optics. Another example of a flat 3D wall is the PowerWall made by Fakespace Systems (a Mechdyne company). PowerWalls are designed to be scalable and can be equipped with a variety of projectors, including DLP, CRT, or LCD projection technologies. PowerWalls can be deployed as either passive or active stereo displays. They use "edge-blending" and "edge-matching" to create high resolution, seamless images.

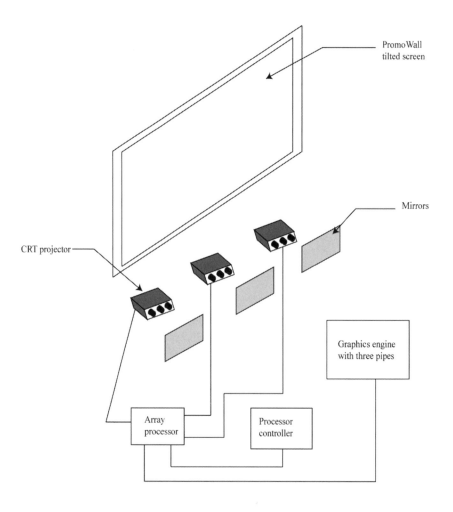

Figure 2.3: Projector array for a 3D wall display

Large scale 3D walls may also be dome-shaped. An example of such a large scale display is the CyberDome created by the Matsushita Electric Works company [Shibano et al., 2003]. In addition to the challenges of flat walls having to do with blending and maintaining uniform brightness and color, curved walls present new challenges associated with projecting onto a curved surface. Dome displays must implement corrections for distortions associated with projecting a planar image onto a curved surface and distortions due to the position of projectors. In the case of a distortion due to a curved surface, a distortion-free image can be displayed by pre-distorting images on the graphics computer before they are sent to the projectors. Distortion due to the position of the projector affects both flat and curved projection surfaces. This type of distortion can often be corrected using the keystone feature of the projector. If the projector lacks adequate support for such a feature or "keystoning" does not provide adequate correction, then again software pre-distortion must be used.

2.4.2   *Workbench Displays*

Workbench displays are a special class of projection-based stereo displays that employ a drafting table style configuration. Workbench displays are designed to foster collaborative 3D viewing. Research in workbench displays originated at the German National Research Center for Information Science. One of the first workbench displays in the United States was the responsive workbench developed at the Naval Research Laboratory based on the work at GMD. The responsive workbench had a table-like appearance with a flat horizontal surface. By wearing shuttered glasses, synchronized with a projector near the table, several viewers could see 3D models on the surface of the table.

One of the earliest commercial workbench displays was the immersive workbench by Fakespace Systems. The immersive workbench used a single CRT projector positioned horizontally outside the table. The images from the projector were directed at a mirror below the diffuser screen. Light was reflected from the mirror up toward the diffuser screen, producing stereoscopic images in combination with active shuttered glasses. The configuration of the immersive workbench is shown in Figure 2.4 [Burdea and Coiffet, 2003]. The dimensions of the immersive workbench were 0.9 meters X 2.5 meters X 3.6 meters.

One drawback of the horizontal surface used in the immersive workbench was that tall virtual objects would get clipped on the side opposite the user. This problem could be overcome by tilting the display screen. Some similar workbench displays that followed incorporated a tilting mechanism that allowed the user to tilt the display screen anywhere from a horizontal to a vertical orientation.

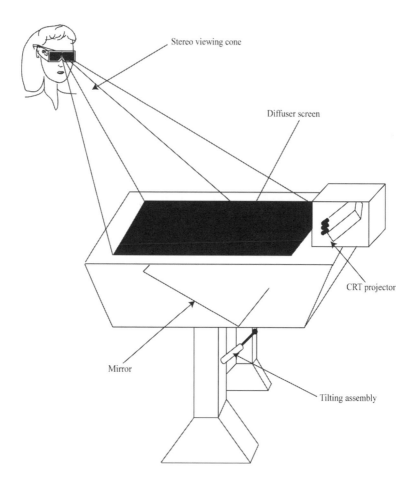

Figure 2.4: The configuration of the immersive workbench

In the late 1990s, Trimension Systems (a division of SEOS as of 2007) came up with a new design. Their workbench display, called V-Desk, incorporated two fixed screens and two CRT projectors instead of an adjustable table. In this L-shaped design, the lower projector is aimed at a mirror below the horizontal diffuser screen as before. A second projector is directed at a vertical diffuser screen. The L-shaped design offers a more compact workbench that is about 1.5 meters X 1.9 meters X 2 meters. The V-Desk allowed several viewers to see 3D images but only one viewer to change perspective by wearing an InterSense tracking device. One drawback to a workbench display, and many other projection-based displays, is that only one viewer can control perspective. If the head positions and orientations of the other viewers are not close enough to the head of the primary viewer, then the other viewers will often see visual artifacts like tilting of tall objects.

As of 2007, Fakespace continues to offer a workbench display similar to the original immersive workbench. The latest workbench is called the M1 Desk. The M1 Desk is small enough to be relatively portable and offers a 1280 X 1024 resolution. It has a 44-inch diagonal visualization screen, which is adjustable. Optional head tracking facilitates the correct perspective of stereo images.

2.4.3   CAVE Displays

A CAVE is a special type of 3D wall display that combines images projected onto several walls to create an immersive and compact virtual room inside of which the viewer can look around to get a panoramic view similar to that of a dome display. CAVE is an acronym for an oddly recursive name - CAVE Automatic Virtual Environment. Motivation for the development of the CAVE technologies came mainly from scientific visualization in the early 1990s. The CAVE was first developed at the Electronic Visualization Laboratory (EVL) at the University of Illinois at Chicago in 1991. Their goal was to use the CAVE as a cube approximation of a sphere in order to reduce the processing time required to generate complex pre-distorted images needed by a dome-like display. This allows the CAVE to respond to user input and run VR applications in near real-time.

A typical CAVE uses four projectors and four projection screens and can accommodate as many as a dozen viewers depending on room size. The configuration of the projectors and the screens is shown in Figure 2.5. One screen is placed on the floor and three other screens are used as vertical walls. Images from the four projectors are reflected off mirrors onto the screens. The mirror that directs an image at the floor screen is oriented in such a way that shadows are created behind the observers rather than in front of them. The projectors generally operate at high refresh rates, alternating the output of images for the right eye and the left eye fast enough for the viewers not to perceive a flicker. LCD-based active stereo shutter glasses are synchronized with the projectors via infrared transmitters to allow the observers to see compelling 3D scenes. Plate 1 (see the color section) shows a 3D scene being displayed inside a CAVE system used by the University of Maryland Virtual Reality Laboratory. The original CAVE developed at EVL used four silicon graphics high-end workstations; each of the four created images for a particular screen. A fifth computer was used for serial communications to input devices and synchronization via fiber-optic reflective memory. The reflective memory was used as a shared cache for all computers.

Reflective memory allows memory pointers to directly access chunks of memory, bypassing the operating system. This was necessary in order to speed up communication between all the workstations. Communication between workstations needed to be very fast in order to enforce tight synchronization of the four screens. If the images generated for two adjacent screens are even one frame out of sync, then a small distortion forms in the corner.

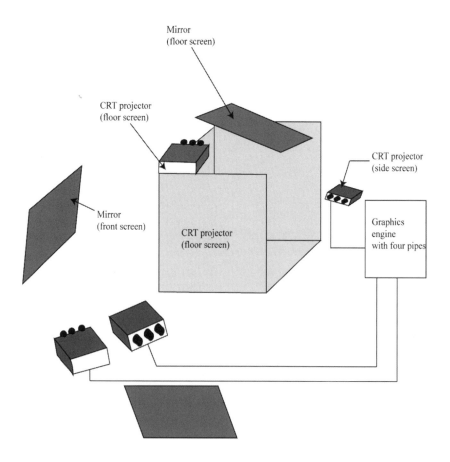

**Figure 2.5: Design of a typical four-sided CAVE system
(three walls and a floor)**

Another implementation of a CAVE system can be found at the Virtual Reality Laboratory at University of Maryland, College Park. This laboratory uses a silicon graphics ONYX2 infinite reality computer and a set of Octane2 workstations. It uses an 8ft X 8ft X 8ft theater composed of three walls and the floor on which images are projected. Users can navigate through the virtual room using active glasses and a wand which are tracked using an Ascension Technology tracking system. The facility can also produce 3D sound by using an array of speakers [Tuncali, 2003].

One limitation of the CAVE system, as in many other 3D wall type displays, is that the perspective is controlled by a single tracked user. Other users in the CAVE environment must stay close to the user controlling the perspective in order to get a good 3D effect. Another drawback is the cost. Due to the hardware requirements of a CAVE system, the cost of the CAVE can typically run into hundreds of thousands of dollars.

Chapter 3

Interacting with Virtual Environments

This chapter provides an overview of the input devices used in virtual environments and examines their effectiveness. Input is generated by the user in the form of position and orientation data for user's head, hands, fingers, or other entities the user might employ to interact with the virtual environment. This chapter also explains the importance of tracking the user's head and hands or entities the user interacts with, in order to generate a realistic and highly responsive virtual environment.

3.1   Tracking Technologies

3.1.1   *The Need for Position and Orientation Tracking*

Three-dimensional visualization and depth perception, described in Chapter 2, is just one component of an immersive virtual environment. Another important component is the interactivity. Interactivity with the human user is supported in the VR application by accepting input from special user interface devices. The most common user interface devices in everyday ordinary computing are the keyboard and the mouse. Unfortunately, very limited data can be supplied with a keyboard and mouse for interaction in a 3D environment. For example, it is a little awkward to describe three-dimensional rotation for a single virtual entity with a mouse. Conveying three-dimensional rotation for two entities simultaneously, such as the user's view and some held virtual object, requires the use of both a mouse and a keyboard. The keyboard is even more problematic than the mouse when trying to convey 3D rotations. Using both simultaneously presents a major challenge to the user. Hence, it is necessary to employ more advanced interface devices which allow the user to generate position and rotation data for multiple objects simultaneously in a convenient and user friendly way. When inside an immersive virtual environment, the user should focus most of the attention on the presented scenes and objects rather than being too preoccupied with interface issues.

This chapter presents many kinds of advanced user interface devices which supply the VR application with positional and rotational data by tracking the user's head, hands, or devices held by the user. Various manufacturers and researchers have come up with a wide variety of technologies that are used to perform tracking. These include devices based on optical, magnetic, ultrasonic, inertial, and mechanical principles. A moving object in 3D space has six degrees of freedom. Three degrees of freedom represent the *x, y, z* positional components of the three orthogonal axes making up a Cartesian coordinate system that is attached to an object or the scene containing the object. The other three degrees of freedom are the object's rotations about the orthogonal axes represented by yaw, pitch, and roll. Some of tracking devices can track only position or only orientation, while others can track both.

3.1.2   *Optical Tracking*

An optical tracker is a position measurement device which uses certain wavelengths of electromagnetic radiation (light) to ascertain the position and orientation of an object. Orientation is often calculated from position measurements. Optical trackers usually work by triangulation. There are two kinds of optical trackers: inside-looking-out and outside-looking-in. The type depends on whether the sensing device is stationary and used to monitor markers on the user's body or the sensing device is mobile and worn by the user. In the inside-looking-out type of optical tracking, the sensor is worn by the user while light is emitted toward the sensor by some sort of a scanner. In the outside-looking-in type of optical tracking system, the user wears one or more light emitting diodes (LEDs), while cameras observe the LEDs and use a combination of image processing and triangulation to determine the position of the LEDs in 3D space. All optical tracking systems require a direct line of sight between the sensors and the transmitters. Optical tracking systems also often require that the tracked area be isolated from sunlight or bright light sources. Advantages of optical tracking systems include very small latency and accommodation of very large work volumes.

An example of an inside-looking-out optical tracking system is the LaserBIRD 2 produced by Ascension Technology Corporation. The LaserBIRD employs a fixed laser scanner with two rotary laser beams. A tracked object, like the user's head, carries a triangular sensor composed of three sensing elements. The laser scanner emits two infrared (IR) light planes, which are offset and may have different orientations. The scanner continuously scans the area while the sensor detects emitted laser beams.

Signals from the sensor are then sent to the scanner, where a built-in microprocessor computes the positions of each of the sensing elements relative to the scanner based on the known triangular arrangement of the three sensing elements, angular difference of the IR beams, and the known arrangement of the two laser scanning heads. The position of the center of the sensor is used as the position of the tracked object. The center position is calculated as the average of the three sensing elements. Orientation is calculated from the three positions of the sensing elements. Finally, the position and orientation of the sensor is sent to the host computer via a RS-232 serial port, for which a USB converter is available. The scanner has a horizontal field of view of about +/-50 and a vertical field of view of about +/- 52 degrees. The LaserBIRD 2 has measurement rate of 240 Hz and a latency of 7.17 milliseconds. It has a maximum range of 1.83 meters, a position measuring accuracy at 1 meter of about 0.7 mm root mean square (RMS), and an orientation measuring accuracy of about 0.5 degrees RMS at 1 meter.

An example of an outside-looking-in optical tracking system is the Precision Point Tracker (PPT) produced by WorldViz LLC [WorldViz, 2004; WorldViz, 2006]. The PPT uses two, four or eight sensors (cameras) to track up to eight targets. The targets are battery powered IR LEDs. Unlike the LaserBIRD, which is a six-degree of freedom (6DOF) tracker, the PPT is a 3DOF tracking system, providing the host computer only with 3D positional data about each target. The PPT uses a combination of image processing and triangulation to calculate the positions of the LEDs. A minimum of two cameras are needed for triangulation to work. The additional cameras provide added accuracy, help avoid line-of-sight occlusion problems, and allow tracking of more targets. Image data from the sensors is sent to the tracking computer for processing and then forwarded to the rendering host computer over a RS-232 serial line. The PPT provides one of the largest tracking volumes of all tracking systems - 10 X 10 X 10 m. It has a latency of about 18 milliseconds and an update rate of 60 Hz. The PPT has an accuracy of less than 0.5 cm over a 3 X 3 X 3 m volume. The two-sensor version costs under USD 10,000 (with academic discount) while the eight-sensor version costs approximately USD 25,000.

3.1.3 *Magnetic Tracking*

A magnetic tracker is a position/orientation measurement device which uses a magnetic field generated by a transmitter to track a receiver. The transmitter is stationary, while the receiver is placed on a tracked object such as the user's head, glove, wand, etc. The transmitter is usually made up of three orthogonal antennas. An example of a 6DOF AC magnetic tracker is the Polhemus Fastrak which has been around in one form or another for more than fourteen years. The Fastrak uses a digital signal processing (DSP) architecture allowing it to have a very low latency of 4 milliseconds. The three antennas of the transmitter are excited with sine wave currents that have a frequency of 8, 10, 12, or 14 kHz. Voltages in the receiver coils, caused by the magnetic currents, are forwarded to low noise amplifiers. Output from the amplifiers is multiplexed to three parallel analog-to-digital converters. The Fastrak has an update rate of 120 Hz for a single sensor. The update rate is cut in half with the addition of a second sensor and reduced to 30 Hz when used with four sensors. The reason for the reduction in update rate with the addition of sensors is the use of multiplexers in the design of this device. Fastrak has a position accuracy of 0.004 cm and an orientation accuracy of 0.15 degrees RMS. The standard range of the Fastrak is 1.5 meters between the transmitter and sensor. Optional long range transmitters can extend the range to 4.6 meters. Four Fastrak systems can be connected to track a total of 16 receivers (4 per system) with an update rate of 30 Hz. Polhemus trackers are not negatively affected by the Earth's magnetic field, power outlets or electric motors – factors that can negatively affect products based on pulsed DC technology. One problem with an AC magnetic tracker like the Fastrak is that the transmitter induces eddy currents in metals nearby. These currents may then produce their own magnetic fields reducing the accuracy of the tracking system. The transmitter must be kept away from the floor and the ceiling, as the metal beams that are part of the structure of the building will degrade the measurement accuracy.

The DC magnetic tracking systems reduce the eddy current problem by replacing the AC magnetic field used by the transmitter with a DC magnetic field. They use a short delay between the time the transmission coils are excited and the time the voltages are sampled in the receiver. The delay allows the eddy currents to subside before measurement is performed. A microprocessor embedded in the transmitter is used to control the amplitude of the magnetic pulses. The microprocessor regulates the amount of current in order to change the magnitude of the magnetic pulse. The current is regulated by sending voltages to current sources connected to the transmitter coils; the higher the voltage, the higher the current. Voltages created in the receiver antennas are sampled sequentially by a microprocessor. Finally, the microprocessor uses a calibration algorithm to determine the position and orientation of the receiver relative to the transmitter.

Another example of a 6DOF DC magnetic tracking system is the Flock of Birds produced by Ascension Technology Corporation. The Flock of Birds can be used to track from one to four sensors with one or more connections to the serial ports of the host computer. Both the transmitter and the receiver are connected to the Flock of Birds control box via cables. Three types of transmitters are available to support short, medium, and long range tracking. The short range transmitter offers a range of about 0.9 meters, while the extended range transmitter can extend the range up to about 3 meters. The Flock of Birds provides a position measurement accuracy of 1.8 mm RMS and an orientation measurement accuracy of 0.5 degrees RMS, although metal objects and stray magnetic fields in the tracking area will degrade performance. Flock of Birds also supports up to 144 measurements per second. The Flock of Birds is a reasonably affordable tracking option which can range from about USD 2,500 with one medium range transmitter and one receiver to about USD 14,000 with four sensors (having long cables) and a long range transmitter.

Magnetic tracking systems tend to be more affordable than the optical ones, but offer much smaller tracking envelopes in general. The biggest problems with magnetic systems are distortions caused by metal objects, and a very rapid decrease in accuracy and resolution with distance. Metal beams in the structure of a building may negatively affect the accuracy of magnetic trackers. Often magnetic tracking systems need to be kept away from floor, walls, and ceiling. Also, the Flock of Birds described earlier is effectively a wired technology with both the transmitters and the receivers being connected to a control unit via cables. The tracked entity is therefore tethered to the control unit. With optical tracking systems, PPT in particular, the transmitters (i.e., LEDs) may be powered by batteries, effectively becoming completely wireless.

3.1.4 *Ultrasonic Tracking*

Ultrasonic trackers employ ultrasonic signals produced by a transmitter to measure the position/orientation of a receiver. Unlike magnetic tracking systems, ultrasonic ones do not suffer from metal and magnetic field interference, although they have their own disadvantages. The design of ultrasonic trackers is similar to that of the magnetic trackers. The system is generally composed of a stationary transmitter, mobile receiver, and an electronic control unit. The transmitter consists of three ultrasonic speakers mounted in a triangular configuration. The receiver is composed of three microphones, also in a triangular configuration. Ultrasonic trackers use the speed of sound to determine distances from the speakers to the microphones. Each speaker is activated sequentially. The distance from each speaker to the three microphones is then calculated for a total of nine distances. Triangulation is then used to calculate the position and orientation of the planar platform holding the sensors (i.e., microphones).

A typical update rate of an ultrasonic tracker is about 50 measurements per second. The update rate is low because a short time delay is necessary between activations of the speakers in order to allow echoes from the previous activation to subside before enabling the microphones. To track multiple targets, ultrasonic tracking systems may use multiplexers to sequentially take measurements for up to four receivers. Unfortunately, doing so further reduces the update rate. With four receivers, the update rate may go down to 12 measurements per second. Using multiple receivers also greatly reduces the operating range of the tracking system. Similar to optical tracking systems, ultrasound trackers require an unobstructed line-of-sight from the transmitter to the receiver. Another drawback to using this type of tracking system is that the microphones may receive interference from background noises, reflections of ultrasonic signals from hard surfaces and other ultrasound devices.

Ultrasonic tracking became a popular choice in the late 1980s for calibration in robotics. Due to the many limitations of ultrasonic tracking, there are not many commercial, pure ultrasonic tracking systems for VR applications. One of the commercial examples, however, is the Logitech Head Tracker. The Head Tracker is a 6DOF motion tracking device that has a range of about 1.6 meters, a latency of 30 milliseconds, an update rate of about 50 measurements per second, and a maximum operating temperature of about 35 degrees Celsius. The Head Tracker's accuracy and range are adversely affected by significant changes in humidity and air temperature because those two factors affect the speed of sound. Hence, the Head Tracker is designed to operate with an accuracy of 30 mm only within a certain temperature range, which is 5 degrees Celsius to 35 degrees Celsius. Both the transmitter and the receiver must be connected to a control box via cables, so the wearer must be tethered to this tracking device. Logitech has combined this technology with a mouse, producing the Logitech 3D mouse. Both the Head Tracker and the 3D mouse cost approximately USD 3,000.

3.1.5   *Inertial Tracking*

Inertial trackers are devices which measure the change in an object's orientation and translational velocity, using a combination of gyroscopes, magnetometers, and accelerometers. Three orthogonal angular rate sensing Coriolis gyroscopes can be used to measure three angular rates to eventually produce the yaw, pitch, and roll values for a tracked object. Unfortunately, use of gyroscopes alone leads to quickly accumulating errors called drift. To perform angular drift corrections, some 3DOF orientation tracking technologies use both magnetometers and linear accelerometers mounted on orthogonal axes along with the gyroscopes.

One such technology is the InertiaCube2 3DOF orientation tracking device produced by Intersense [Intersense, 2006].

The InertiaCube is a monolithic part that is based on micro-electro-mechanical systems (MEMS) technology. This technology does not use any spinning wheels, which may be a source of inertial forces, mechanical failures and noise. For each orthogonal axis, the InertiaCube measures linear accelerations, angular rates, and magnetic field components. Micro-miniature vibrating elements, solid-state magnetometers and integral electronics are used to measure all nine values. The gyroscopes provide fast, dynamic, high resolution measurements of orientation. The accelerometers and magnetometers are used to make corrections relative to Earth's gravitational and magnetic fields. When processing accelerometer data, the InertiaCube uses an adaptive algorithm to remove the portion of accelerometer measurements that represents actual motion instead of gravity. The accelerometer values associated with gravity are used to perform roll and pitch corrections. Magnetometer data is used to perform yaw corrections by keeping track of the magnetic north.

The InertiaCube2 measures orientation across the entire 360 degree range with an update rate of 180 Hz, accuracy of 1 degree RMS, and a latency of about 2 milliseconds. The InertiaCube2 is not susceptible to line-of-sight issues. It is also not nearly as susceptible to interference from metals and magnetic fields in the area as magnetic tracking systems. The range of the InertiaCube2 is limited only by the length of the cable that connects it to a RS-232 serial port of the host computer. It is small, highly portable, and, at approximately USD 1,700, a very affordable orientation tracking solution. A newer version called InertiaCube3 also offers a wireless tracking capability, allowing the InertiaCube to communicate wirelessly with a receiver and be powered by a single 9V battery. The wireless InertiaCube3 costs approximately USD 3,000.

In addition to performing pitch and roll corrections, accelerometers can be used to perform position tracking, producing a complete 6DOF tracking system. To get position, three orthogonal linear accelerometers measure the total acceleration vector of the moving object. This vector can then be converted from object coordinates to world coordinates using the known instantaneous orientation of the object determined by the gyroscopes. The effect of gravity is then subtracted from the measured acceleration. Finally, to get the new position, double integration is performed starting from a known initial position.

One major problem with pure inertial 6DOF tracking systems is the drift in the linear position, which is very difficult to reduce to a satisfactory level. One source of large drift in the linear position is the accelerometer errors such as bias stability, scale factor stability, nonlinearity, and misalignment. Another source is the use of double integration when calculating position. The position drift error can be easily calculated [Foxlin et al., 1998] and is seen to grow quadratically in time. The last source of position drift is the errors in orientation produced by the gyroscopes. Since the acceleration vector of a tracked object is converted to world coordinates, using the orientation of the object, any errors in orientation will result in the integration of the acceleration vector in the wrong direction. In order to have reasonably low position drift, the gyroscopes must be extremely precise and have a very small rotational drift. This requirement vastly increases the cost, complexity, and size of the inertial tracking system. As a result of this major limitation, inertial tracking systems are often used in combination with other technologies in order to track six degrees of freedom. Such tracking systems are called hybrid inertial.

3.1.6   *Hybrid Inertial Tracking*

A hybrid inertial tracking system combines inertial trackers with another tracking technology to produce accurate and fast 6DOF measurements. The key is distributing the tracking tasks between the two technologies so that each technology focuses on what it does best instead of trying to accomplish all measurements and calculations with a single technology. Often using the hybrid approach is more cost effective than trying to use a single technology where performing certain types of measurements results in an increased latency or increased cost. One example of such a hybrid tracking system is the Intersense IS-900. The IS-900 tracking system is composed of SoniStrips, tracked devices (stations), and a processor unit. Both the stations and the SoniStrips are connected to the processor unit via cables. The stations are composed of a subset of InertiaCube hardware described earlier combined with a number of ultrasonic rangefinders. The rangefinders contain an IR LED, a microphone, and some electronics. The IR LED of the rangefinder is used for synchronization with SoniStrips, which are an array of ultrasonic speakers. When a station emits a uniquely encoded LED signal, one of the speakers is activated based on the unique ID of the signal. The signal is received by the microphones and a time-of-flight measurement is used to determine range to the ultrasonic rangefinders on the station. The range measurements are used to calculate the amount of drift and make corrections to the orientation and position data reported by the InertiaCube hardware.

The IS-900 provides 6DOF tracking with a latency of 4 milliseconds, a positional accuracy of 2.5 mm, and a rotational accuracy of 0.25 degrees. Optionally, the stations and the SoniStrips may communicate with the processor unit wirelessly, but at the cost of reduced accuracy. Distance between SoniStrips and the stations may not exceed 4 meters.

3.2   Touching and Feeling Virtual Objects

Section 3.1 presented some of the advanced VR interface devices which may be used to allow a user to interact with a virtual environment. These interface devices work by tracking objects that are physically controlled by the user. The user uses these objects to manipulate virtual entities or to navigate in the virtual worlds. One example of such an object is a wand.

A wand is usually a remote control-like device with several buttons. Depending on the type of tracking system, sensors or transmitters can be attached to the wand to measure its position or orientation. Inside the virtual world, the wand may control a virtual laser pointer, such that the wand's position and orientation are reflected by the virtual laser pointer. The user may then pick up virtual objects using the laser pointer and move them around by moving the real wand.

Other real objects that the user may use in order to navigate in virtual worlds and manipulate virtual objects are the user's head and hands. If the user is wearing an HMD, then a transmitter or sensor can be attached to the HMD to track its orientation and position. The user can then change the perspective in the virtual environment by walking around and turning the head.

Sometimes, it is useful to enable the user to interact with the virtual environment with his hands. Tracking the user's hands often requires more specialized tracking devices. To enable the user to use the fingers to interact with virtual objects, the tracking device must be able to measure finger flexure or even detect contact between fingers. If the system allows the user to manipulate virtual objects with his hands, then it may also be useful to provide force feedback to the user's hands. This section presents various hand tracking devices and haptic technologies which provide touch or force feedback to the user's hands.

3.2.1   *Glove-Based Hand Tracking and Haptic Feedback*

Glove-based tracking and feedback technologies incorporate a set of sensors into a glove-like structure in order to keep track of the fingers. Glove-based tracking devices generally work by measuring finger joint angles. Measurements produced by the sensors can be used not only for gesture recognition, but also to update the finger positions and rotations of the virtual hand in the virtual environment. Tracking gloves can range from sophisticated technologies which have many finger joint sensors to simpler ones which may have only a single sensor per finger. The 5DT Data Glove 5, shown in Figure 3.1, is an example of the latter.

Figure 3.1: Photograph of the 5DT Data Glove 5

The Data Glove 5 contains a fiber optic loop for each of the five fingers. The loop is a highly flexible cable that spans the entire finger. An LED is placed at one end of each fiber optic loop. The other end of the loop is connected to a phototransistor. The walls of the fiber cable are treated to change the index of refraction upon bending, so that light will escape as the fingers are bent. When the fiber optic cable is straight, most of the light remains within the cable since the refractive index of the walls is less than that of the core material. The Data Glove estimates finger bending by measuring the amount of returned light. The Data Glove also has a tilt sensor to measure wrist orientation. 5DT offers a wired and wireless version of the glove. The wireless version has a higher latency and is more expensive. Figure 3.2 shows the design of the 5DT Data Glove 5.

Like most tracking gloves, the Data Glove requires configuration before use to adjust the estimated finger bending to account for different hand sizes. The user does the calibration by flexing his hand several times. The calibration needs to be performed at the beginning of every VR session.

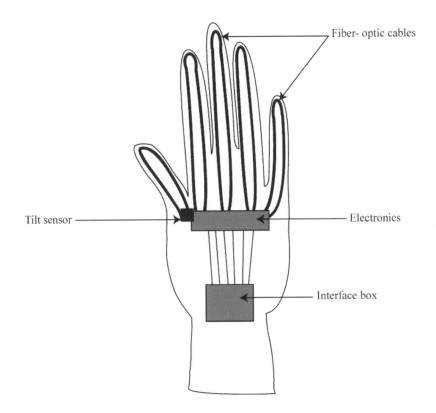

Figure 3.2: Design of the 5DT Data Glove

Another example of a finger tracking glove is the Immersion CyberGlove, shown in Figure 3.3. Unlike the 5DT Data Glove, the CyberGlove uses electrical sensors instead of fiber optic ones [Burdea and Coiffet, 2003]. Each glove contains between 18 and 22 sensors that are embedded in an elastic nylon material. The sensors measure joint angles by using pairs of strain gauges, which change their resistance as they are bent. When a finger joint is bent, one strain gauge is under tension while the other is under compression as shown in Figure 3.4. The change in resistance causes a change in the sampled voltage. Precise measurement of finger bending is carried out with two to three such strain gauges per finger. In addition to measuring a bend in fingers, the CyberGlove is also capable of measuring wrist yaw and pitch, palm arch, and bending of the thumb toward the palm around the ball joint. Use of many sensors and good quality supporting software make the

CyberGlove one of the best hand tracking systems. However, the high fidelity measurements of the CyberGlove come at a high cost. While the 5 sensor version of the 5DT Data Glove may cost approximately USD 1,000, the CyberGlove, depending on the chosen options, may cost between USD 10,000 and USD 20,000.

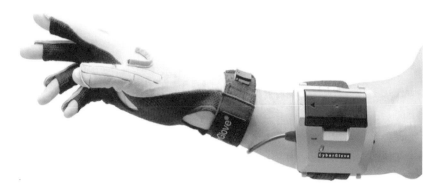

Figure 3.3: Photograph of the Immersion CyberGlove II (Reproduced by permission of Immersion Corporation, Copyright © 2007 Immersion Corporation. All rights reserved.)

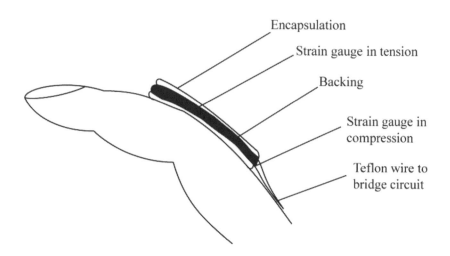

Figure 3.4: Configuration of electrical strain gauges used by the CyberGlove

In addition to tracking hands, glove-based technologies may also offer some form of haptic feedback to the hands. The feedback is often in the form of vibrations or small forces. Such feedback adds a sense of touch to a virtual reality application, which may already provide a sense of vision through the use of stereo images and a sense of hearing through the use of realistic 3D sound. Haptic feedback may especially be useful in the field of medicine to train minimally invasive surgeries.

The Immersion Corporation offers a product called the CyberTouch glove, which combines the CyberGlove technology described earlier with vibrotactile stimulators for each finger. The stimulators can generate varying degrees of vibration to each finger. Such vibration may be useful in signalling to the user when contact has been made in the virtual environment between a virtual hand and some other virtual object.

Yet another Immersion product, called the CyberGrasp Exoskeleton, goes a step further. The CyberGrasp Exoskeleton builds on top of the CyberGlove to apply forces on the fingers of the wearer by using a mechanical exoskeleton, a set of cables and five electrical actuators. After collision detection between the virtual objects is performed, data is sent to the force control unit (FCU) by the host computer. The FSU converts the digital data into analog currents, amplifies them, and sends the currents to the actuators. The actuators transmit torques to the user's fingers through the exoskeleton and a set of cables. The exoskeleton applies forces in the direction opposing hand closure. The actuators are capable of applying a force of 12N on each finger. The main drawbacks of the CyberGrasp, or any such system, are the tendency to cause wearer fatigue due to weight and the high cost of system at about USD 50,000.

3.2.2   3D Mouse and 3D Probe Hand Tracking and Haptic Feedback

Glove-based tracking and feedback technologies are a great way to track the user's hands and add a sense of touch to the virtual world, but sometimes a simpler and more affordable solution will suffice. This section presents some alternatives to glove-based tracking technologies. These alternate tracking systems are often a good choice for desktop-based virtual reality applications where the user sits in a chair and does not need to walk around. For a desktop application, the user may take advantage of a 3D mouse or a mechanical arm to navigate in the virtual environment, manipulate virtual objects, or get touch feedback.

A 3D mouse is a user interface device similar to a standard 2D mouse, but designed to support navigation and manipulation in 3D environments. A 3D mouse is very similar to the concept of a wand mentioned earlier. In fact, the only real difference may be the shape of the 3D mouse. Unlike the usual wand, which has an elongated stick-like shape, the 3D mouse usually has the shape resembling a standard 2D mouse, allowing it to be placed flush on the table and used as a standard 2D mouse. Both a 3D mouse and a wand are normally 6DOF tracking devices, which allow the user to change the translation and rotation of the view or virtual objects. Wands and 3D mice can track the position and orientation of the entire hand, but unlike glove-based trackers, they do not track individual fingers. Usually, a 3D mouse will have several buttons that can be used to toggle manipulation modes in the VR application or perform other application specific tasks.

One example of a 3D mouse is the Ascension 6D mouse sold as an add-on to one of Ascension's magnetic tracking systems like the Flock of Birds. The 6D mouse contains an embedded magnetic sensor which detects magnetic fields coming from a transmitter, allowing it to measure all six degrees of freedom of the user's hand. Another example is the Logitech 3D mouse described earlier. The Logitech 3D mouse uses ultrasonic technology to provide 6DOF tracking. Both 3D mouse systems have a very limited range and are best used with desktop VR applications, which do not require the user to move around much. Like their glove-based counter parts, 3D mouse technologies are capable of offering haptic feedback. One example is the Logitech iFeel Mouse, which can be instructed by the application to vibrate, providing the user with a sense of touch.

Another alternative to the glove-based tracking and feedback system is the 3D probe [Burdea and Coiffet, 2003]. A 3D probe is a small sensorized mechanical arm that is mounted on a support. A 3D probe, like the 3D mouse, is capable of tracking six degrees of freedom, but unlike a 3D mouse, it can provide better haptic feedback by offering force feedback instead of mere vibration. 3D probe devices generally provide six degrees of freedom by using multiple joints where each joint gives one degree of freedom. The user moves and rotates a stylus at the end of the arm. Readings from the joint sensors are combined with the known data about the structure of the mechanical arm and the lengths of the segments. The position and rotation of the tip is then calculated relative to the base.

A good example of this type of device is the PHANTOM Desktop produced by SensAble Technologies. The PHANTOM Desktop can track six degrees of freedom and can exert a maximum feedback force of about 8N. Three degrees of freedom are active, providing translational force feedback. Since the orientation of the stylus is passive, torques cannot be applied to the user's hand. The PHANTOM uses linearity potentiometers to measure yaw, pitch, and roll of the arm segments. It uses digital encoders for position sensing. Force feedback is provided via cables and pulleys. By taking advantage of the PHANTOM's stiffness capabilities, the VR application can prevent virtual objects from going through walls.

Chapter 4

Geometric Modeling for Virtual Environments

Virtual environments utilize geometric models of a physical object. This chapter provides an overview of the main concepts from the geometric modeling area that are utilized in the virtual environments. Section 4.1 describes different ways for modeling geometric objects. Section 4.2 describes how these models can be transformed in the space. Section 4.3 describes trajectory specifications, which involve the use of curves to define non-linear object travel. Section 4.4 describes the process of rendering 3D objects. Finally, section 4.5 describes how collision detection can be performed on the geometric objects.

4.1   Representing Geometric Objects

Before virtual objects can be loaded into a virtual environment, they must be created using a computer-aided design (CAD) system. Although certain simple objects may be modeled programmatically by the software running the virtual environment, this approach limits the complexity of the object and usually takes much longer than using a professional CAD system where 3D entities can be created interactively. Various CAD systems use different methods of modeling 3D objects. This section describes several methods of representing 3D geometric objects. Since virtual environment applications mainly use solid models, this section also presents the underlying representations and operations used in solid modeling.

4.1.1   *Wireframe Models*

Any 3D object may be modeled as a collection of points and line segments connecting the points. Such a model is called a wireframe model because it resembles a wire mesh. In addition to line segments and points, a wireframe model may be composed of a list of curve equations, describing curves of the wireframe, and connectivity data, describing the relationships and adjacency between the lines and vertices. CAD systems which perform wireframe modeling often allow modification of the 3D shapes by letting the user interactively modify lines and points or change the values fed into the equations associated with the shape. Figure 4.1 shows an example of a wireframe model.

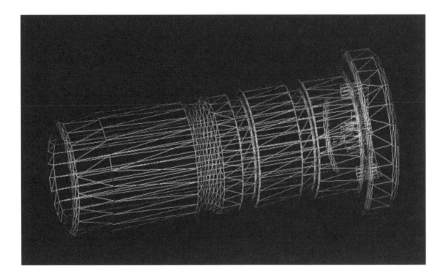

Figure 4.1: Wireframe model of a part

Wireframe modeling was mainly used in the early days of computer-aided drafting systems. Their simplicity made it easy for users to create and modify models of 3D objects and to develop similar systems independently. Wireframe models, however, have many limitations. One limitation that can be especially problematic in virtual environment-based applications is the fact that complex wireframe models are difficult to visualize. A wireframe model does not have any surfaces; it is merely a complex mesh of wires. Another limitation is the lack of information within a wireframe model about the outer and inner boundary surfaces. This data is necessary in the development of tool paths, calculation of the object's mass properties and moments of inertia, and execution of finite-element analysis [Lee, 1999]. These calculations are sometimes necessary in virtual environment-based applications, but they are especially useful in the engineering design process. Hence, wireframe modeling systems have been for the most part superseded by solid and surface modeling systems.

4.1.2 *Surface Models*

Surface models contain information about a 3D object's surfaces in addition to the points, lines, and curve equations contained in the wireframe model. The surface data includes surface equations and often information about surface connectivity. The surface equation includes attributes such as direction of the center axis, location, and radii of cylindrical surfaces. Surface connectivity describes how surfaces are connected and how the surfaces are adjacent to each other. The adjacency information is useful in calculating tool paths and predicting possible gouging of neighboring surfaces [Lee, 1999]. As the user manipulates the 3D object interactively using the surface modeling CAD system, surface equations, curve equations, and coordinates of vertices are updated internally by the CAD system. Surface modeling CAD systems often do not display the surfaces, so the graphical representation of the 3D object may look similar to the graphical representation of a wireframe model. Three methods may be used by the surface modeling CAD system to construct surfaces:

- Interpolation of input points
- Interpolation of input curves
- Translation or revolution of an input curve

Surface models serve mainly two purposes. Their graphical representation is used for visualizing the 3D shape and their mathematical representation is used to calculate tool paths for machining the surfaces of the modeled object.

4.1.3 *Solid Models*

Solid models contain more data than what is stored in wireframe and surface models. The surfaces of the solid model contain information about not only the shape of the surface but also which side of the surface face is inner and which side is outer. This is an important piece of information, because it allows one to determine if a given point in space is outside, inside, or on the solid. This enables the CAD system to derive a lot of volume-related information, which may later be used to perform operations at the level of a volume instead of at the level of a surface [Lee, 1999]. In addition to these benefits, knowing what side of the surface is facing the outside of the solid, rather than the inside of a solid, allows for better rendering of the surface.

A requirement of a solid model, however, is that volume represented by the model be closed. This means that two faces, for example, may not be connected with a single point and two distinct closed volumes may not be joined with a single face, edge, or vertex. There should not be any dangling edges or faces, and the shape represented by the solid model may not have any two-dimensional sides. These requirements make solid models manifold models, as opposed to nonmanifold models, which are allowed to have such characteristics. The manifold requirement ensures that the models created by a solid modeling CAD system can be manufactured.

Creation of solid models requires a lot of data. In order to avoid burdening the user with inputting every required piece of information, solid modeling CAD systems do their best to employ convenient user interfaces and modeling functions for users to create models with. Some of these functions include Boolean operations, sweeping, lifting, skinning, rounding, and creation of primitive shapes, as detailed in section 4.1.6. In the process, these CAD systems automatically generate much of the required data and perform a lot of mathematical computations behind the scenes. As a result, solid modeling CAD systems tend to be large, complex applications which often have high hardware requirements.

Solid models are the most popular method of representing 3D shapes and objects, so they will be presented in greater detail than wireframe or surface models. The basic elements that make up the boundaries of a solid model are vertices, edges, and faces. In the context of a solid model, a face is a portion of a boundary surface such that the boundary between two faces represents a significant change in the normal vector of one face relative to the neighboring face. Each face is defined by a series of edges listed in a counterclockwise or clockwise order and each edge is defined by two points. Listing the edges in a consistent order, like counterclockwise, conveys information about which side of the face points to the outside of the solid and which side points to the inside of a solid. This allows the CAD system or some other application to later regenerate the face normals and point them toward the outside of the solid.

In addition to the boundary information, solid models often contain histories of Boolean operation which were used to create the final shape and the primitives (basic shapes) which were used in the Boolean operations. The solid model may also store a structure of primitives, such as a cube, which approximates the solid model. Such a structure of simple shapes often makes certain computations easier or more efficient.

4.1.4   *Polygonal Models*

Polygonal models can be thought of as simpler versions of solid models; they contain a large subset of the information stored with solid models. Like solid models, polygonal models consist of vertices, edges, and faces. In a polygonal model, any two faces may share at most one edge. Unlike in a generic solid model, where a face may consist of many edges, in a polygonal model each face generally consists of only four or three edges. This connotes that a polygonal model generally consists of triangles or quads. Triangulated polygonal models are probably the most common. Since any three points define a plane, triangles always lie on a single plane. This may not be true for polygons with more than three sides. The fact that triangles lie on a single plane makes it easy to calculate the surface normal by taking the cross product of two of the edges. The clockwise or counterclockwise order of the vertices may then be used to point the normal toward the outside of the solid. Such surface normals allow for proper rendering of the 3D shape; shading in particular.

Small faces of the polygonal model can be combined into groups to represent larger surfaces. Curved surfaces can also be approximated with triangular faces. The errors in the curve approximations can be made arbitrarily small by reducing the size of the faces [Banerjee and Zetu, 2001]. The drawback of doing this, however, is that the storage requirements of the polygonal model increase significantly. The advantage that polygonal models have over generic solid models is speed of rendering. Modern graphics cards allow rendering of complex polygonal models in a scene at a frame rate of 60 frames per second or higher, permitting near real time interactivity by the user with a virtual environment.

Figure 4.2 shows the contents of a stereolithography (STL) file used to represent triangulated polygonal models. Each triangular polygon is defined by the coordinates of three vertices. Each face also has the x, y, and z components of the face normal associated with it. When storing such data internally, software applications generally create a single list containing all the vertices used in the polygonal model. A separate list of faces then uses references to the elements of the vertex list. This strategy avoids redundant storage of vertex coordinates since each vertex may be shared by many faces. Figure 4.3 illustrates this concept. It shows two connected polygons and the two tables used to represent them. Notice that vertex references in the face list have a counterclockwise order.

The simple format of the STL file allows only one normal per face. However, normals may be associated with each vertex in a polygonal model. Per-vertex normals permit smooth shading of curved surfaces via the Phong shading algorithm. Figure 4.4 and Figure 4.5 illustrate the differences between flat shading performed with per-face normals and smooth shading performed with per-vertex normals.

4.1.5   *Assembly Models*

All models mentioned up to this point have focused on the computer representation of a single 3D object. Assembly modeling systems, on the other hand, combine the geometry data of other types of models (mainly solid models) with relationship data which describes how several parts may be combined to form an assembly. Very often CAD systems provide both the functionality to model individual parts and the functionality to combine them into an assembly.

Q2 - Notepad

File Edit Format Help

```
solid ascii
        facet normal -0.842763 -0.526727 -0.110952
                outer loop
                        vertex 2.41481 -7.5 0.647048
                        vertex 0 -3.5 1.46642e-013
                        vertex 2.5 -7.5 1.04744e-013
                endloop
        endfacet
        facet normal -0.78533 -0.526727 -0.325294
                outer loop
                        vertex 2.41481 -7.5 0.647048
                        vertex 2.16506 -7.5 1.25
                        vertex 0 -3.5 1.46642e-013
                endloop
        endfacet
        facet normal -0.674378 -0.526727 -0.517468
                outer loop
                        vertex 2.16506 -7.5 1.25
                        vertex 1.76777 -7.5 1.76777
                        vertex 0 -3.5 1.46642e-013
                endloop
        endfacet
        facet normal -0.517468 -0.526727 -0.674378
                outer loop
                        vertex 1.76777 -7.5 1.76777
                        vertex 1.25 -7.5 2.16506
                        vertex 0 -3.5 1.46642e-013
                endloop
        endfacet
        facet normal -0.325294 -0.526727 -0.78533
                outer loop
                        vertex 1.25 -7.5 2.16506
                        vertex 0.647048 -7.5 2.41481
                        vertex 0 -3.5 1.46642e-013
```

Figure 4.2: Contents of an ASCII STL file

Relationship data stored with the assembly models often includes mating conditions, instancing information, orientations and positions of individual parts within the assembly, allowable tolerances, parametric constraint relationships between parts, and a tree structure representing the child-parent relationships between subassemblies and parts. Mating conditions between parts convey how parts are connected to each other. For instance, mating conditions may state what two faces of a pair of parts are in contact or what cylindrical surfaces are aligned [Lee, 1999]. Instancing information defines various locations where an instance of an object should be inserted. Instancing enables the CAD system to avoid storing multiple copies of the same geometry of a part like a common screw or a nut for every location in the assembly where such a part must be present. Allowable tolerances make it possible for the assembly modeling system to declare the range of motion a part may have within the assembly or the number of degrees a part may rotate. Parametric constraint relationships represent the relationships between the dimensions of different parts of the assembly. They are useful for defining the interfaces between connected parts. Parametric constraint relationships permit the assembly modeling system to automatically change the dimensions of one part after changes are made to the dimensions of the connected part. Finally, the tree structure of the assembly parts aids in the visualization of the assembly and the parent-child relationships between parts. Often assembly modeling CAD systems allow the user to interactively collapse or expand the branches of the tree in order to change the level of detail or to find and select parts within the geometry of the assembly by clicking on the tree nodes. Figure 4.6 shows an assembly displayed in a CAD system called ProEngineer by PTC.

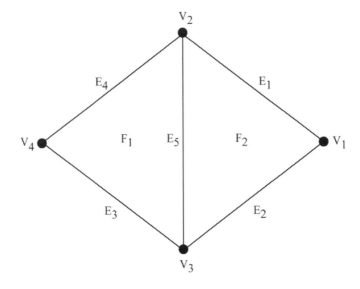

Face	Vertices
F1	V3, V2, V4
F2	V1, V2, V3

Vertex	Coordinates
V1	x1, y1, z1
V2	x2, y2 ,z2
V3	x3, y3, z3
V4	x4, y4, z4

Figure 4.3: Sharing vertex data

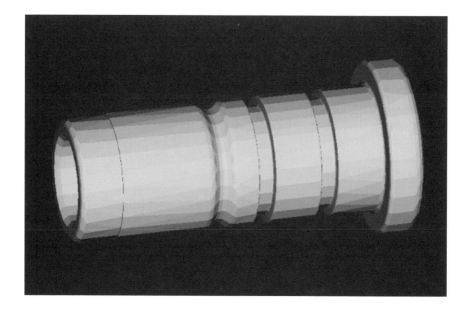

Figure 4.4: Flat shading performed with per-face normals

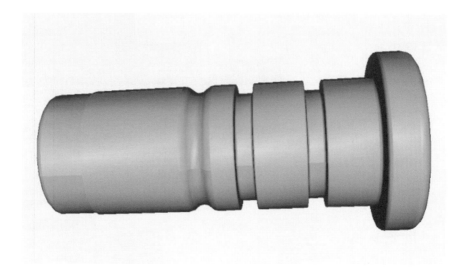

Figure 4.5: Smooth shading performed with per-vertex normals

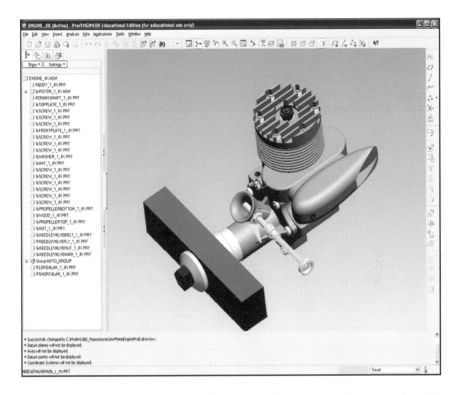

Figure 4.6: Assembly model of a model airplane engine loaded with ProEngineer

The motivation behind the development of assembly modeling systems has been the desire to foster collaboration between different groups of engineers working on the same product. Prior to the arrival of assembly modeling systems, engineers would focus on the design of individual parts and assembled them to assess proper fit and function later in the development cycle. Assembly modeling systems enable engineers to perform these tasks earlier in the development cycle. Assembly modeling systems make it easy for different organizations or different groups of engineers to work on different parts of the overall assembly and later combine all the parts into a complete product. Assembly modeling systems often implement check-in/check-out mechanisms which control access to various parts of the assembly and prevent multiple engineers from modifying the same part design simultaneously. In the context of virtual environment-based training systems, assembly models also often make it easier for the tutorial designer to specify how a set of parts is to be assembled if the assembly representation for those parts exists. If, in the virtual environment-based application, it is known in advance how the parts come together, then the tutorial designer is only required to provide insertion paths.

4.1.6   *Techniques Used in Solid Modeling*

Since solid models are the most common representation of 3D objects, this section will present some details on the techniques and data structures used with solid model representations. As was briefly mentioned in section 4.1.3, solid models can be constructed with the aid of a set of intuitive and relatively easy to use modeling functions. Modeling functions provided by most solid modeling systems can be categorized into five groups [Lee, 1999].

The first group of modeling functions consists of primitive solids and Boolean operations on those solids. The primitive solids are simple 3D shapes such as cubes, spheres, pyramids, cones, and cylinders which are built into the CAD system. The user can modify and combine these primitive solids in order to create an approximation of the desired solid. Various dimensions of primitive solids may be adjusted via user-specified values to system declared parameters. Boolean operations like union, intersection, and subtraction can then be used to manipulate the shapes of primitives. Boolean operators employ set theory to manipulate primitive solids that are effectively sets of points. Figure 4.7, Figure 4.8, and Figure 4.9 give visual examples of union, intersection, and difference of two primitive solids. The user must usually specify the positions and orientations of the solids involved in the Boolean operation. Users may use the result of one Boolean operation as an input to another Boolean operation. Modeling functions belonging to the first group make it easy for an engineer to quickly create prototypes and approximations of the final model, but they often lack the power to precisely model complicated 3D objects.

Figure 4.7: Union of two primitive solids

The second group of modeling functions contains functions which modify an existing solid by using rounding or lifting. Rounding is a technique which takes a sharp corner and replaces it with a smooth, curved surface such that the normals of the curved surface are an interpolation of the normals of the planar surfaces which connect at the corner. Figure 4.10 illustrates rounding where a sharp corner of a pyramid is replaced with a curved one. Lifting is a function which takes a face of an existing solid and translates it in a user-specified direction to create a new solid defined by the volume spanned by the translated face. Figure 4.11 shows an example of lifting.

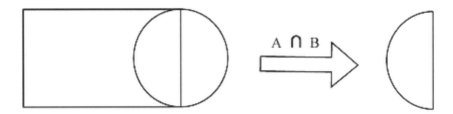

Figure 4.8: Intersection of two primitive solids

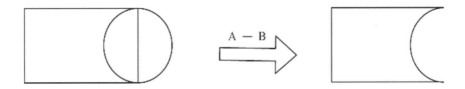

Figure 4.9: Difference of two primitive solids

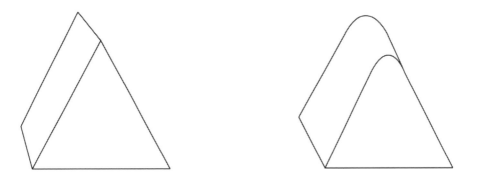

Figure 4.10: Rounded sharp corner in the rounding technique

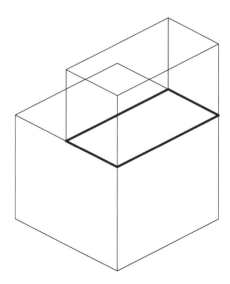

Figure 4.11: An example of the lifting technique

The third group of modeling functions allows the user to create an object by moving a surface. Functions which belong in this group are surface sweeping, rounding, and skinning. Sweeping involves taking a planar surface of a user-specified shape and translating it into a certain distance. The volume traversed by the 2D planar surface defines a new 3D shape. Swinging is similar to sweeping except that rotation of the planar surface is used instead of translation. Figure 4.12 and Figure 4.13 illustrate sweeping and swinging respectively using a 2D shape resembling a capital letter "I". The user may use geometric constraints like values of the dimensions or relationships between 2D shape elements to create swinging or sweeping surfaces. This technique is called parametric modeling and it is also a member of the third group. Parametric modeling can be used to create a set of cross-sections and apply a skinning function on the cross-sections, which encloses the volume defined by the cross-sections with a closed surface. Modeling functions in this group give the user the power to create solids which are very close to the final representation.

The fourth group consists of boundary modeling functions. Boundary modeling functions give the user the power to create or modify individual vertices, edges, and faces similar to the procedure used in a surface modeling system. Unlike a surface modeling system, the created model must represent a closed volume. The user interactively creates vertices and line segments, while the CAD system creates and maintains the low level connectivity information and data structures. Since creation of solids using this method alone is very tedious, boundary modeling functions are normally used to create a 2D face, which can then be swept. Boundary functions are also very useful for modifying existing solids. Equations may also be applied to give straight edges a curved shape.

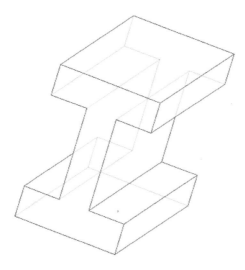

Figure 4.12: 3D shape formed by sweeping a 2D "I" shape

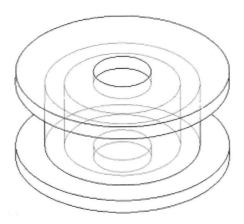

Figure 4.13: 3D shape formed by swinging a 2D "I" shape

The fifth and final group of modeling functions permits the user to modify solids by applying a predefined set of features on them. Some examples of common predefined features are pockets, fillets, holes, and slots [Lee, 1999]. Feature-based modeling allows the CAD system to record the presence and characteristics of common features and the geometries representing them. Features may later be used to perform many kinds of automated tasks and analyses. For instance, process plans may be generated automatically. The VTS, a virtual environment-based training system developed by the authors, is capable of using feature data, amongst other kinds of data, to automatically generate highly detailed text instructions.

Three representations are commonly used in solid modeling. The first one is called the constructive solid geometry (CSG) representation. The CSG representation employs a tree structure to record a history of Boolean operations. Each non-leaf node represents a Boolean operation while each leaf node represents a primitive solid shape. The benefits of the CSG data structure are its simplicity and compactness, the validity of the solids stored in the CSG tree, and easy integration of parametric modeling for adjustment of primitives. The CSG tree does have some drawbacks. It only allows Boolean operations in the modeling process, which limits the power to create complex 3D objects. The CSG representation requires extensive computations in order to derive information about boundary surfaces, like vertices, edges, and faces – data that is required for many applications. Consequently, the CSG tree is often used as supplementary data structures rather than stand-alone representations.

The decomposition representation uses simple solids like cubes to approximate a solid model. Two data structures commonly used in decomposition models are voxels and octrees. A voxel representation divides the bounding box containing a solid model into many little cubes or voxels. A three-dimensional array may then be used to store individual voxels. Geometric calculations are used to determine which voxels are intersected by the solid model. Array elements are then given a value of 1 or 0, depending on whether an intersection with the corresponding voxel exists.

A more efficient management of voxels can be achieved with an octree. Using the octree data structure, the bounding box may be recursively subdivided into eight hexahedra, where each hexahedron becomes a node in the octree such that each node has either zero or eight children. If a hexahedron is completely inside a solid model or completely outside of it, then it becomes a leaf and has no children. If, on the other hand, the hexahedron is partially inside the solid model, then it will have eight children. The recursive subdivision of the solid model bounding box continues until the size of the hexahedron matches the minimum dimensions assigned to voxels. By storing hexahedrons of variable sizes, rather than a large set of small voxels of equal dimensions, the octree representation reduces the memory requirement.

Decomposition models like voxel representations make it easy to make certain kinds of calculations. For example, calculation of volume, mass, or moments of inertia for a solid model represented by voxels can be accomplished simply by adding up the individual values of all the primitive shapes. Decomposition representations also make it easy to perform Boolean operations because all that is needed is a check for intersections between the individual voxels of the two voxel representations. However, there are some drawbacks to the decomposition representations. Voxel representations are only an estimate of a solid model and decreasing the size of the voxels dramatically increases memory requirements. As a result of these limitations, decomposition representations, like CSG trees, are used primarily as supplementary data structures to speed up certain kinds of geometric calculations.

The most common representation of solid models is the boundary representation (B-Rep). Various kinds of data structures, like half-edge or winged-edge, may be used for the boundary representation, but the most common is the half-edge data structure. The half-edge data structure stores the vertices, the edges, the faces, and the connections between them. It gets its name from the fact that each edge is represented as two components. If an edge is defined by points A and B, then it can be represented as a directional edge (half-edge) from A to B and a directional edge from B to A. Each of these two components participates in a loop which defines a unique face. Loop in this context means a doubly linked list where the last element in the list has a pointer to the first element. If faces F1 and F2 share an edge E1, then each half-edge of E1 participates in the definition of a different face through participation in a loop. So, each non-directional edge has two pointers to each of its half-edges, and each half-edge also has a pointer to its non-directional edge. Each vertex has a pointer to one of the half edges that are connected to it. Each half edge also has a pointer to its starting vertex [Lee, 1999]. If a half-edge is defined as a directional edge from vertex A to vertex B, the vertex A is its starting vertex. This kind of strategy allows for efficient traversal of the data structures when performing certain kinds of geometric calculations like analysis of adjacent edges or faces.

4.2   Geometric Transformations

Geometric transformations are an important component in computer graphics and virtual environment-based applications. Transformations may be combined with a solid model of an object to construct the object in a virtual environment. For example, the solid model may be used as the initial representation of the object and a transformation can then be applied to the solid model in order to make the object bigger, smaller, or stretch it along certain dimensions. Geometric transformations can also be used to move and rotate objects in 3D space. This is a necessary functionality for animations or interactive simulation inside a virtual environment-based application. Transformations are widely used in geometric modeling and reasoning. The following examples illustrate needs of geometric transformation:

- Transformation is needed during construction of objects. For example, if the users want to create a hole on an object, they usually first create a cylinder, then translate it to its proper location, and then by subtracting the cylinder from the initial object, they create the hole.
- In order to assess the geometric similarity between two objects, the two objects need to be aligned with respect to each other by using geometric transformations.
- Transformation is used in visualization. A designer may want to view a geometric object from different angles. Therefore, geometric transformation is needed to achieve this effect.

In this section, we introduce the basic concepts and techniques of geometric transformations. A geometric object can be considered a set of points in two-dimensional space or three-dimensional space. A geometric object is constructed and manipulated within a particular coordinate system. For any point in space, a transformation maps it into a new point. Theoretically, we can transform a geometric object by transforming each of its underlying points.

In order to apply geometric transformations, points in space can be represented as position vectors. A vector is a directed line segment having a direction and magnitude. Vectors are defined in the context of a particular coordinate system. A standard two-dimensional coordinate system has two orthogonal axes with the y-axis being vertical and the x-axis being horizontal. Three dimensional spaces can be represented with three-orthogonal axes: x-axis, y-axis, and z-axis. Vectors are generally represented with a 3 X 1 matrix. Each element of the matrix represents a magnitude of the vector along each of the axes of the coordinate system.

A simple linear transformation involves applying a matrix on a vector in order to produce another vector. Since points defining objects may be represented as position vectors, a transformation maps a point in space into another point. Most transformations used in geometric reasoning are linear in nature. Following are some typical linear transformations:

- Rigid Body Transformations: Examples of these transformations include rotations and translations. We often describe these transformations as rigid-body motions, because they resemble physical movements. Rigid body transformations preserve the metric properties (i.e., distances between points, angles, areas, volumes, etc.) of the geometric objects.
- Isotropic Transformations: This type of transformation is a uniform expansion or contraction of the geometric object about some fixed point or center. Isotropic transformations preserve angles.
- Anisotropic Transformations: Anisotropic transformations include anisotropic dilation and shear. An anisotropic dilation is an expansion or contraction of the geometric object whose ratio is dependent on orientation. This indicates that although two line segments are of equal length, if their directions are different, then in general under an anisotropic dilation, the lengths of their transformed versions are not equal. However, parallel lines remain parallel after anisotropic transformations.
- Projective Transformations: Projective transformations are important for many reasons. For example, they allow us to produce two-dimensional images of three-dimensional objects. Projective transformations preserve straight lines and intersections. However, they do not preserve properties such as parallelism, angles, and distances.

Translation transformation involves moving a geometric object along a line and can be viewed as vector addition. Rotating an object which is composed of many points is equivalent to rotating each of the points. In 2D space, the simplest form of rotation is the rotation about the origin. If a rotation is applied on a point that is at the origin, the position of the point does not change. However, if a rotation is applied on a point that is not at the origin, the point is translated around the origin in a circular path. Therefore, rotation can be modeled, using the laws of *sines* and *cosines* and basic trigonometry.

Rotations in three dimensions are very common. Sometimes it is useful to rotate an object or the camera to get a different perspective. The rotation of geometric objects in three-dimensional space is more complex than rotations in the two-dimensional plane. The reason for this is that in three dimensions, an object is rotated around an axis, represented by a 3D vector, rather than a point. What further complicates things is the fact that often rotations need to be carried out sequentially around different axes. Rotation involves matrix multiplication, which is not commutative. So, when performing successive rotations, care must be taken to carry out transformations in the correct order. Three-dimensional rotations can be expressed as three 2D rotations often referred as yaw, pitch, and roll.

The rotation of a point or other geometric object in space can be specified as the product of successive rotations about each of the three principle axes. It is important to establish some kind of convention describing how it can be done. Here is one way:

1. Rotation about z-axis
2. Rotation about y-axis
3. Rotation about x-axis

Up to this point, we discussed the rotation of objects within a fixed global coordinate system. Now, we will define a local frame that is rigidly attached to the object. A sequence of three rotations is performed with respect to the local frame so that when we rotate an object this frame rotates with it. The local and global frames initially coincide, and the rotation angles are called Euler angles. The first rotation is simply a rotation about the z-axis in the global frame, leaving the z-axis of the local frame unchanged, and rotating the local x- and y-axes along with the object. The second rotation is about the rotated x-axis, which no longer coincides with a global axis. The third rotation can be about the rotated z-axis.

4.3   Trajectory Specifications

In order to facilitate training, objects need to move inside the virtual environment. Hence, trajectories of objects need to be defined in space to show complex motions. Often trajectories get defined by spatial curves. Spatial curves can be represented in many different forms. Parametric form is the most popular form and it combines benefits of explicit and implicit forms.

Two commonly used types of curves are the Bezier curves and B-Spline curves. B-Spline curves and Bezier curves have many advantages in common. For both curves, control points influence curve shape in a predictable and natural way, making them good candidates for use in an interactive environment. Both types of curve are axis-independent and multivalued.

The Bezier curve is defined by the vertices of a polygon that enclose the resulting curve. Bezier curves have a number of shortcomings. First, a high degree of polynomial is required to accurately fit complex shapes. Second, the influence of the control points is not sufficiently local. A solution to overcome these problems is to use piece-wise polynomial curves.

B-Spline curves are piecewise polynomial curves defined by a set of control points. The degree of its polynomial basis function is defined independently of the number of control points. Local control of curve shape is possible, because changes in control point location do not propagate shape change globally, and control points influence only a few of the nearby curve segments. B-Spline curves are invariant under affine transformations of the control points. The local control of curve shape possible with B-Splines gives this form an advantage over the Bezier technique, as does the ability to add control points without increasing the degree of the curve.

B-Spline curves do have some shortcomings. For example, ordinary B-Spline curves cannot represent many interesting spatial curves, such as conics, exactly. A more general form of B-Spline curves has been developed to increase their expressive power. This form is called rational form. In the rational form, a set of weights are attached to the control points. These weights provide extra degrees of freedom to control the shape of the curves. Using the rationale form, all conic curves can be represented exactly.

4.4   Rendering

In the context of this chapter, rendering refers to the process of taking virtual 3D objects and drawing them on a 2D screen such as a computer monitor. No matter what display hardware is used, be it a conventional desktop monitor, an HMD, or a set of projectors, the final rendering is always done on a 2D surface. Objects drawn on the monitor are represented at the lowest level by a two-dimensional array of pixels, each pixel having some combination of the three basic colors: red, green, and blue. It is the job of the graphics card and the software running a VR application to transform 3D virtual objects into a set of pixels for the monitor, or some other display device, to display. The drawing process consists of several steps. The first step is the set-up of the position and the orientation of an abstract camera in 3D space and the specification of its viewing volume. Next, the virtual 3D objects are added to the virtual world. In the process, the computer performs shading and texture calculations to ascertain, for each vertex, the color intensities of each of the three color components. Next, clipping is performed on the 3D objects inside the camera's viewing volume. Hidden surfaces are then removed and the 3D objects are then projected onto a plane within the viewing volume. The image on the plane is then translated to a set of pixels to be displayed on the hardware device.

The set up of the virtual camera and its viewing volume is the first step in the process. The virtual camera is defined by providing the graphics software with the position and direction of the camera. Additionally, the shape of the viewing volume emanating from the camera must be defined. The viewing volume may either have the shape of a parallelepiped or a rectangular pyramid. The use of a parallelepiped camera shape results in a parallel projection. The parallel projection refers to the idea of projecting a 3D object onto a 2D surface such that some or all of the dimensions of the 3D object are preserved. Parallel projections are very useful in engineering drawings where the drawing conveys the true dimensions of the object. The use of a rectangular pyramid camera shape results in a perspective projection. Perspective projections often distort the dimensions of the object in order to convey a better sense of depth and offer a more realistic view of the object.

After the camera has been specified, 3D objects are added to the scene. Section 4.1 described the modeling techniques that may be used to represent 3D objects. Once the 3D models have been added to the virtual world, they are transformed, using techniques described in Section 4.2. Next, color is added to the vertices based on the position of the light source, the characteristics of the object surfaces, camera perspective, and the specified textures. In a process called shading, the light intensities across the surfaces of the 3D object are calculated based on the angle between the normal vector at each vertex and the vector from the vertex to the light source. This relationship between the brightness of the surface and surface orientation is called Lambert's Law.

Next, clipping is performed to remove objects or surfaces which lie outside of the viewing volume of the abstract camera. During the clipping stage, the graphics software examines all the edges of the individual surfaces making up an object. If the entire edge lies inside the viewing volume, it is left alone. If a portion of the edge leaves the viewing volume, then the point of intersection is found and used as the new vertex defining the edge. In a process called hidden surface removal, parts of solid objects which are obscured by other objects are also removed.

The final step is the transformation of a 3D scene onto a 2D surface. The graphics software first projects all the points and lines onto the view plane within the viewing volume. The view plane is normally the side of the parallelepiped or the rectangular pyramid that is closest to the origin of the virtual camera and whose normal vector is parallel to the direction of the abstract camera. At this point, the vertices are finally passed through a viewport transformation which maps them to screen coordinates. The viewport is an abstract representation of the screen. The final result is a two-dimensional array of pixels which contains the luminosity values for the red, green, and blue color components of each pixel. Each pixel may also have an alpha component which dictates the degree of transparency of a particular pixel. The combination of the three-color values can represent a vast spectrum of colors.

4.5   Collision Detection

Collision detection is an important functionality in virtual environment-based applications. It is used in physics-based modeling to produce realistic behaviors for colliding objects or combined with gravitational force calculations to simulate realistic motion when an object is dropped on the floor or on the table. Collision detection is also heavily used in the implementation of interactive simulation, where the user manually assembles a device using either virtual hands controlled by tracked gloves or using a laser pointer. In the case of virtual hands, the system must check for collisions between the virtual fingers and the grabbed object to determine if the object may be picked up or how the object is to move. In the case of a virtual laser pointer, the system, upon detection of collision between a held object and a stationary object in the environment, must determine how a held object and the stationary object will behave, depending on where collision occurred, the direction of motion, and other factors. In addition to virtual environments, collision detection is used in robotics mainly for planning collision free paths. It has also been used in computer aided design applications, virtual prototyping, engineering analysis, and gaming.

In our discussion of the most popular collision detection techniques we will assume that triangulated polygonal models are being used. Polygonal models are the most commonly used representations in computer graphics and modeling mainly because they have simple representations, they are versatile, and due to the widespread availability of hardware accelerated polygon rendering [Lin and Gottschalk, 1998]. Given two polygonal models M and N containing m and n facets (triangles) respectively, collision between M and N may be detected by checking for intersections between n and m.

The problem with performing pairwise polygon comparisons between polygons of M and polygons of N is that the computation time is O(nm), which becomes very high as n and m increase. This is a serious problem, because very often collision detection may have to be performed many times per second as the object moves through an environment and possibly interacts with other objects. For this reason, many approaches have been developed in order to reduce the number of necessary computations at each time increment. One type of approach, which many researchers have chosen, is enclosing each polyhedron in different kinds of bounding boxes and performing initial collision checks on these bounding boxes. Polygon intersection tests are later performed on a very limited set of polygons.

Three collision detection systems employing various bounding box techniques are presented in this section. They are I-COLLIDE [Banerjee and Zetu, 2001], SOLID [van den Bergen, 1997], and RAPID [Gottschalk, 1996]. I-COLLIDE and SOLID make use of axis aligned bounding boxes (AABB), while RAPID uses oriented bounding boxes (OBB).

In order to achieve interactive rates, I-COLLIDE performs pruning of objects before carrying out pairwise collision testing. Each object in I-COLLIDE is surrounded by a three-dimensional bounding volume representing a box. The dimensions of the bounding box are aligned with the coordinate axes, hence the name axis-aligned bounding box. An advantage of the AABB type of bounding box over the oriented bounding box (OBB) is the simplicity and speed of calculation of the box. The drawback of the AABB type of bounding box in comparison to the OBB is the inferior fit to the shape of the solid it encloses. An OBB is designed to produce a tightest-fitting box around a solid, taking into account the orientation of the solid. The tighter fit of the OBB reduces the possibility of false positives – reports of collision when no collision is taking place.

When the collision detection mechanism is activated, I-COLLIDE first checks for overlaps between all the boxes in the environment. This results in a computational time of $O(n + m)$, where n is the number of stationary objects and m is the number of moving objects. If a set of bounding boxes overlap, then further collision checking is needed. If a bounding box does not overlap with any other bounding boxes, then the facets contained by the bounding box do not need to be checked during exact collision detection. The check for overlap is done by projecting the bounding boxes onto the coordinate axes. Projection of the axis aligned bounding boxes onto the coordinate axes results in intervals on the coordinate axes. These intervals must then be checked for overlaps. This strategy relies on the fact that if two bounding boxes are in collision, then all three of the coordinate axis intervals of one bounding box must be overlapping with the three intervals of another bounding box. After overlaps between bounding boxes are checked, I-COLLIDE enters the exact collision detection phase.

I-COLLIDE's exact collision detection mechanism entails the use of Voronoi regions to locate the closest features of two polyhedra. According to Banerjee and Zetu, "The Voronoi region of a feature is the set of points closer to that feature than to any other feature in the set" [Banerjee and Zetu, 2001]. The Voronoi regions form cells around features where each cell has a pointer to neighboring cells. Voronoi regions allow I-COLLIDE to quickly locate a feature on one object that is closest to a feature on another object. Feature is defined here as a small set of triangular polygons. Once a pair of features is found, polygon intersection tests can be performed.

Another well known collision detection package is called Software Library for Interference Detection (SOLID). SOLID makes use of a hierarchal model of AABB bounding boxes. In SOLID, the dimensions of each bounding box are aligned with the axes of the local coordinate system of a solid. For each polyhedron, SOLID creates a binary tree of AABB bounding boxes. The bounding box hierarchy is created top-down, starting with a tightest-fitting coordinate axis-aligned bounding box which encloses a single solid model. This bounding box represents the root of a binary tree. The bounding box is then partitioned into two halves which become children of the root with the facets classified to the two child bounding boxes. The parent bounding box is split by a plane orthogonal to the longest axis of the AABB. Primitives (facets) are assigned to bounding boxes depending on whether they are labeled as positive or negative. Assuming that the plane partitioning the longest axis intersects it at coordinate δ, a primitive is classified as positive if the midpoint of its projection onto the longest axis is greater than δ and negative if the midpoint is less than δ.

Intersection tests between two models are carried out by recursively comparing pairs of nodes belonging to the binary trees of the two models. For each visited pair of nodes, the bounding boxes represented by the nodes are tested for overlap. Only nodes whose bounding boxes are found to be overlapping with some other bounding box are further traversed. If both nodes found to be intersecting are leaf nodes, then the primitives which are assigned to the leaf nodes are tested for intersection. If a leaf node overlaps an internal node, then the leaf node is compared to each of the children of the internal node. If the overlapping nodes are both internal, then the node with the smaller volume is further compared to each of the children of the node with the larger volume.

Since the AABB bounding boxes in SOLID are aligned with the local coordinate system of the model and the local coordinate system may be arbitrarily oriented in the world coordinate system, SOLID uses a technique by Gottschalk [Gottschalk, 1996]. This technique is called the separating axes test (SAT). The separating axis is an axis such that the projection of two bounding boxes onto the axis creates intervals on the axis which do not overlap. Finding such an axis immediately proves that the two bounding boxes do not intersect in 3D space. It has been found that such an axis, if it exists, may be found by testing all axes which are either orthogonal to a facet of one of the polytopes or orthogonal to an edge from each polytope. For a simple box, this means that in order to find a separating axis, a total of 15 potential separating axes must be checked – 6 axes corresponding to the 3 uniquely oriented surfaces of each box and 9 pairwise combinations of edge directions. The search for the separating axis stops as soon as a separating axis is found. If all 15 potential

separating axes have been tested and a separating axis is not found, then
the corresponding bounding boxes intersect.

The last collision detection library discussed here is called RAPID.
The techniques used by RAPID are very similar to those used by SOLID.
The biggest difference is the fact that RAPID employs object-oriented
bounding boxes (OBB) instead of axis-aligned boxes. By using OBB trees,
RAPID is able to traverse fewer levels of its hierarchy to process a
collision query for objects in close proximity to each other in comparison
to hierarchies (trees) of AABBs. In fact, an AABB tree usually requires
approximately twice as many bounding box intersection tests as an OBB
tree [van den Bergen, 1997]. The drawback is that the computation of an
OBB is longer than that of an AABB. Figure 4.14 and Figure 4.15 show
how RAPID constructs an OBB tree hierarchy.

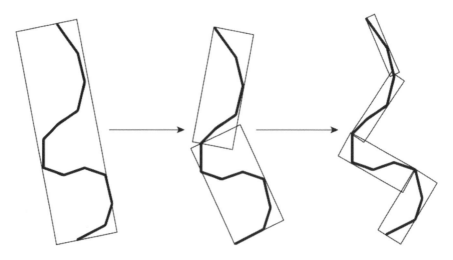

**Figure 4.14: Partitioning of oriented bounding boxes in the RAPID
collision library**

An OBB-based collision detection algorithm uses statistics
summarizing vertex coordinates to build an oriented bounding box around
a set of triangular polygons. The statistics include mean and a covariance
matrix [Gottschalk, 1996]. Since the eigenvectors of the symmetric matrix
are mutually orthogonal, they can be normalized and used as a basis.
External vertices along each axis of the basis can then be found and the
bounding box can be sized to enclose those vertices, making sure the
bounding box is oriented with the basis vectors.

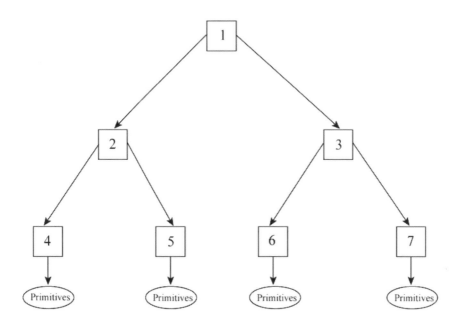

Figure 4.15: Hierarchy of OBBs in the form of a binary tree. Each OBB is partitioned into two parts, which become its children.

One issue that arises with OBBs is that internal vertices of the polyhedron, which are densely arranged, may have a negative influence on the eigenvectors that are used as the basis of the bounding box. Since it is undesirable for internal vertices to influence the orientation of the bounding box, a convex hull can be formed around the polyhedron and used in the calculation of the bounding box instead of the polyhedron itself. This significantly improves the fidelity of the bounding box, but densely arranged, nearly collinear vertices on the convex hull may cause misalignment of the OBB. To overcome this problem, a dense sampling of the convex hull can be performed by integrating over the surface of each triangle. The covariance and the mean can later be computed based on the sample points.

Chapter 5

Use of Virtual Environments in Training Applications

This chapter describes representative research and associated systems that have investigated learning from visual instruction and use of virtual environments in training and assembly planning. Representative virtual environment-based training tools are described in Section 5.1 to demonstrate some of the technologies being developed. The research on the ability to transfer skills from the virtual environment to the real world is discussed in Section 5.2. The research on the effect of presence, memory, and spatial abilities on learning is presented in Section 5.3. Work on the use of virtual environments to analyze device assembly design and process is detailed in Section 5.4. Finally, Section 5.5 describes work related to the development of intelligent tutoring systems for training applications.

5.1 Virtual Environment-Based Training Tools

Over the last few years many different training applications have emerged where the use of virtual environments is being explored. A significant amount of research in this field is devoted to teaching of motor skills. Representative areas where VE-based training research has received recent attention is in the medical field, where VE-based surgery training is growing [Peng et al., 2003; Morris et al., 2004; Tendick et al., 2000; Keehner et al., 2004; Chen and Marcus, 1998; Wiet et al., 2002; Lu et al., 2005] and in areas where mistakes in the assembly process are dangerous or expensive [Hodges, 1998; Gamberini et al., 2003; Duffy et al., 2003]. VE-based training is also finding use in preflight training operations to simulate certain aspects of microgravity and to be an effective countermeasure for space motion sickness and spatial disorientation [Stroud, 2005]. This section will describe representative applications from civilian and defense applications areas.

Two representative tools have been selected from the civilian domain to be discussed in detail in this section. Their ideas and designs, in some ways, parallel some of the design goals of VTS. One of these systems is virtual reality-based while the other is augmented reality-based.

He et al. point out that the conventional methods for the training of assembly and disassembly operations are carried out in the real world on physical prototypes in order for technicians to develop skills [He et al., 2003]. For training involving STEs (special type equipment), which may include radiant, explosive, or hazardous materials, this type of conventional training is largely inappropriate because of the inherent danger to trainees as well as the exceeding cost of prototypes. In response to this realization, researchers have proposed a virtual reality operation-training simulator featuring artificial intelligence to assist trainees in acquiring the highly technical assembly and disassembly skills necessary for maintenance of STEs.

In this work, three goals are established for their system. The first goal is to provide an immersive training environment. The second goal is to act as an operational tutorial and dynamic aid for assembly/ disassembly processes. The third goal is to provide force feedback in the virtual environment to allow the user "a kinesthetic sense of when he/she interacts with the virtual object." In order to accomplish these goals, the authors have described the groundwork and features necessary to develop such a system, which include an intelligent kinematics modeling system, a VE manager capable of hosting and categorizing interactions with the user, and an operation monitoring system capable of identifying difficulty with the assembly/disassembly process and providing the appropriate dynamic cues to assist the user.

The proposed kinematics modeling system works by dividing the part motion into two kinds: the motion controlled by the user's hand and the uncontrolled motion such as dropping or sliding an object. By using information from the virtual environment to provide an estimation of how the parts should act while part of a controlled or uncontrolled motion, the modeling becomes an economical approach and allows for a reasonably accurate representation of the physics of the parts within the VE while saving computational power. The virtual environment manager described by the authors is responsible for defining the assembly relations and the correct order for the assembly/disassembly process in order to assure the validity of the training program. Both the assembly relations and the order of the processes are defined within the manager using semantic constraints that identify how the assembly is named, how it is performed, and what entities are involved in the process (i.e., ID, description, constraint-set, entity-set). In order to provide the trainee with feedback and assistance during assembly sessions, the VE manager also includes the ability to detect the recurrence of incorrect assembly/disassembly motions by comparing them to a predefined set of ideal movements and to act on them by providing the user with some type of dynamic cue (video, audio) to help the trainee correctly complete the task.

The discussion of this proposed STE virtual reality training system identifies features that are important in order for virtual environments to be effective training aids for assembly/disassembly processes. By developing and describing their own system to deal with STEs, the authors have demonstrated that their vision of an appropriate VE includes a smart system with the ability to adapt to users with different skills, physical feedback, and efficient modeling of part physics. Their system is interesting because of their first two goals, to create a fully immersive environment and to allow their system to act as a dynamic aid for assembly/disassembly training, along the same lines as VTS's Virtual Author and Virtual Mentor. The force feedback is interesting but not in the scope of the work planned for VTS in order to maintain a low cost.

Yuan et al. describe an augmented reality (AR)-based system [Yuan et al., 2005]. A characteristic of many augmented reality systems in use today is the need for sensor systems or markers in order to keep track of the components being used and ultimately track the progress of the user within the assembly sequence. They propose an AR system with a predefined, easily accessed assembly sequence that uses a unique technique to track an interactive pen used to access the assembly data, all without the assistance of markers or sensor systems. The proposed system features a virtual interactive tool, Virtual Interactive Panel, which hosts virtual buttons that provide meaningful assembly information in addition to a visual assembly tree structure (VATS) to manage information and access assembly instructions.

The input device of the proposed system consists of an interactive pen featuring a segmented image map and an interactive point extracted as the input device. Using a neural network, the Virtual Interactive Panel is able to visually track the position of this interactive pen, which allows the user to select virtual buttons (by holding the interactive point on the pen over the desired button) that assist in the assembly process without the need of any sensing devices. These virtual buttons are capable of accessing different directories within the VATS so that users can provide themselves with additional information concerning a specific assembly step. The VATS is composed of organized, predefined instructions that allow the user to start the assembly process from the beginning or access data referring to specific parts and subassemblies. They used the assembly of a 'fun train' in order to demonstrate the AR system using both HMD and desktop configurations. The user is able to employ the interactive pen to select the assembly database, and through the use of confirmation Virtual Interactive Panel, continue through the assembly process, visually displaying the subsequent assembly steps by confirming the completion of the prior step.

They have demonstrated that it is possible to create a functioning AR system that does not need object markers to guide the user through an assembly task. With further development of the Virtual Interactive Panel software, the possibilities for AR training without the need for sensor systems make it a prime candidate for complex assembly procedures where numerous markers make the standard AR approach too difficult to monitor. The design presented here is not directly related to the VTS system because of the inherent differences between VR and AR. However, its implementation of the VATS may be of interest in a future iteration of the VTS.

In addition to the above described civilian applications, many applications have emerged in the defense-related areas where virtual reality-based tools and simulations are being used to improve training. The remainder of this section will describe representative training applications from defense-related domains.

Knerr and Lampton describe a system for training dismounted soldiers using virtual simulations [Knerr and Lampton, 2005]. They also conducted detailed evaluation of the system. As per their results, activities that can be performed well during simulations include identification of people, identification of tactically significant areas, and individual weapons use. On the other hand, activities such as indoor maneuvering and identification of the source of fire are difficult to perform during simulations. They concluded that the virtual simulation technology is now sufficiently mature to be included in the mix of training technologies.

Pelz et al. have developed training system simulation software for parachute mission planning using virtual reality simulations [Pelz et al., 2003]. This system models the terrain and winds. Multiple participants can interact with the same virtual space. Using this system, jumps can be rehearsed in unfamiliar territories. Users can create detailed models of the jump sites using terrain data, imagery, and forecasted wind speeds. According to the authors, this system is now available commercially. Further advances in their system allow multiple networked jumpers to coordinate their jumps and also enable use of a simulated navigational aid system [Hogue, 2003].

Lee presents a review of research in the area of immersive learning environments [Lee, 2007]. In addition to the immersive learning environments, a number of closely related technologies, such as intelligent tutoring, distributed training, and team training, are also covered in this work. The feasibility of integrating different learning technologies has been evaluated. Virtual environments are found to be realistic for individual and team training. In addition, virtual environments are found to be useful for virtual interaction between trainees and instructors. However, more thorough assessments are necessary to better understand the role of virtual environments.

Bachelder describes a system for helicopter aircrew training using fused reality [Bachelder, 2007]. Fused reality is defined to be a combination of live video capture, real time video editing, and simulation in virtual environments. A combination of these technologies is expected to enhance training realism significantly. This environment supports training for a wide variety of tasks, including door gunner targeting, cargo hook operations monitoring, and hover position control. The training environment has been constructed using off-the-shelf video hardware.

Andre et al. describe a training system for aircraft maintenance training application [Andre et al., 2003]. The initial system is called Virtual Environment Safe-for Maintenance Trainer. This system provides apprentice technicians with an opportunity to practice maintenance procedures associated with F-15E model aircraft. This system decreases the use of actual aircraft in training and hence creates new training opportunities. The system enables interactive experiences with front and rear crew stations, weapons stations, and the ground. The system evaluation results have indicated that improvements should be made in the areas of graphical representation and the joystick pointer. These improvements are planned to be incorporated in the new version of the system called Generalized Operations Simulation Environment.

Singer et al. describe experiments that were conducted by the US Army to determine the effects of VE system characteristics and instructional features in training applications [Singer et al., 2006]. The goal was to establish the benefits and problems associated with VE-based training and rehearsing complex activities and tasks. Detailed experiments were conducted to examine the effects of interrogative coaching and attention direction instructional features on the tasks involving recognition and decision skills. The analysis of experiments showed significant improvement on complex tasks related to Bounding Overwatch and Landing Zone. The interrogative coaching helps in skills acquisition, but at the same time, it increases the time to perform the task.

Badler and Allbeck describe a system called Advanced Visual and Instruction Systems for Maintenance Support [Badler and Allbeck,

2006]. This system explores the use of an HMD, wearable computers, new input devices, and augmented reality software in a training application. As a part of this system, instructions are generated from expert demonstrations. First, expert performance is captured via multi-media during demonstrations. Second, multi-media tracks are interactively cleaned up to generate task segments. Third, individual task segments are linked to entries in a parameterized action representation database. Fourth, parameterized action representations are returned as output for the interactive presentation. Finally, instructions are presented to the user via interactive manuals, augmented reality, or virtual reality.

5.2   Transfer of Knowledge

The transfer of knowledge from the virtual environment is a very important aspect of the VTS. It is also important to review the work that other researchers have performed and discuss their findings. There are several works that are discussed in this section. Even though some of these works do not discuss virtual reality-based training systems, all talk about skill transfer and/or assembly tasks from non-conventional 3D training systems and are, therefore, relevant to the development of VTS.

Boud et al. investigated whether various types of virtual (VR) and augmented (AR) reality training sessions are effective for the training of manual assembly tasks, such as assembly of a water pump [Boud et al., 1999]. They studied the mean completion times of the pump for five distinct training methods. The first method was conventional engineering drawings for the individual to study. The second method was a desktop VE application that included a monitor and 2D mouse. The third method was a desktop VE application that included stereoscopic glasses in addition to a monitor (to provide 3D images) and 2D mouse. The fourth method was an immersive VE environment that included an HMD, tracking system, and 3D mouse. The fifth method was a context-free AR system that included a see-through monocular HMD that provided a static display of the engineering drawings. Once the training sessions were completed, participants were then directed to assemble the water pump in the real world, and the mean times for assembly by each training method were used for comparison.

In order to conduct the experiment, 25 students with engineering backgrounds were divided into five groups of five and each group was trained for 10 minutes using a different method as discussed above. The group that trained with the conventional engineering drawings was given the full 10 minutes to study the drawings while the groups that trained with the VE systems were given 2 minutes to study the conventional engineering drawings and an additional 8 minutes to practice the assembly process within the virtual environment. Those individuals who were trained using the AR system were given 2 minutes to study the conventional drawings and an additional 8 minutes to view the drawings through the monocular viewing screen.

The experiments revealed that users who trained with the conventional method averaged a completion time of approximately 4 minutes while users who trained with the VE systems averaged a completion time of approximately 45 seconds. Furthermore, users who trained with the AR system averaged a completion time of approximately 15 seconds. Although it was clear that VR and AR systems were superior training methods when compared to the conventional method, it was also statistically proven that there existed a significant difference between the fastest VR (stereoscopic) and AR system results.

These findings again support the hypothesis that VR and AR training systems aid the learning process and lead to shorter assembly times when compared to the conventional methods of training through engineering drawings and written assembly procedures.

Boud et al. also introduce the concept of utilizing real instrumented objects (IOs) in order to provide the user with "tactile, force, and kinesthetic feedback" while immersed in the virtual environment [Boud et al., 2000]. For this study, the IOs used were constructed from wooden discs fitted with magnetic tracking devices. By tracking the IOs, positions and orientations of the virtual objects representing IOs could be updated. The goal of the investigation was to determine whether the implementation of a "hybrid, haptic-augmented VR system" would improve user performance when compared to real and virtual environment settings.

To achieve this, the experimenters selected four individuals having six months experience with the VR system and had them complete a simple ring and peg puzzle ("Tower of Hanoi") as a basic simulation of an assembly process. The five conditions under which the subjects had to operate were: "immersive VR and 3D mouse, immersive VR and IOs, desktop VR and conventional 2D mouse, real environment with real objects, and real environment, but blindfolded." The mean performance times to complete the puzzle under each condition were recorded from the data and compared. Additionally, a movement analysis was performed to compare the speeds with which the tasks were performed.

From the data collected, it was shown that there existed significant differences between the times of completion for the conditions. The 2D and 3D mouse conditions required an average of 35 seconds for completion while the IO condition required an average of approximately 22 seconds. The real condition required an average of 15 seconds, and the blindfolded required approximately 20 seconds. Additionally, a

Tukey pairwise comparison test identified significant differences between the IO and 2D, IO and 3D, real and 2D, real and 3D, real and IO, and blindfolded for both 2D and 3D. When a movement analysis of the small ring was conducted and compared between the real and IO conditions, it was revealed that movement onto and off the pegs was 3.5 times faster. Inter-peg movement was almost two times faster for the IO condition when compared to the real condition.

The assembly time superiority demonstrated by the IO condition over the standard immersive VR condition gives reason for the continued research and development of haptic systems to improve the viability and effectiveness of virtual environments for use in assembly training. By allowing users to rely on tactile feedback rather than visual feedback alone, virtual environments that feature haptics have the potential to decrease assembly times through faster learning curves. These results were interesting but are out of the scope of the current design and capabilities of VTS.

Pathomaree and Charoenseang discuss an augmented reality (AR) system to show that it was capable of transferring the skills of an assembly process more effectively than conventional methods [Pathomaree and Charoenseang, 2005]. In order to carry out the investigation, the authors gathered 20 participants to complete two sets from one of four experiments which included 2D assembly task with AR training, 2D assembly task without AR training, 3D assembly task with AR training, and 3D assembly task without AR training. During the 2D and 3D assembly tasks without AR training, the participants were asked to complete the puzzle given to them after witnessing a single complete build. Once the first unassisted build was completed, the participants were asked to build the 2D or 3D puzzle a second time. (Both completion times for the builds were recorded.) For the 2D and 3D assembly tasks with AR training, the participants were provided the assistance of augmented reality for the first build and then were asked to complete the build a second time without the aid of AR. Both completion times for the builds were recorded.

The completion times with the assistance of AR training were 85 percent shorter than those without it for the 2D puzzle on the first build, while completion times with AR were 61 percent shorter than those without it for the 2D puzzle on the second build. For the 3D puzzle, the reduction in times using the AR system was even better, with time savings of 96.2 percent and 92.6 percent for the first and second builds, respectively. Additionally, the total number of steps performed to complete the puzzle was recorded. With AR training for the 2D puzzle, 80 percent fewer steps were used to assemble during the first build while 65 percent fewer steps were used during the second. For the 3D puzzle,

AR training led to 93 percent and 84 percent fewer steps during the first and second builds, respectively. As a result of this data, the percentages of skill transferability were calculated to be 81.5 percent for the first build in 2D, 61.5 percent for the second build in 2D, 96.2 percent for the first build in 3D, and 92.6 percent for the second build in 3D. Lastly, it was calculated that on average, users of the AR training system made 0 excessive assembly steps on the 2D puzzle and 0.4 on the 3D puzzle.

As the results show, the utilization of an AR system to train an assembly sequence greatly improves user retention and performance. Not only did the AR quicken the user's ability to complete the puzzles provided, but it also demonstrated that it was an effective teaching tool through the minimization of unnecessary steps completed by users trained on the AR, as well as the users' ability to perform at the same level during the second build after the AR was disengaged.

Valimont et al. state that although AR clearly affords trainees various physical associations with the training information they are provided, it has yet to be proven that AR is an effective means to convey training information when compared to conventional methods [Valimont et al., 2002]. Their hypothesis states that through the support of multi-sensory interaction while training, users of AR systems are more likely to retain the information provided to them over conventional methods of training via video or paper manuals.

In order to conduct an experiment to validate their claim, these authors gathered 64 participants and divided them into four groups of 16 in order to train each group using four distinct methods: video instruction (observe group), interactive video instruction (interact group), AR instruction (select group), and print-based instruction (print group). The subject of the training sessions was the assembly of a Lycoming T-53 turbine engine vane-type oil pump. During training, the select group was allowed interaction with the disassembled oil pump and was shown the technical information through the AR system.

The observe group was provided a 3-minute video of the pump and its disassembled components. The interact group was provided the same video with the inclusion of the AR annotations. The print group was provided 9 freeze frame photos from the AR session with the necessary technical information. For the training sessions, individuals were given eight minutes to study the oil pump using their assigned group method, after which they were immediately tested (three minutes after the training was complete) on their comprehension of the functions, locations, and assemblies of the various oil pump components. An additional long-term retention test was also administered a week after the training session. Both tests were scored on a scale of 0 to 100 based on the individual's comprehension of the device.

For the short term recall test, the select group yielded the highest score of 88.3, followed by the observe group with 82.9, followed by the interact group with 78.3 and the print group with 77.5. The overall average of all of the groups was 81.8. On the long term recall test, the select group again yielded the highest score of 80.0, followed again by the observe group with a 72.5, the print group moved up one and came in third with a 71.3 followed by the interact group with a 69.2. The overall average for all the groups was 73.2.

Based on the results of the experimentation, an ANOVA analysis of the mean test scores for all four training groups failed to find a statistically significant difference for either test. Although this was the outcome, it is clear from the data provided by the authors that the individuals trained with the AR system were able to initially absorb more information than the other groups and interestingly enough, were able to retain more of their information later in the week than other groups. (The difference between the select and observe group in the 2nd test grew wider by the end of the week.)

The results from this study are encouraging, because they continue with the trend that AR systems are more effective at conveying information than conventional methods. Additionally, the fact that at the end of the week the select group which trained with the AR system was retaining more of the information than other groups may be evidence that training with AR encourages the storage of information in long-term memory.

Rose et al. set out to understand whether training in virtual reality offers the true potential for skill transfer when compared to that in the real world [Rose et al., 2000]. Additionally, the study was an analysis of whether training in the virtual environment (VE) is cognitively simpler than that in the real world. In order to study these comparisons, the authors gathered together 250 participants to perform three distinct experiments that were based on the completion of a steadiness test. The steadiness test was selected because it allowed for the equivalence of sensory and motor aspects of the real and virtual training worlds. The steadiness test involved the navigation of a deformed length of wire using a wire loop that signals the user when contact is made, much like the kind one would find at an amusement park. The first experiment was designed to study the extent of training transfer from the VE to the real world and was conducted by training three different groups of individuals (one group trained using VE, one group trained using real objects, and one group had no training) and recording the number of errors made while navigating the wire length. Using the outcome from the first experiment, the authors set out to determine whether there existed any significant differences in the way people learn from the VE and real world training exercises and what portion of their cognitive resources they used during the training through the second and third experiments. In order to do this, the second experiment was conducted by dividing the VE and real world trainees into two sub-groups: motor interference and cognitive interference. Members of the motor interference sub-group were required to tap on a Morse code key to the cue of a tempo at two beats per second while completing the steadiness test. Members of the cognitive interference sub-group were required to listen for the names of predetermined fruits interspersed within strings of random words and say 'yes' when they occurred during the testing. The third experiment was conducted by subjecting the participants in the two training groups (real and VE) to visual (5 colors displayed on a nearby TV screen) and auditory (3 distinct tones) cues to be recalled at the completion of the steadiness test.

After the results from the second experiment were analyzed, it was determined that the motor interference during testing had a more disruptive effect than the cognitive interference for both the VE and real training sessions. Additionally, it was determined at the statistically significant level that the VE-trained participants were less influenced by the introduction of interference than those who were trained in the real world. As for the third experiment, it was determined through independent t-tests that there existed no discernible difference between the real and VE trained participants for either the visual or audio cues recalled.

Although the results from experiments two and three appear to oppose each other (the reasoning is that the conclusion from experiment two points to the fact that VE training is less cognitively taxing and therefore should lead to higher performance recalling cues for experiment three, which was not the case), there exists a theory that may explain the trends of the data. As theorized by the authors, in VE training, the disconnect of visual feedback from other sensory feedbacks that are commonplace in real world training make the task in the virtual environment more difficult and cognitively taxing than its counterpart in the real world. As a result, when VE trainees move into the real world to test their trained skills, they are graced with a surplus of cognitive capacity allowing them to cope with interference as was supplied from experiment two. The significance of this outcome might suggest that all complex or dangerous assembly tasks should be trained within VEs in order to ensure that trainees have the maximum cognitive capacity while working on the real world task.

Hamblin evaluated the transfer of knowledge and training efficiency of virtual environments (HMD and screen display-based) for a complex manual assembly task [Hamblin, 2005]. The two tasks selected for the completion of the investigation were the post training assembly of a Lego forklift model as well as that of a Lego race car that utilized the same parts as the forklift model but with a different configuration (to determine the transfer of learning). During the study, 48 participants of comparable assembly skills were divided into two groups of fast and slow builders to ensure an even distribution of build times. These groups were further broken down into four divisions within each of the fast and slow build groups in order to administer the different training methods: immersive virtual environment using a HMD and a pair of touch gloves, PC-based virtual environment using a monitor screen and 2D mouse, real world, and none at all. With regards to the three active training methods, participants of these groups were trained a total of four times over four days in order to familiarize them with the technologies they would be using to complete the training, as well as observe and interact with the assembly sequence they would be tested on at the end of the study. Each training session consisted of the participant completing the assembly of the forklift one time within their assigned environment as quickly and accurately as possible. Time used for familiarization with the hardware used was not counted as training.   During the experiment, the participants were asked to perform an initial build, pre-training, and an additional post-training build for the forklift model. The assembly times for these builds were recorded for analysis between build and training groups.

From the data collected, it was determined through a 2 X 4 between-subjects ANOVA that there existed a significant difference in improvement times (post-training assembly time subtracted from pre-training assembly time) across the training methods. A comparison analysis using Tukey's HSD revealed that the real world training group improved the most while the HMD and PC-based virtual environment training methods were similar to one another and showed significant improvement over the group with no training. In terms of transfer of training, it was demonstrated through a 2 X 3 between-subjects ANOVA that there existed a significant difference across the training methods. Again the real world training method was at the top with the highest ratio of transfer of training at approximately 225 percent, while the virtual reality training methods both achieved moderate, insignificantly different levels at approximately 140 percent. The transfer of learning study conducted with the assembly of the race car after the forklift assembly provided inconclusive data due to a high amount of variance, but the author claims that visual inspection of the data shows that some learning did occur for individuals within the slow builder group trained using virtual environments. The conclusions that can be drawn from this study from data presented above are: (1) VE training is an effective method for training real world tasks, although not as effective as real world training itself, and (2) real world training is more efficient than VE training at teaching skills that may be transferred to other tasks, although VE does an effective job in this area as well. Due to this outcome, it seems fair to say that VE training is better suited to training dangerous or otherwise costly tasks in the real world, whereas if safety and cost are not a concern, real world training is the way to go.

There have been a number of other studies which suggest that certain elements of virtual environments are conducive to the transfer of knowledge. In many applications, visual instructions are significantly more effective than textual instructions. Research has confirmed that animations showing the step-by-step procedures have facilitated the learning of procedural knowledge [Mayer, 2001; Sweller, 1999; Zacks et al., 2001]. Considerable progress has been made in the area of investigation of the role of visual media in learning based on cognitive load theories. The use of virtual environments for training has been shown to increase cognitive stimulation over traditional training methods [Mikropoulos, 2001; Camachon, 2004; Ashby and Maddox, 2005; Romano and Brna, 2001; Tracy et al., 2003; Green and Flowers, 2003; Kalyuga et al., 2004; Hsi et al., 1997]. Studies have also been performed to measure effectiveness of visual instructions and the role of multimedia instructions (i.e., instructions that either include text or audio in addition to visual instructions). Recent representative studies in this area show that cueing effects increase the effectiveness of multimedia instructions in terms of better learning results or less mental effort spent [Tabbers et al., 2004; Bodemer et al., 2004; Klatzky et al., 2002; Piburn et al., 2005].

5.3   Effects of Presence, Memory, and Spatial Abilities on Learning

Virtual reality has emerged as a technology capable of training users to perform specific tasks. While virtual reality is not a new technology to the scientific community, only recently has the hardware finally been developed to a performance level that allows the full potential of virtual reality to be realized. Because virtual systems are immersive, they can act as learning environments for the user, affecting the cognitive and spatial learning of the user.

Because of the ability for virtual reality to provide audio/visual/haptic feedback to the user, while still being flexible enough to control the situation presented to the user, virtual reality can serve as an important tool for training. However, in order for these senses to be fully utilized and for knowledge to be transferred from the virtual environment to the real world, a high sense of presence must be experienced by the user.

Romano and Brna investigated the importance of presence within a virtual world. They propose that to achieve a strong sense of presence, the type of interface selected is important [Romano and Brna, 2001]. While desktop interfaces are inexpensive and the most accessible of the interfaces, they do not allow the user to navigate within the virtual world using natural body movements, which will affect the amount of learning that takes place. Therefore, more immersive displays, such as HMDs, may provide better learning experiences for the user. But while immersive displays may be better suited for object manipulation systems, desktop displays, through which immersion and learning can still be achieved, better minimize the effects of motion sickness.

In addition to the interface, they also look at the set-up of the virtual world itself. The virtual environment need not be created to exactly replicate the real world. It should, instead, be altered in order to take advantage of the ability of the program to account for various, possible real-life situations. The world should first be created to fully meet the learning requirements desired of the program, as this is its main purpose.

The system analyzed by Romano and Brna, called ACTIVE, is a virtual environment used to train fire-fighters. ACTIVE will provide both a 3D virtual world and also what the authors call "superpowers" - situational awareness that the user would generally not have available to him in the real world, such as the ability to change the time within the simulation and to change points of views in the world. In the end, though, it is inconclusive as to whether these superpowers available to the user, that are not available in the real world, affect the person's sense of presence within the virtual world.

Bystrom and Barfield also investigated the effect of presence on learning [Bystrom and Barfield, 1999]. They claim that two main factors exist in determining how useful a virtual environment is in regards to learning: high level of presence within a virtual environment and the ability for participants to collaborate with each other in the virtual environment. Collaboration within a virtual environment can be either in the form of a distributed virtual environment or a "copresent" virtual environment. A distributed virtual environment consists of multiple users that are in different locations and have different points of view with respect to each other within the virtual world. In contrast, the users in a "copresent" virtual environment share the same tracking perspective within the environment and physically close to each other. Three aspects of collaborative virtual learning in their experiment were identified: the effects of copresent collaboration on the sense of presence and on task performance, the effect of control of movement on users' learning, especially in copresent virtual environments, where different participants may experience different sense of presence, and finally the effect on task performance in a copresent virtual environment.

In order to test these aspects, the authors examined three aspects of collaborative learning. The first aspect was the effect of copresence examined by comparing the results of one participant working alone to the results of two participants working collaboratively. The second aspect was the level of control of movement and navigation. The third aspect was the effect of head tracking on the sense of presence and task performance. According to questionnaire responses, sense of presence was not affected by shared or singular experiences within the virtual environment. Sense of presence was also not affected by use of head-tracking. Based on participants' responses, the use of head-tracking only affected the participants' sense of realism of movement within the VE. This may be because it was realized that few people fully utilized the capability that comes from the head-tracking device. Also, a slower update rate may have affected the person's sense of presence in the virtual environment. Based on this, it was determined that head-tracking would be most beneficial in a copresent world that only required one viewpoint for all participants.

Copresence made a significant difference in task performance, as more objects were found during the partner trials. Also, having no head-tracking ability slightly affected task performance with fewer items found. The trial with a singular participant using only the pre-determined guided tour resulted in the lowest results — much lower than the other trials with fairly similar results. Copresence did not affect the individual's own sense of presence within the virtual world, but people who knew each other before the experiment and then worked together for the partner trials had a slightly higher sense of presence in the virtual environment.

Based on the results of this experiment, it was determined that developers of virtual environments should focus simply on creating a realistic virtual environment for one person because they do not have to focus on the copresent aspect, as it does not lead to higher levels of presence and does not necessarily result in greater task performance results.

Mania and Chalmers assert that memory is another significant aspect of learning associated with virtual reality [Mania and Chalmers, 2001]. They focus specifically on the differences that arise between memory learning in the real world and virtual worlds. They first distinguish between the terms immersion and presence as used in virtual environments. They refer to immersion as being the "quantifiable description of technology" and presence as being more like a "state of consciousness." Presence can be considered the "illusion of nonmediation"; the user is unaware that he is learning through a different medium. He believes that he is actually experiencing the event. Mania and Chalmers also distinguish between realistic virtual worlds, which are realistic simulations of the real world that focus on "means over ends" to allow for transfer of information to the real world, and magical virtual worlds, which are simulations of the real world that tend to ignore some real world "rules" and have no final real world application.

Because the authors believe that "one way of getting an objective baseline for effectiveness of an application is to evaluate that against the real world," the experiment addressed in this work focuses on comparing experiences in the real world to experiences in the virtual world, viewed through shutter glasses and a desktop monitor.

It was determined that there was no real difference in task performance between the two types of displays within the virtual world. Memory recall was higher, however, for the real world experience. In regards to presence, those in the real world set-up experienced higher levels of presence, which was expected. The authors attribute the main difference in results between the real world and the virtual world to the current limitations of technology.

Waller discusses the importance of the transfer of spatial ability and that it is necessary to allow for learning to take place in the real world [Waller, 2005]. In order for a person to acquire spatial information about a particular environment, the person must obtain the ability to manage changes that take place regarding objects in the environment and the person himself and also the ability to detect spatial relationships that have not been directly provided by the environment.

To test a person's spatial ability, a desktop virtual reality program called the WALKABOUT was created. The purpose of the WALKABOUT was to test these two factors in spatial ability, calling them UPDATE and PERSPECTIVE, which measured the person's ability to infer spatial information. Errors in PERSPECTIVE were fairly accurate at predicting a person's ability to accurately locate unknown locations within an environment, as much as a person's own sense of direction. Errors in UPDATE were also related to a person's ability to locate positions in the environment. The experiment demonstrated that, of the two characteristics related to spatial knowledge, neither was more closely related to spatial knowledge ability than the other. Virtual reality was useful in conducting this test because it allowed for greater control over the experiment and its variables. However, one limitation that arose was the virtual environment's inability to incorporate other sensory features that could add to a person's acquired spatial knowledge.

Johansson and Ynnerman look at the different options in virtual interfaces and then assess each to determine which interface is the best to use, based on detection time and the number of successful trials [Johansson and Ynnerman, 2004]. According to their experiment, visual content accounts for about 80 percent of the information processed by the brain. This means that vision will have a large impact on the user's sense of immersion in the virtual environment presented to him. Three types of visual interfaces were studied in the experiment: an immersive workbench, a desktop virtual environment, and a desktop-based non-immersive display.

The purpose of the experiment was to find errors in a product presented on each display. Results of the experiment showed that the Desktop-VE was the medium which produced the shortest detection times, while the use of the immersive workbench showed the greatest improvements in time. In terms of the number of successful trials, all three displays showed improvements, while the desktop display showed the greatest number of successful trials. The experiment also showed that, as users became more familiar with the displays, the results improved. It was also observed that the non-immersive desktop display provided the most learning at the beginning of the experiment, but the desktop-VE and immersive workbench, which showed similar learning curves, provided the best learning overall. The reason for this is speculated to be because people were more familiar with the desktop display than the other two methods, meaning that they did not have to learn it as they performed the experiment. At the same time, the differences in learning may not be enough to make up the significant differences in cost. Overall, there seemed to be little difference between the three displays. If more training was provided for the desktop-VE and the immersive workbench methods, better results may have been achieved in the end because they showed greater overall learning.

5.4   Assembly Design and Planning in Virtual Environments

Virtual environments have a great potential to improve the assembly design and manufacturing process. By analyzing the assembly process for a device inside a virtual environment, the engineer can detect problems in the design early in the design process. After the individual components of an assembly have been modeled in a CAD system, the engineer must perform assembly planning to come up with the most efficient and reliable way for operators to assemble the device. In the absence of a virtual environment, the engineer must perform the assembly planning either using the CAD system, which is difficult and error-prone, or using a physical prototype, which can be expensive. If the designed device is very large, then a scaled down version of the prototype may have to be created. The scaled down prototype may conceal assembly issues that affect its full scale version. The CAD system often does not provide a convenient interface to experiment with different assembly possibilities. Engineers generally interact with CAD systems using keyboard and mouse. The virtual environment allows an engineer to duplicate a shop floor environment and load full scale virtual models into an environment where the engineer can quickly try out different assembly possibilities using an intuitive, realistic interface composed of data gloves, trackers, and stereo display. This allows the engineer to detect accessibility and part interference problems early in the manufacturing process. It also allows the engineer to quickly explore many assembly possibilities in order to come up with a good assembly plan in an environment which mimics reality with physics-based modeling and collision detection.

A significant amount of recent research on virtual environments has been dedicated to simulation of spatial manipulation tasks in the context of mechanical design, assembly planning and assembly evaluation. Such applications are often very similar to the virtual reality-based applications designed specifically for assembly training. The primary focus on this work is development of new algorithms and software to support real-time and accurate collision detection, physics-based modeling, and assembly path planning. Recent representative works in this area include Detailed Virtual Design System [Arangarasan and Adh, 2000], Design Synthesis Virtual Environment [Maxwell et al., 2001], Virtual Assembly Design Environment [Taylor et al.; 2000], Multi-Modal Immersive Virtual Assembly System [Wan et al., 2004; Jayaram et al., 2004], Prototyping and Design for Assembly Analysis Using Multi-modal Virtual Environments [Gupta et al., 1997], Modeling of Flexible Components for Assembly Path Planning [Mikchevitch et al., 2003], and Virtual Reality Based Decision Support Framework for Manufacturing Simulation [Banerjee and Cecil, 2003]. The secondary focus in this area is the development of new user interfaces for humans to interact with the virtual environments. Representative work in this area includes [Kim and Vance, 2003; Jayaram et al., 2000]. Other references of interest to spatial manipulation tasks include the following work [Chun and Jiang, 2003; Endo and Takeda, 2004; Mania et al., 2003; Wilson and Peruch, 2002; Holl et al., 2003; Wann and Monwilliams, 1996; Bischof, 2004; Klatzky et al., 2002]. In the remainder of this section we will describe representative work in the area of assembly planning and analysis.

One example of a virtual reality system which was built to assist in assembly planning is called the Virtual Environment for General

ASsembly, (VEGAS) [Kim and Vance, 2003]. This VR application uses a six-sided CAVE as its platform that is 10 ft. X 10 ft. X 10 ft. VEGAS uses six rear projected surfaces that make up the walls, ceiling and floor. It uses stereo shutter glasses that are synchronized with the graphics computer to alternately display images for the left eye and the right eye. The graphics computer is a 24 processor Onyx2 Reality Monster, which provides six InfiniteReality2 graphics pipes. A magnetic tracking system is used to track the user's head and hands. The initial version of VEGAS used a wand; however, the later version used two wireless 5DT Data Gloves.

VEGAS relies on fast collision detection and physics-based modeling. For this purpose, it uses a software called Voxmap PointShell (VPS) developed at Boeing. VEGAS uses geo file format as the graphic model input. The models are first loaded into Engineering Animation's VisModel software to perform polygon decimation in order to decrease the number of polygons. The VPS package then converts the polyhedrons into a voxmap that is made up of small voxels or cubes. The voxmaps are used to perform collision detection and physics-based modeling. Use of voxmaps allows the collision detection software to be very fast, but reduces the accuracy of collision detection. Users pick up virtual parts by using certain gestures and by causing collisions between hand and part models. When a part is picked up, its new location is calculated based on the external force or torque. The external force is a combination of the spring force, the collision force, and the viscous force. The new position is used to update a new spring force and torque. VEGAS allows engineers to analyze assembly paths for part interference and accessibility.

Another virtual reality system called VADE has been developed at Washington State University [Jayaram et al., 1999]. Unlike VEGAS, which uses the CAVE method of stereo display, VADE uses a head mounted display (HMD). VADE uses a magnetic tracking system called Flock of Birds to keep track of the user's head and hands. It also uses the CyberGrasp glove to track finger positions and provide haptic feedback. A six processor SGI Onyx2 machine uses two Infinite Reality pipes to send stereo image output to the HMD.

VADE assists engineers in assembly design evaluation, assembly plan analysis, maintenance verification, and on-the-fly part modification inside the virtual environment. Physics-based modeling algorithms were developed using friction, number of contacts, and direction of force to allow users to perform fine motor manipulations of virtual parts using one or two hands. VADE's real-time hand-to-object interaction involves checking for intersections between the polygons of a part and the "hair sensors" of the virtual hands. The hair sensors are lines projecting from the triangles of a hand along the triangle normals. The number of hair sensors used can be adjusted based on the computer's processing power. For attachment of parts, VADE uses constraints extracted from the CAD system – ProEngineer. During insertion, a part is allowed to move only along certain axes and planes in order to avoid computationally expensive numerical methods. VADE provides tight integration with the CAD system by allowing certain parameters like hole radius and chamfer angle tagged in the CAD system to be dynamically adjusted inside the virtual environment using menus. In addition to the capabilities mentioned so far, VADE offers real-time collision detection, simulation of dynamic behaviors of objects held in the user's hand, simulation of ballistic motion, and simulation of behaviors of a part that is constrained by a base or container part. Test cases performed with VADE showed that the overall assembly process can be simulated realistically using the virtual environment.

A system called VEDA developed by Gupta et al. explored the viability of using VR applications to estimate ease of part handling and insertion [Gupta et al., 1997]. VEDA offered a multi-modal virtual environment with visual, auditory, and haptic senses given to the user. VEDA employed two PHANTOM 3D probes (6DOF mechanical trackers) for interaction with the virtual environment and StereoGraphics CrystalEyes shutter glasses for stereo viewing. A Silicon Graphics Indigo Extreme computer with a 100MHz processor was used to run the application. The PHANTOM devices were used to track two points representing the user's index finger and thumb. PHANTOM devices were also used to provide force feedback to the user.

VEDA analyzed how users carried out a simple "peg-in-hole" task in both the virtual environment and the real environment. This work was limited to investigating interactions between two-dimensional polyhedral objects. Due to the simplicity of the task, physics-based modeling was performed in only two dimensions. Only two force components and one torque component in the plane could be generated by contact between the peg and the hole or between the virtual fingers and a peg. Users were asked to insert pegs into holes inside the virtual environment and in a real environment. Using time of assembly as the main performance measure, this research found that trends in the variation of assembly time with parameters such as friction, chamfer, clearance, and handling distance were the same in the real world and VE. Specifically, assembly completion times in the virtual environment conveyed subtle differences in clearance, handling distance, and other parameters.

Ye et al. compared the use of virtual environments in assembly planning to some of the conventional methods of assembly planning [Ye et al., 1999]. They used fifteen volunteers to carry out assembly planning using three different methods: traditional engineering environment (TE), where paper drawings were used to analyze and plan the assembly; a non-immersive desktop VR environment (DVR); and an immersive virtual environment using a CAVE (CVR). The DVR environment was run by a Silicon Graphics workstation executing a VRML browser plug-in called CosmoPlayer. CAD models were converted to VRML format and displayed by the browser plug-in. The CVR environment was run by a CAVE system developed at the Electronic Visualization Laboratory, University of Illinois at Chicago. A magnetic tracking system was used to track the user's head and a wand. In the CVR environment the subject used a wand to interact with 3D virtual models. In the DVR environment, a mouse was used for interaction.

An air-cylinder assembly consisting of 34 parts was used in the testing of the three environments. To evaluate the performance of the subjects, the researchers used the following metrics to measure the "goodness" of the generated assembly plans: reorientation, handling difficulty, similarity, and stability. The reorientation metric measured the number of excessive part reorientations. The handling difficulty metric measured the number of difficult assembly operations, often resulting from instability of the assembly. The similarity metric measured whether similar parts are put together in a similar manner to ensure efficiency. Stability measured whether the components of a subassembly were securely or loosely attached to each other. The experiments revealed that using the two VR environments, subjects were able to achieve significantly better scores in the reorientation, handling difficulty, and similarity criteria when compared to the TE environment. The visualization of the entire assembly and the ability to manipulate and move parts around allowed the volunteers to produce better assembly plans.

5.5 Development of Intelligent Tutoring Systems for Training Applications

Generating instructional material for intelligent tutoring systems is a very challenging task. Hence, recent work in this area is focused on the use of interactive demonstrations as a means for conveniently creating tutorials. An example of this type of authoring tool is the Cognitive Tutor Authoring Tool (CTAT) [Koedinger et al., 2004]. CTAT builds math tutorials by demonstration. The author performs a scenario using a windows based GUI, while the system records the procedure. The author must also manually demonstrate all alternative correct and incorrect solution paths. With CTAT, the author manually annotates steps with hint and error messages. Another example of this type of authoring tool is RIDES [Munro and Towne, 1992], which can train nurses to use medical equipment, among other uses. In simple mode, RIDES allows an author to "record" a procedure that students must learn, simply by carrying out the procedure in a window-based user interface. During training the student is asked to carry out the correct sequence of actions. While training, the student receives meaningful generated feedback. In a more advanced authoring mode the author can write event-based behaviors to achieve special effects using a procedural script like language. VIVIDS is a more advanced descendent of RIDES which can build lessons for use in Virtual Reality and employs an autonomous agent that can observe and critique student actions. Other representative examples include [Hsieh et al., 1999; Jong and Van Joolingen, 1998]. Existing applications in this area so far have not been based on demonstrations of motions in PVEs. Interactive demonstrations in PVEs require new types of algorithms for automated tutorial authoring.

Detecting errors made by trainees during training sessions and generating hints to provide them meaningful feedback is an important aspect of intelligent tutoring system. An example of a system that uses these techniques is the Georgia Tech Visual and Inspectable Tutor and Assistant [Chu et al., 1995], a tutoring system designed to teach satellite control and monitoring operations. Lessons can be assigned one of many styles of tutoring ranging from demonstration via animation with little control of the lesson by the user to system monitoring of trainee progress with only occasional intervention by the system. In effect, the tutor "fades" as the trainee progresses through the curriculum. Each lesson specifies performance requirements, which the student must satisfy to proceed to the next lesson. Another example of this type of system is "Steve" [Rickel and Johnson, 1999], an animated agent who helps students learn to perform procedural, physical tasks in a virtual environment. Steve can demonstrate tasks, monitor students and provide basic feedback when prompted by the trainee. Steve signals mistakes with shaking of the head and saying "No". Other representative examples include [Paiva and Machado, 1998].

Recent advances in this area are focused on the development of the next generation tutorials that can adapt their instructions based on users' capability and progress. Such systems, which adapt instructions to specific users, often use machine learning techniques from the artificial intelligence community. An example of this is AgentX [Martin and Arroyo, 2004], which uses Reinforcement Learning to cluster students into learning levels. AgentX chooses subsets of all hints for a problem (instead of showing all possible hints) based on student's learning level. Students are grouped into levels based on pretests and their subsequent performance. If pretest data is not available for a student, then that student is automatically placed in level L4, which represents students who perform in the 50th percentile of the performance distribution. Other works in this category include [Aimeur et al., 2002; Gertner et al., 1998; Beck and Woolf, 2000; Beck et al. 2000, Hsieh and Hsieh, 2004; Woolf, 1996; Murray et al., 2004; Heffernan et al., 2004].

Intelligent tutoring systems are also being used in defense-related applications. As an example, we will discuss an intelligent tutoring system called Virtual Sand Table [Wisher et al., 2001]. This system was developed for use in Army training applications. The system enables instructors to conduct remote training. An evaluation was conducted to compare the performance of users who trained using the conventional methods with the performance of users who trained using the intelligent tutoring system on sand table exercises. The evaluation results demonstrated superior performance by those who trained using the intelligent tutoring system. The training tasks included higher order cognitive skills such as analysis, synthesis, decision making, and evaluation.

Chapter 6

Virtual Training Studio

In this chapter, the authors discuss the development of the Virtual Training Studio (VTS), a virtual environment-based training system developed at the Center for Energetic Concepts Development at the University of Maryland, which allows training supervisors to create training instructions and allows trainees to learn assembly operations in a virtual environment. The authors were the primary developers of the system. VTS is mainly focused on the cognitive side of training so that trainees can learn to recognize parts, remember assembly sequences, and correctly orient the parts during assembly operations. VTS enables users to train using the following three training modes: (1) interactive simulation, (2) 3D animation, and (3) video. We will discuss the hardware requirements and selection, software architecture and design, and the rationale for certain hardware and software decisions. In this chapter, we will also present a core component of the VTS called Virtual Workspace.

Section 6.1 provides background information. Section 6.2 presents hardware requirements that were put together for VTS. It also discusses selected hardware components which were chosen to satisfy the requirements. Section 6.3 discusses software architecture and, in particular, software requirements, software design, Virtual Workspace and its design rationale.

6.1 Background

The workforce in most industries requires continued training and updating. Current training methods, for the most part, involve a combination of paper-based manuals, DVD/video-based instructions, and/or hands-on master/apprentice training. Due to the rapid influx of new and changing technologies and their associated complexities, accelerated training is a necessity in order to maintain an advanced and educated workforce. Existing training methods can be further improved in terms of cost, effectiveness, time expenditure, and quality through the use of digital technologies, such as virtual environments (VE). The advent of personal virtual environments offers many new possibilities for creating accelerated training technologies.

Our exploratory studies indicated that people preferred to utilize the virtual environment differently for training purposes, based on the task at hand and the individual training styles of the user. Sometimes, it is useful to get 3D visual clues from 3D animation; sometimes, it is useful to see images of real parts; and sometimes, practicing assembly tasks in the virtual environment helps facilitate training and aids in transferring that knowledge to real life. To meet this requirement, VTS supports three different training modes.

The virtual environment-based training system we have developed is called Virtual Training Studio (VTS). The VTS aims to improve existing training methods through the use of a virtual environment-based multi-media training infrastructure that allows users to learn using different modes of instruction presentation, while focusing mainly on cognitive aspects of training as opposed to highly realistic physics-based simulations. The VTS is composed of the following three modules: Virtual Workspace, Virtual Author, and Virtual Mentor. Virtual Workspace provides the underlying VE multi-modal infrastructure. It provides the platform for the other two modules to function and integrates the hardware and software into a cohesive package. Virtual Author is a component of the VTS that allows non-programmers to quickly create new tutorials. Virtual Mentor is a module, running on top of the Virtual Workspace, which checks for user errors, assists users in the training process and provides additional details to further clarify the action required.

The VTS system has two main goals. The first goal is to ensure that virtual environment-based instructions for training personnel in the manufacturing industry can be created quickly, so an overall training cost reduction can potentially be realized through the use of our system. The second goal is to accelerate the training process for the trainees through the use of multi-modal virtual environment-based instructions. With VTS, training supervisors have the option of using a wide variety of multi-media options such as 3D animations, videos, text, audio, and interactive simulations to create training instructions. The virtual environment enables trainees to practice instructions using interactive simulation and hence reduces the need for practicing with physical components. The system is mainly geared toward cognitive skills –

training workers to recognize parts, learn assembly sequences, and correctly orient the parts in space for assembly. The VTS was designed to be an affordable personal virtual environment (PVE) for training. We developed a low cost wand design and used an off-the-shelf head mounted display (HMD). The level of physics-based modeling that has been implemented as well as the hardware selected reflects this design decision. The VTS system architecture is shown in Figure 6.1.

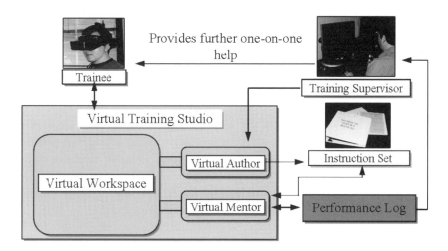

Figure 6.1: Virtual Training Studio architecture

6.2   Hardware

6.2.1 *Hardware Requirements*

The first requirement was to create an interactive training environment that would afford trainees the opportunity to interact, learn and make mistakes in a safe, controlled environment. This requirement pushed us towards virtual reality (VR) as the platform for this research project. We believe the VR interface is more intuitive than the interface of a desktop personal computer (PC)-based application. Another benefit to using VR technology is that it offers stereo vision which helps in the visualization of the assembly process, part recognition, and part alignment. Unfortunately, virtual reality can also be somewhat costly. For this reason, there has to be both a VR version and a desktop PC version of Virtual Training Studio. The desktop version must be able to run on a modern PC running a Windows operating system. This allows organizations operating with smaller budgets to realize most of the benefits of the Virtual Training Studio without the added cost of the hardware required to be fully immersed in the virtual environment. The base system can easily be upgraded to a fully immersive VR environment at any time.

Taking into account the types of organizations and users that might utilize VTS in the future, we came up with the following requirements for the hardware:

- Stereo vision
- Low cost
- High fidelity
- Ease of maintenance, configuration and use
- Large tracking area

Stereo vision is important for VTS because it improves navigation in the virtual environment and, more importantly, we believe it will help the trainee visualize the assembly process more realistically. Because of the inherent difficulty of depth perception on a 2D PC monitor, viewing 3D animations on a 2D monitor could make it challenging for some trainees to determine the path of parts in motion during animation.

Another important system design criterion is that it should be possible to build Virtual Training Studio on a modest budget. The system should not be very expensive to purchase, use or maintain. Many organizations already have relatively low cost training processes in place, so if the cost of the system is too high, fewer organizations will be willing to replace or supplement their current training practices with a more expensive virtual reality-based system.

The decision to make fidelity as well as ease of maintenance and configuration a requirement has to do with our perception of who will most likely use our system. Broadly speaking, there are two types of potential users of VTS. The first type of user is the trainer – training supervisors and experienced engineers who will create the tutorials. These people will most likely make up a minority of all those who would use VTS. The other type of user is the trainee – personnel who would use the system to learn an assembly/disassembly process and would use that knowledge and training to perform that operation. The latter users will most likely make up the majority of all those using our system. The personnel in training will not necessarily have a significant amount of computer and software experience. As a result, it is likely that many personnel will face difficulties in the event the system requires reconfiguration or a malfunction occurs. For this reason, it is important to reduce the chance for malfunctions as much as possible. Hence, we decided to acquire hardware that is reliable, stable, and easy to configure. In the event of interference from objects/forces in the tracking area, the system must be either easily reconfigurable or the interferences must be easy to eliminate.

It was also decided that VTS requires hardware that is capable of accommodating a potentially large tracking area. Certain training situations may require the operator to walk significant distances. For example, the operator might need to walk from one room to another to activate a machine or to walk from one large machine tool to another large machine tool. In the case of using multiple rooms, it may be possible to scale down the size of the actual rooms inside the virtual reality environment, but the user would still need to walk significant distances in the virtual reality environment.

6.2.2 Selected Components

To implement the Virtual Reality interface and to satisfy the requirements mentioned in the previous section, we chose to use the following hardware components:

- Precision Position Tracker (PPT) by WorldViz using four cameras, two infrared lights, and one tracking computer
- Two Intersense InertiaCubes
- Wireless wand (mouse/presenter) by Targus
- Virtual Research V8 Head Mounted Display
- Application computer (high end PC) by DELL

The Precision Position Tracker is an optical tracking system, composed of four cameras and a dedicated PC for processing the data from the cameras [WorldViz, 2004; WorldViz, 2006]. The four cameras track infrared markers (lights) to determine their X, Y, Z position. One marker is placed at the tip of the wand while the other is mounted on top of the HMD worn by the user. The PPT system uses a triangulation algorithm to determine the location of the markers. The tracking computer then transmits the data to the application computer, which executes the training program and generates graphics for the HMD. The PPT system can also be purchased as a dual camera version; however, the dual camera version is susceptible to occlusion problems and is not as reliable as the four camera setup. The PPT is immune to most forms of interference such as metals in the area and magnetic fields and it supports a very large tracking area (10 meters X 10 meters). It is important to prevent the four cameras from moving in any way after they have been set up and configured, otherwise reconfiguration will be necessary. For this reason we mounted the four trackers securely to the walls. High intensity infrared light, such as sunlight coming from a window or incandescent lamps, in the tracking area can interfere with the PPT, but those forms of interference, we found, are easy to eliminate by covering windows with curtains and using fluorescent bulbs to illuminate the tracking area.

The orientation of the wand and the orientation of the user's head are measured by two InertiaCube2 inertial tracking devices [Intersense, 2006]. These devices were selected for their low cost and ability to be easily integrated into the system. One of the InertiaCubes is attached to the top of the HMD and the second is attached to the front of the wand. It should be noted that the magnetometers inside an InertiaCube2 are susceptible to interference from metal objects in close proximity to the device. Aside from the problem of metal interference, which is easily overcome, the Intersense InertiaCubes work reasonably well and do not require much skill to set up, maintain or to reconfigure in the event of metal interference.

Next, an interface to allow the user to grab and manipulate objects in the virtual environment was necessary. A wireless mouse/presenter was chosen, manufactured by Targus, to use as the wand. This device was selected for several reasons. The presenter does not require an unobstructed line of sight with the wireless receiver. This capability allows trainees to walk around a large room and face any direction while using the wand. No additional software was required to utilize the device and the presenter's cost of approximately USD 60 made it a good low cost solution.

After receiving and processing the information from the PPT, the InertiaCubes, and the wand, the application computer, a high end PC, generates graphics and transmits them to the V8 HMD. The V8 HMD contains two individual lenses and two liquid crystal displays (LCDs), one for each eye, that are used to create a stereo effect. The resolution of the virtual research V8 HMD is 640 X 480.

Earlier in the project, we attempted to use 5DT Data Gloves (one sensor per finger - for measuring finger flexure) as our physical interface with the virtual environment. Unfortunately, the five sensor version of the 5DT Data Glove turned out to be very unreliable and imprecise. The gloves made it very difficult to perform gesture-based control. Although gloves of much higher quality could have been purchased for this project, one of the requirements was to keep the cost of the system as low as possible. After some testing, we found that for training purposes, the wand-based interface is simpler and more user friendly. Even if gesture recognition could be made reliable with a glove of higher quality, we felt that the trainee would be forced to memorize certain gestures in order to efficiently issue commands inside the virtual environment.

Figure 6.2 shows the hardware schematic for the chosen equipment, including a photograph which shows some of the actual hardware components (the V8 HMD, the InertiaCube2, a wand, and markers).

6.3   Software Architecture

6.3.1   *Software Requirements*

We had a number of project goals in mind when we compiled a list of software requirements. First, the system needed to accommodate two types of users. The first type is the trainer (instructor). The second type of user is the person who will use the system as a learning tool – the trainee. Trainees will need to have the ability to train either by using the PC-based version or by using the fully interactive version for training in the virtual environment.

Second, it was necessary to make sure that new multimedia/VE tutorials could be created quickly. Programming each VE tutorial manually could be too costly and time-consuming for the training method to be practical. In addition to that, most organizations probably could not afford to have a team of programmers dedicated to tutorial creation, and it would actually offset any cost savings realized by implementing this training system. Because of this, it was decided that a tool to help non-programmers create new tutorials was an important requirement. Many organizations already create text-based documentation or training material and most of those organizations may not be willing to completely abandon their existing training methods and solely adopt virtual environment training. Therefore, VTS had to be designed to supplement existing training methods and not replace them completely. At the same time, it would be inconvenient to force the engineers and instructors to do twice as much work by generating a VE tutorial and then composing all the required text, as well as compiling it into a conventional paper-based manual with illustrations. The system needed to aid in generating some of the instructional material in order to ease the burden on the engineer.

Third, the system needed to create highly effective tutorials as far as maximizing comprehension and retention of the assembly process. To accomplish this, VTS would have to monitor trainees in the virtual environment and provide them with constant feedback as well as highly detailed error messages and highly effective hints. The VTS would also have to support multiple correct part placements in order to mimic real assembly scenarios. If a certain part attachment operation is allowed and yet the system gives an error when the trainee attempts it, then the trainee's training may be slow or confusing.

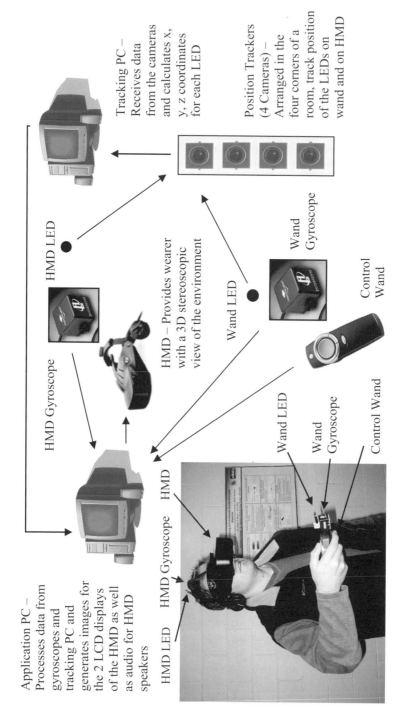

Figure 6.2: Hardware components of the VTS

Application PC – Processes data from gyroscopes and tracking PC and generates images for the 2 LCD displays of the HMD as well as audio for HMD speakers

HMD Gyroscope

HMD LED

Tracking PC – Receives data from the cameras and calculates x, y, z coordinates for each LED

Position Trackers (4 Cameras) – Arranged in the four corners of a room, track position of the LEDs on wand and on HMD

Wand Gyroscope

Control Wand

Wand LED

HMD – Provides wearer with a 3D stereoscopic view of the environment

HMD LED   HMD Gyroscope   HMD

Wand LED

Wand Gyroscope

Control Wand

Keeping these goals in mind, we compiled the following list of requirements:

- The application should be separated into multiple modules with unique tasks.
- One of the system tasks must be to assist the instructor in creating VE-based tutorials and to make it possible for the instructor to create tutorials without writing code.
- One of the system tasks must be to monitor the trainees and perform error checking.
- System must be able to offer hints with a range of detail levels.
- System must speed up training material generation by automatically generating at least some of the training material.
- System must support part symmetries and alternate attachments.
- System must support a desktop PC interface and a VR hardware interface.

6.3.2 *Software Design*

To satisfy the requirements in Section 6.3.1, we created the design for the Virtual Training Studio that distributes the various tasks among three main components:

- **Virtual Author** – This module assists the instructor in quickly building new tutorials, which are later executed inside the virtual environment. The instructor creates tutorials by loading CAD models into a virtual environment and performing a virtual demonstration of the assembly process. The Virtual Author also generates text instructions by analyzing the instructor's motions, collisions between objects, and feature alignment. Chapter 7 discusses the Virtual Author in great detail.
- **Virtual Workspace** – This module loads tutorials created by the Virtual Author and executes them inside the virtual environment. The Virtual Workspace breaks down the assembly process into individual steps and allows each step to be completed using an animation sequence, interactive simulation, or video of the actual process. Details of the Virtual Workspace are provided in Section 6.3.3.
- **Virtual Mentor** – This module is responsible for monitoring trainees in the virtual environment, providing them with error messages and adaptive hints. This module is responsible for not only the content of the messages sent to the trainee, but also the

appropriate presentation of content to the user. Virtual Mentor is described in detail in Chapter 8.

VTS was built with the help of a graphics library/engine called Vizard developed by WorldViz [WorldViz, 2006]. Vizard uses the Python (interpreted) programming language as its interface to the programmer and has a very convenient library for loading and manipulating VRML objects [Lutz, 1999; Python Manual, 2006]. One of the biggest benefits of using Vizard is productivity. Vizard allows the software developer to focus more of his efforts on the logic of the system and less of his efforts on production of graphics and integration of VR equipment into the system. Much of the productivity gain may be due to the Python language itself, which contains a very rich library and produces very readable and compact code. Vizard also has an extensive collection of what WorldViz calls "sensor plug-ins" – Python wrappers of drivers for VR hardware. The speed of Python and Vizard has been more than acceptable for our application thus far.

For implementation of graphical user interfaces (GUIs) for use on a desktop PC, VTS employed wxPython, a Python wrapper around a popular cross platform library called wxWidgets. Due to Vizard's use of Python, integration of GUIs built with wxPython into the rest of VTS has been relatively straightforward. Figure 6.3 shows the software layers and components of the Virtual Training Studio.

6.3.3 *Virtual Workspace*

The goal of this component of the VTS is to provide the basic infrastructure for multimodal training and to incorporate the appropriate level of physics-based modeling consistent with the operation of a low cost PVE. Virtual Workspace houses the necessary framework to allow manipulation of objects, collision detection, and execution of animations, and it integrates the hardware with the software to provide the user an intuitive, easy to use interface to the virtual environment. Virtual Workspace also acts as the platform for the Virtual Author and the Virtual Mentor.

The current version of the Virtual Workspace places the user in a furnished room with a table at the center and a projector screen on one of the walls. Parts used in the tutorial are placed on the table, while video as well as text instructions are displayed on the projector screen. The user interacts with the VE using a single wand, represented in the VE as a virtual laser pointer, to pick up, move, and rotate objects and to click on buttons located on the control panel at the front of the room. The implementation of the Virtual Workspace also includes the option to interact with the VE through a desktop personal computer (PC) interface.

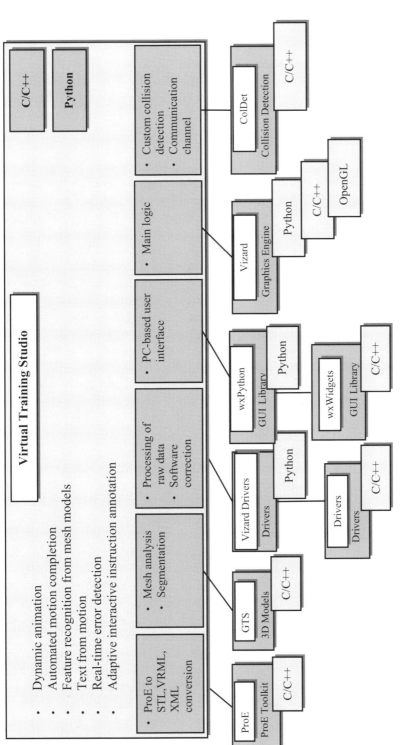

Figure 6.3: Software infrastructure and libraries of the VTS

Virtual Workspace offers three primary modes of training: 3D animation mode, which allows users to view the entire assembly via animations; interactive simulation mode, which is a fully user driven mode that allows users to manually perform the assembly tasks; and video mode, which allows users to view the entire assembly via video clips. Trainees can switch between these modes at any time with the click of a button. The Virtual Workspace environment is shown in Plate 2 (in the color section).

While inside the Virtual Workspace the user can pick up parts using a virtual laser pointer. A button on the wand toggles "hold" mode on and off. When the hold mode is on, any object that is intersected by the laser pointer is attached to the laser. Only one part can be picked up at a time. If the part is a component in an assembly, then the entire assembly is attached to the laser. Once a part or assembly is attached to the laser, the user can move the part using one of two methods. One method of moving the object is rotating and moving the wand itself. Since the wand is tracked, the virtual laser pointer moves and rotates with the wand, causing the attached object to move with it. The other method of moving parts that are attached to the laser is by rotating a trackball that is on top of the wand. A second button on the wand toggles the wand mode between rotation and translation. When the wand is in translation mode, rotating the track ball back and forth brings the held part closer or moves it away from the user along the laser beam. When the wand is in rotation mode, rotating the trackball rotates the held part. If a part is released in mid-air, the part remains in mid-air.

When a held object collides with a stationary object both objects become translucent and the held object is allowed to pass through the stationary object. The only exceptions to that are the walls and the table. Upon collision with any of these entities, the held object is stopped and possibly detached from the laser. On collision, Virtual Workspace also produces the appropriate sound effect. Virtual Workspace is aware of the materials of various objects and maintains an internal interaction table, which it consults to produce one of the pre-recorded sound effects. Currently, Virtual Workspace has a list of sound effects for interactions between metal, wood, rubber, and concrete objects (e.g., a wall). The materials of parts are declared in Virtual Author. Plate 3 (in the color section) shows a screen shot of two parts colliding inside VTS.

In the most interactive mode, called interactive simulation, the user first positions and orients a part so that the interfaces align and the components can be assembled. The user can then click on a "Complete" button. If the part is positioned and oriented correctly, allowing for a certain margin for error, the assembly of the part is completed via animation. If the orientation or position of the part is incorrect, an error message, generated by the Virtual Mentor, is given, and the user must realign the part so that assembly can be completed.

The animation mode requires very little input from the user and simply shows the process of assembling a part to another component by animating the movement of the part to its final position and orientation within the container subassembly. During this animation, the user can walk around and change his perspective simply by walking in the tracked workspace. Since the user's head is tracked, the view is appropriately updated inside the virtual environment. If the objects being animated fall out of the user's view, the animation pauses until the user looks at the animated parts.

The Video mode also requires very little input from the user and shows a video clip of the real part being attached to a real assembly. The user can repeat, pause, rewind, and fast forward the video clip as they desire. The video clips, which are optional, are added to the tutorial in the Virtual Author.

Two buttons on the virtual control panel allow the user to skip to the next step or go back to the previous step. Each time one of these buttons is pressed certain parts on the table are rearranged to reflect the new step. A button on the control panel also allows the user to reset the tutorial, bringing it to the initial state. Parts in the Virtual Workspace are usually about four times larger than their real counterparts. Increasing the size of the virtual parts is necessary due to resolution limitations of most HMDs. Small parts are difficult to visualize in the virtual environment. To give the user a sense of true size, a virtual quarter is placed on the table scaled to match the virtual parts.

Both the 3D animation mode and the interactive simulation mode are dependent on the dynamic generation of animations. In interactive simulation, users place one part near another and signal to the system to complete the assembly. If placement is correct, the system takes over and completes the assembly using animation. Many virtual environments utilize static animations where all the information about the animation is generated only once and stored in volatile or non-volatile memory. The positions and paths of the objects cannot be altered in static animations. For our system, it was necessary for the animation to be dynamic because the trainees are given the freedom to place parts anywhere prior to activation of the animation. For dynamic animations, it is necessary to perform some re-planning each time the animation is activated.

The Virtual Workspace is responsible for generating dynamic animations. The Virtual Workspace allows two forms of animation. In the first type, the attaching part is first gradually rotated until it matches the orientation of the entry marker. The attaching part is then gradually translated to the position of the entry marker. Finally, the attaching part is gradually translated to the position of the final marker. In the second form of animation, the Virtual Workspace follows the same procedure as the first except for translating the part to its insertion location. Instead of drawing a direct route, the Virtual Workspace first translates the part along the Y axis (top-down) until the part's y component matches the y component of the insertion marker. Next, the part is gradually translated along the Z axis (forward-back) and finally along the X axis until the part reaches its insertion location.

We discovered that using the second animation method allows us to decrease the chance of collisions without using a more computationally expensive path planning algorithm (as long as the room is along the standard x,y,z, axes and the front of the room is at the positive z). The instructor can use the second animation method to reduce chance of collisions during animations by placing parts on the table in a certain arrangement. The instructor can further reduce the chance of collisions during animations by requiring the Virtual Workspace to reset the positions of the parts to certain default positions on the table prior to beginning the animation, in effect making the animation static instead of dynamic. However, realizing the importance of sophisticated path planning for our application, an efficient and robust path planning algorithm is currently in development.

6.3.4 *Virtual Workspace Design Rationale*

The following design decisions were made for the Virtual Workspace:

- Elimination of gravity
- Use of a wand interface instead of gloves
- Multiple methods of rotating held objects
- Lack of auto release of held object on collision

In order to speed up the system development, we decided to reduce the level of realistic physics-based modeling. This trade-off was made because of the belief that for training purposes, highly realistic physics-based modeling may not always necessary. We believe that high level of physical realism is necessary for tasks such as assembly verification, design analysis, or accessibility testing. However, we felt that for cognitive training that emphasizes process comprehension, geometric modeling will be adequate for the first version of the system.

Gravity is an excellent example of added realism that reduces convenience and adds few or no benefits to our system. Currently, using a single wand, the user is able to pick up one part, release it and leave it in mid-air, then pick up another part and attach it to the first one. Had gravity been supported, a dual wand interface would have been required to assemble parts in virtual reality, which would have made the interface more complicated for many trainees and would have raised the cost of the system.

As was mentioned earlier, we initially tried using a glove-based interface. Unfortunately, the glove-based user interface made it difficult to efficiently issue commands to the system from inside the virtual environment. To use the gloves to communicate with the system, one could take three different paths. First, the user could memorize multiple gestures. Second, instead of memorizing gestures the user could push buttons on a virtual control panel inside the virtual environment. Third, the user could click on buttons on a wall using a laser beam coming from the top of the virtual hand (similar to our current wand interface), and at the same time, manipulate objects using fingers. The first option was unattractive, because trainees may not all use the system often enough to memorize the required gestures. We have implemented and tried the second option, and it significantly slowed down the user, because the user not only had to reach for buttons, but also had to aim with the finger to touch them. The third option, though the best of the three, was still not as convenient as the wand interface due to the "screw driver effect" problem.

The screw driver effect is the reason why we decided to implement multiple methods of rotating held objects. To rotate an object clockwise or counterclockwise with a virtual hand controlled by a glove, a user would normally have to twist the hand while holding the object, then release the object, then rotate the hand in the opposite direction, grab the object and twist again, repeating this process as many times as necessary. With a wand in VTS, the user is able to rotate a trackball on the wand in the appropriate direction and the held object will continuously rotate clockwise or counterclockwise. We discovered that this sort of rotation was used quite a bit by users who tested VTS to either assemble parts or to bring an object close to the view for observation of all of its features.

Initially, the system forced the wand to release a held object when the object collided with something in the environment. This, however, annoyed many testers, due to the fact that testers tended to be more "clumsy" in the Virtual Reality environment than they are in reality. As a result of this problem, Virtual Workspace was modified to not cause an automatic release of a held object when it collided with something in the environment. Parts are allowed to pass through each other, but those that collide become translucent. The only exceptions to this rule are the walls and the table. We did not want to allow users to put objects through walls, because that makes the objects inaccessible. Allowing objects to pass through the table also has the undesirable side effect of objects being hidden under the table.

6.4   Benefits of VTS

We foresee a number benefits from the use of the Virtual Training Studio. First, we believe that the number of personnel required to become trainers will be reduced, since the system will perform the bulk of the training. Second, the system will provide a convenient mechanism for depositing assembly process knowledge into a central repository for later retrieval by trainees, trainers, and managers. Third, the VTS will assist instructors in the creation of VE-based tutorials and paper-based documentation by generating an instruction set from the animation sequence and by providing a convenient way of generating 2D illustrations. Fourth, the system will provide an affordable Personal Virtual Environment. Finally, we believe that the most important benefits will be an accelerated learning process as well as a reduced probability of worker error.

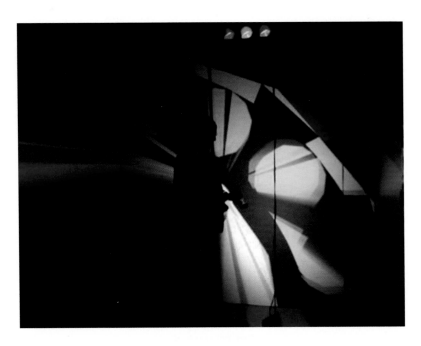

Plate 1: 3D scene being displayed inside a CAVE system at the University of Maryland Virtual Reality Laboratory

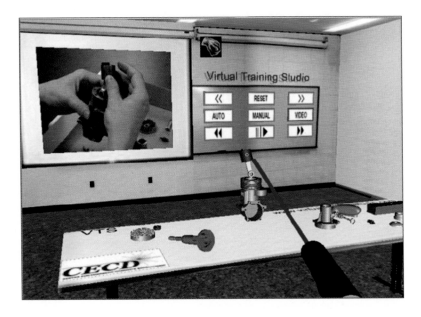

Plate 2: VTS environment as the user would see it through the HMD

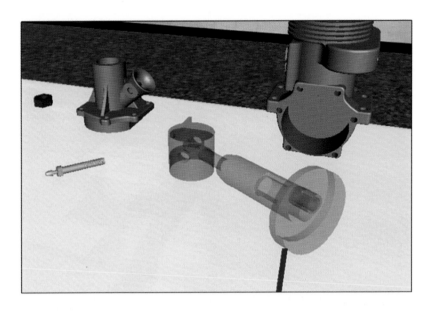

Plate 3: Two colliding parts become translucent, but movement is not restricted.

Plate 4: Parts are being animated dropping down on the table. Random positions were automatically generated by Virtual Author.

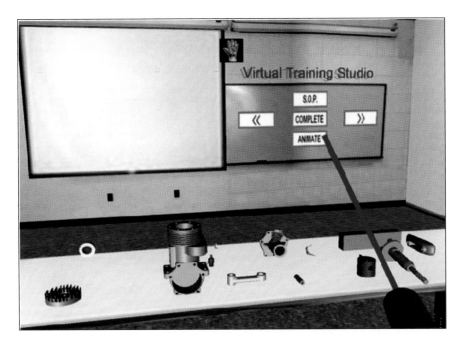

Plate 5: Instructor's view of the virtual environment run by Virtual Author

Plate 6: Virtual demonstration of attachment of engine cover to top of engine case

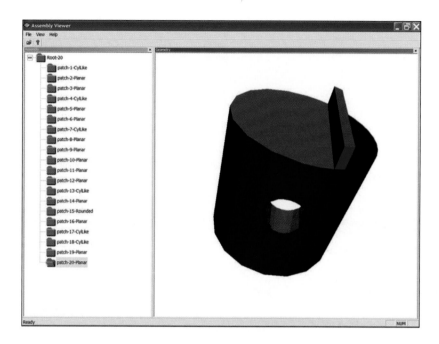

Plate 7: Segmentation performed on model airplane engine piston

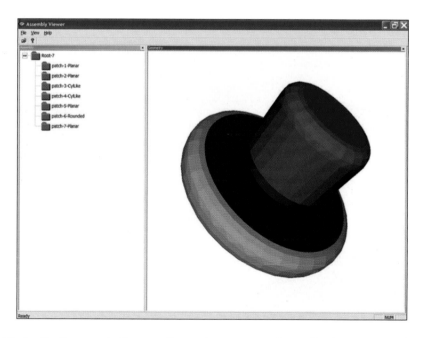

Plate 8: Segmentation performed on a parachute deployment device cartridge

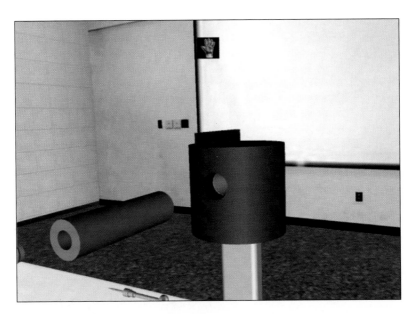

Plate 9: An example of subtype B4 symmetry where the pin can be inserted from two different positions (either side of the piston hole). For each position either the alternate or the primary orientation around the secondary axis may be used.

Plate 10: Animation of nut sliding onto threaded crankshaft rod can be made more efficient by taking advantage of the symmetry of the nut around the main axis (axis of the nut cylinder).

Plate 11: Placement of propellant grain at its alternate position

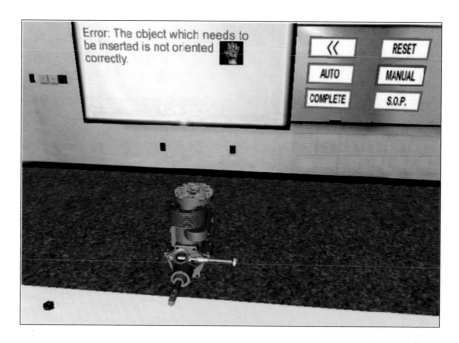

Plate 12: Virtual Mentor detects an orientation error.

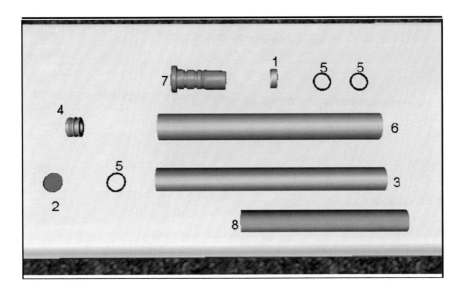

Plate 13: Components of a navy rocket motor assembly

Plate 14: Small cap must be attached to the side of the nozzle with a relief.

Plate 15: Rubber o-ring must be rolled on top of the rightmost rectangular groove.

Plate 16: Detail in the form of flashing arrows is added to animation of small cap attachment to nozzle.

Chapter 7

Virtual Author

In this chapter, we discuss the development of a virtual environment (VE) instruction generating tool called the Virtual Author, which is the main component of the Virtual Training Studio (VTS). The Virtual Author tool is designed to allow an instructor to perform virtual demonstrations using CAD models in the virtual environment, in order to quickly generate VE-based training instructions for use in VTS. This chapter describes the algorithms used to carry out motion smoothening of instructor's actions, automated text instruction generation based on part and assembly motions, and extraction of alignment constraints from 3D CAD models to support instruction generation. This chapter also describes the step by step process of generating a VR tutorial and a paper manual. Also presented are examples to illustrate how the use of the Virtual Author tool leads to a significant reduction in the training instruction generation time.

Section 7.1 provides background information. Section 7.2 presents the step-by-step procedure for creating new training materials using the Virtual Author. Section 7.3 presents the algorithms and techniques used by the Virtual Author to accomplish its tasks. Specifically, Section 7.3.1 discusses the extraction of part surfaces and alignment constraints from polygonal models. Section 7.3.2 discusses automatic generation of text instructions. Finally, Section 7.3.3 discusses motion smoothening and feature alignment.

7.1   Background

One of the major challenges in the deployment of PVEs in training applications is the time necessary to generate high quality instructions. Currently, it takes an experienced programmer several days to weeks to generate PVE-based training instructions. Our goal is to develop a highly automated authoring capability which can generate high quality instructions through a virtual demonstration of the task, without any programming effort by the author. We are utilizing the virtual environment as the user interface to assist in the creation of the training instructions. In our framework, the person authoring training instructions will not be required to perform any programming or be familiar with geometric transformation operations. This work is automatically performed behind the scenes to speed up the creation time of training instructions and allow anyone familiar with the task to easily author instructions.

Some have used interactive demonstrations as a means of conveniently creating tutorials. An example of this type of authoring tool is the Cognitive Tutor Authoring Tool (CTAT) [Koedinger et al., 2004]. CTAT builds math tutorials by demonstration. The author performs a scenario using a windows-based GUI while the system records the procedure. The author must also explicitly demonstrate all alternative solution paths both correct and incorrect. Another example of this type of authoring tool is RIDES, which can train, amongst other things, nurses to use medical equipment [Munro and Towne, 1992]. In simple mode RIDES allows an author to 'record' a procedure that students must learn, simply by carrying out the procedure in a window-based user interface. Another example of virtual authoring is a system called UVAVU [Ritchie et al., 1999], which generates assembly sequences by observing an author perform an assembly in a virtual environment. UVAVU makes use of known information about final part locations within the assembly to perform snap-ons upon collision during the author's demonstration. Testing conducted with UVAVU showed that assembly plans produced in virtual reality were similar to those produced in a real environment.

The Virtual Author is the main component of the Virtual Training Studio (VTS). VTS is a virtual environment-based training system that allows instructors to create training instructions and allows trainees to learn assembly operations in a virtual environment. The most novel aspect of the Virtual Author is the automated instruction generation based on demonstrations of motions in the virtual environment by an instructor. The Virtual Author allows an instructor to import CAD models of parts belonging to a product into the virtual environment and to define a dictionary by naming parts and certain features on those parts. The instructor then simply picks up CAD models in the virtual environment and assembles the models in the order they want the assembly process to be taught to trainees. The system monitors and records the instructor's actions and then performs motion smoothening and alignment adjustment to account for the fact that the instructor's motion and placement may not be precise. The Virtual Author then automatically generates (1) text instructions, (2) 3D animations, (3) 3D interactive simulations, and (4) a paper manual. These training instructions are generated based on observed motion, feature and part alignment, and collision detection during the virtual demonstration. The generated training material consists of two parts: an HTML document containing text and figures, representing a paper manual, and a script file containing hundreds of lines of Python code, which can later be loaded by the Virtual Workspace component of VTS during training sessions.

The greatest benefit of the Virtual Author is the rapid creation of VE-based training instructions without the need for coding. This reduces the time and the cost of building new tutorials. Demonstrations in VE also make the system user-friendly and allow the process expert, who is most likely a mechanical or manufacturing engineer, to directly control how the instructions for device assembly are generated without relying on programmers. Another benefit of the Virtual Author is the consistency of the generated tutorials. Hard-coding the data for each tutorial may often lead to inconsistent tutorials with slight differences in either the look and feel or the behavior of features. Generating training instructions automatically from virtual demonstrations also ensures that the instructor can visually verify that the training instructions being generated are complete and no step is missing in the sequence. Consistent tutorials are expected to streamline the training process for trainees once they have become accustomed to the system.

7.2   Training Material Creation Process

The goal of the Virtual Author is to enable the instructor to quickly create multi-media training instructions for use in the Virtual Workspace without writing any code. The Virtual Author automatically generates VR tutorials for use in Virtual Workspace as well as paper-based manuals consisting of text instructions and figures. This material is generated by monitoring the demonstration of the assembly process by the instructor within the virtual environment. The Virtual Author performs motion smoothening on the instructor's actions and then generates the training material. Before a demonstration of the assembly can be carried out, the instructor must import polyhedral models of the appropriate format into the Virtual Author. This process is discussed in Section 7.2.1. Next, the instructor must declare a dictionary for the Virtual Author to use when automatically generating text instructions, and the instructor must arrange parts on the virtual table. Dictionary declaration and initial part placement are discussed in Section 7.2.2. Once a dictionary has been declared and parts have been given initial locations on the table, the instructor demonstrates the assembly of a virtual device inside the virtual environment. This procedure is explained in section 7.2.3. Finally, the instructor must declare part symmetries. This information is later used by the Virtual Workspace to allow multiple correct part attachments for a given step in the assembly process during interactive training simulation inside the virtual environment. It is also used to generate more efficient animations. Declaration of part symmetries is presented in section 7.2.4.

7.2.1 *Importing Polyhedral Models*

The Virtual Training Studio was designed to work with CAD models created in a wide variety of CAD systems. This is accomplished by working with relatively simple CAD model representations in the form of Stereolithography (STL) files and Virtual Reality Modeling Language (VRML) files. STL format stores the CAD model as a set of triangulated facets and facet normals. It may be in either binary or ASCII form. The vast majority of CAD systems are capable of exporting to this very simple format. Most CAD systems are also capable of exporting their native models to VRML format. If in some cases that is not possible, simplified VRML files can be generated from STL files by approximating vertex normals, which are not available in STL files. Vertex normals allow curved surfaces like a cylinder or a torus to be rendered as a smooth surface as opposed to being rendered as a set of planar surfaces if an STL file is used in rendering. VRML files can support complicated object hierarchies and textures. One drawback to working with VRML files, however, is that they can be difficult to parse and process. For this reason, VTS uses VRML files for rendering of CAD models in the virtual environment and parses corresponding STL files to load all facets and their normals for additional processing. The technical details of the processing that is performed on the loaded triangulated facets are discussed later in Section 7.3.1. VTS uses a commercial graphics library/tool called Vizard, made by WorldViz, to perform basic loading and transformation of VRML files.

The VTS package includes a plug-in for a popular CAD system called ProEngineer (ProE). The plug-in is implemented using ProE Toolkit and allows an engineer to load an assembly into ProE and export it to the file formats used in the VTS – VRML and STL. The plug-in also generates an XML file describing the structure of the assembly. The engineer may also export individual parts from different CAD systems, import those parts into the Virtual Author, and put together a complete assembly.

7.2.2   *Dictionary Declaration and Table Setup*

The instructor uses a desktop PC-based application to load parts into the Virtual Author, declare a dictionary, and give initial placement for parts on the virtual table. Once all polyhedral models have been loaded into the Virtual Author, the Virtual Author performs face-based feature recognition on the polyhedral models and extracts alignment constraints. The next step is dictionary declaration. The dictionary consists of part names and feature names that will be used by the Virtual Author to automatically generate text instructions. As each part is loaded, the instructor is asked to give it a descriptive name. The instructor has the option to accept a default name, which is simply the name of the file without the extension. Figure 7.1 shows a screen shot where parts are being named by the instructor. Once the parts have been named, the instructor must declare a set of features and give them descriptive names. To declare a feature for a part, the instructor first selects a part and then selects the "Add Features" item from a menu. The selected part is then loaded into a separate window where it is broken down into a set of surfaces, each displayed with a unique color. The instructor selects a set of surfaces, representing a single feature, and gives them a name. Figure 7.2 shows a screenshot of feature declaration. The instructor may declare multiple features for a given part or none at all. Later, during the assembly demonstration process, the dictionary is automatically expanded, when the Virtual Author generates names for subassemblies by taking the name of the subassembly component with the largest surface area and appending the word "assembly" to it. The instructor later has the option to modify such automatically-generated names.

After the initial dictionary has been declared, parts must be given initial positions on the table. The Virtual Author automatically generates a random position on the table for each part by taking into account the table area and the part's bounding box. Parts are then placed at a certain height above the table and animated, dropping down until all parts come in contact with the table. The instructor has the option of clicking on a "Redo" button to generate new random positions for all parts. Physics-based modeling is being developed as of this writing, but has not yet been integrated into the Virtual Author. Consequently, the system does not generate ideal rotations for each part on the table, but instead keeps the default orientation of each part. In order to adjust orientations, the instructor must later manually adjust the rotations inside the generated configuration file. Plate 4 (in the color section) shows the parts being animated toward the table. After the dictionary has been declared and initial positions on the table have been generated, the instructor signals to the Virtual Author to generate a configuration file.

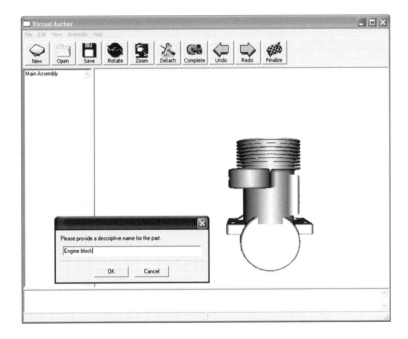

Figure 7.1: Naming of parts in the desktop-based part of Virtual Author

Figure 7.2: Declaration of selected part feature as crankshaft rod

The Virtual Author generates a configuration file in the form of a Python script and presents a dialog box to the instructor, asking whether the instructor wishes to load the VR-enabled portion of the Virtual Author or just save the configuration file. If the instructor chooses to load the generated configuration file into the VR-enabled part of the Virtual Author, then the instructor initializes the VR hardware and signals to the Virtual Author to proceed. The Virtual Author then launches another one of its component applications, which communicates with the VR hardware, initializes the virtual environment, and allows the instructor to put on an HMD and continue the authoring process in virtual reality.

7.2.3   *Virtual Demonstration*

Upon entering the Virtual Author-run virtual environment, the instructor sees a scene that is very similar to what trainees see in the virtual environments run by the Virtual Workspace. There is a large table in front of the instructor with prearranged parts on top of it. There is a projector screen at the front of the room where generated text instructions are displayed, and there is a virtual control panel with several buttons on it on the front wall. A virtual laser pointer, which is controlled by a physical wand held by the instructor, allows the instructor to pick up parts from the table, rotate parts using various buttons on the wand, and activate virtual buttons on the control panel. The virtual environment as the instructor sees it is depicted in Plate 5 (in the color section).

Once inside the virtual environment, the instructor demonstrates the first step to the Virtual Author by picking up a part from the table and inserting it into another part. Instructor's motions are completely unrestricted. Virtual parts are allowed to pass through each other, but parts are stopped if the instructor tries to move them through the table. If the geometry of one part intersects the geometry of another, both become translucent. Gravity is not enabled inside the virtual environment in order to permit the use of a single wand. The instructor can leave one part in mid-air and attach another part to it. After the instructor attaches one part to another, he signals to the Virtual Author to perform motion smoothening and more precise alignment of matching features and surfaces. Motion smoothening is necessary, because the demonstrated insertion path is most likely somewhat circuitous, indirect, and imprecise. The system must also generalize the final insertion path so that the generated animations can work no matter what position or orientation the two parts have later. Motion smoothening allows the Virtual Author to estimate the final insertion vector and the insertion point. Alignment of matching surfaces is necessary because part placement, just like the insertion path, is most likely not very precise. This is due to the fact that the instructor's motions are not restricted by part collisions and because limitations of the VR hardware used by VTS make it difficult for the user to do precise attachments. The technical details of motion smoothening and surface alignment are discussed in Section 7.3.3. After the Virtual Author aligns the nearest matching surfaces, the instructor can either accept the Virtual Author's alignment simply by demonstrating step two, or the instructor can reject the Virtual Author's alignment by clicking on the "<<" (Back) button on the virtual control panel with the virtual laser pointer. If the "Back" button is pressed, the Virtual Author disassembles the two assembled components and places them back on the table. The instructor repeats this process until the entire assembly has been put together. Plate 6 (in the color section) shows a virtual demonstration in progress.

After the assembly of a device has been demonstrated, the instructor can have the Virtual Author automatically generate text instructions using the previously declared dictionary and the generalized insertion produced by motion smoothening. The instructor does this by using the "Back" button again to go all the way back to the initial state where all parts are on the table. Then, by continuously clicking on the "Animate" button, the instructor signals to the Virtual Author to generate the animation and highly detailed text instructions for each step. Finally, by clicking on the "S.O.P." button, which stands for standard operating procedure, the instructor tells the Virtual Author to generate a paper manual and a VR tutorial to be used within the Virtual Workspace.

7.2.4 *Declaration of Part Symmetries*

During the interactive simulation mode inside the Virtual Workspace, where the user manually assembles a virtual device, the system must monitor how the trainee is attempting to attach parts to each other and report errors. Sometimes when one part is attached to another, it may have more than one correct attachment orientation or more than one correct insertion location. An example of this is one tube being inserted into another tube. The tube being inserted may be rotated around its axis by any angle and the insertion would still be correct. This is also the case if the tube is flipped 180 degrees, end over end. Therefore, the system must recognize these numerous insertion possibilities as correct and avoid reporting an error. To aid the system in determining if a particular assembly operation is correct or incorrect, the instructor must declare the symmetries for the parts or subassemblies involved in an assembly operation. The system can then use information about part and assembly symmetries to infer alternate correct orientations and insertion locations in addition to the primary orientation and position declared by the instructor during the virtual demonstration.

The Virtual Mentor, a module embedded in Virtual Workspace, is responsible for enforcing correct attachments and insertions involving part/assembly symmetries, though the Virtual Author is used to declare and categorize the symmetries. In order to declare part symmetries, the instructor once again uses a desktop-based application. This is the same application that was used to create a dictionary and generate initial part positions on the table. This time, instead of loading a set of parts, the instructor loads the Virtual Author-generated tutorial, which the instructor can edit using this desktop application.

The desktop tutorial editor allows the instructor to navigate through all the assembly steps which were previously demonstrated in a virtual environment and edit those steps by making changes to the text instructions, associating audio and video files with a step and declaring symmetries for each step. To declare symmetries for a particular step, the instructor brings up a dialog box which allows him to select a set of axes describing the symmetry of a part or assembly, define rotations around those axes, define how those rotations are to be enforced, and declare the type of attachment. Figure 7.3 shows the desktop tutorial editor and the symmetry specification dialog box.

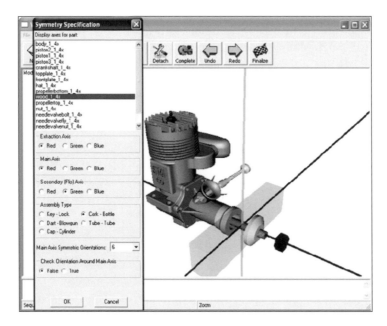

Figure 7.3: Desktop tutorial editor and symmetry specification dialog box

Section 8.2 of Chapter 8 describes in great detail how symmetry information declared within the Virtual Author is used to infer alternate correct orientations and positions.

7.3   Technical Challenges and Solutions

7.3.1   *Extraction of Part Surfaces and Alignment Constraints from Polyhedral Models*

In order to generate proper text instructions and perform motion smoothening, The Virtual Author needs location and orientation information about parts' faces. In order to make the Virtual Author independent of any specific CAD system, we use STL and VRML models. Both of these file formats represent parts as a collection of triangles (also called triangulated meshes) and do not maintain part surface information. Hence, we need to extract part surface location and orientation data by analyzing a triangulated mesh of each part. The required data consists of the following: extracted surfaces, which are classified as cylindrical, planar, and curved; axes associated with planar and cylindrical surfaces; and areas of the surfaces.

As a part of the Virtual Author, we have developed a module which is capable of performing segmentation of part geometries and extraction of axes of planar and cylindrical patches. In order to extract axes of parts, the system must first perform segmentation on all the parts the instructor has chosen to use in the VE tutorial. Our current algorithm classifies all extracted patches into three categories: planar, cylindrical, and curved. All patches that are not determined to be planar or cylindrical are placed in the generic curved category. Segmentation and classification is conducted in three stages. In the first stage, the algorithm calculates angles between all adjacent facets and places all adjacent, coplanar facets into planar groups. In the second stage, the algorithm visits all planar groups (patches), converting connected planar groups into curved groups. For example, the Virtual Author may take multiple small planar patches which are not co-planar and convert them into a curved patch based on a set of heuristics such as area of a planar patch relative to total part area, area of planar patches relative to the area of neighboring planar patches, and angles between neighboring planar patches. Cylindrical patches are extracted in the third stage. Our algorithm for finding cylindrical surfaces involves going through each patch labeled as curved and ascertaining whether the facets that make up the curved patch have a mostly cylindrical arrangement. That algorithm first visits every facet and places the area of each facet into a bucket that matches the facet's normal. The buckets are sorted in descending order based on surface area. The algorithm then chooses the largest bucket and uses it as a reference. It then visits every other bucket and computes the cross product between the normal of the reference bucket and the normal of each visited bucket. The results of the cross products (resulting vector and the surface area of visited bucket) are placed in a separate set of buckets which are sorted by surface area in descending order. If the largest bucket contains at least 70 percent of the surface area, then the patch is mostly cylindrical and the vector associated with the biggest bucket is used as the axis. The axis of a planar patch is simply the normal of the surface. Axes of curved patches are not extracted.

Plates 7 and 8 (in the color section) show how two representative parts were automatically segmented into patches by our system. For the part shown in Plate 7 (in the color section), a model airplane engine piston, the segmentation algorithm correctly produced 13 planar patches, 6 cylindrical patches and 1 generic curved patch. For the part shown in Plate 8 (in the color section), a parachute deployment device cartridge, the segmentation algorithm correctly produced 4 planar patches, 2 cylindrical patches and 1 generic curved patch. Tests of this algorithm on a large number of parts with varying shape and complexity revealed good extraction accuracy. We have also conducted extensive performance testing of this algorithm with respect to file size. The computational results indicate that our algorithm can support interactive applications. These tests were conducted on a machine with a dual-core Intel processor (1.8 GHz) and 1GB of RAM. For a set of 5 MB stereolithography (STL) files in ASCII format, the extraction of alignment constraints was completed on average in 5.50 seconds. For 10 MB STL files in ASCII format, the algorithm completed on average in 39.74 seconds. For a set of 20 MB STL files, the algorithm completed on average in 64.94 seconds. Note that segmentation and extraction of alignment constraints is a one-time operation performed when parts are loaded in the system.

7.3.2 *Automatic Generation of Text Instructions*

Automatic generation of highly detailed text instructions is one of the ways in which the Virtual Author augments the trainer's productivity. The instructor later has the option of editing generated text and adding new text, but most of the work is done by the Virtual Author. Automatic generation of text instructions also insures that the generated text matches the generated animations and reduces the probability of the instructor forgetting to mention certain training details when generating text. Text is an important component of training instructions, because it can be used not only during training in the virtual environment, but also as a reference, along with 2D illustrations, on the shop floor.

   The Virtual Author generates text instructions during the replay phase of the authoring process after the instructor has demonstrated a particular step and the system has performed all the necessary motion smoothening. In the replay phase, Virtual Author plays the animation of the assembly for a step the way a trainee would see it. While the animation is playing, the system performs collision detection between virtual parts, assemblies, and instructor-declared features. At the end of the animation, it determines which features are aligned and what parts are internal or external. All the gathered information is combined to choose an appropriate set of instruction templates. The instruction templates are then completed with the insertion of part, feature, and assembly names in appropriate places and combined into sentences. A list of template groups for assembly text instructions is shown in Figure 7.4.

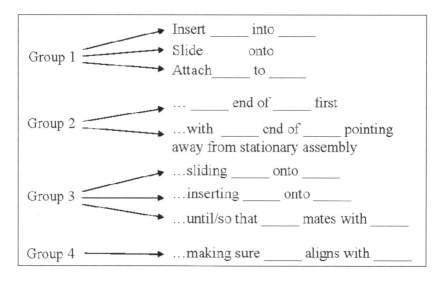

Figure 7.4: Text instruction template groups

   The blanks represent part names or feature names which are inserted into the template dynamically. Each template has certain rules or conditions associated with it. The Virtual Author picks templates by determining which conditions were met during the animation of a particular step. Virtual Author always picks a single template from Group 1. This is done by recording the position at which the moving assembly collided with the receiving assembly and recording the position where the moving assembly came to a stop. A vector is then calculated from the point of collision to the stop point. Next, Virtual Author creates three axes which are aligned with the mobile assembly's three bounding box dimensions and determines which of those axes has the smallest angle with the insertion vector. The Virtual Author divides the distance between collision point and stop point by the length of the dimension associated with the nearest axis. If the ratio is greater than a certain number, then either a "slide on" or an "insert into" template must be chosen. Otherwise, the "attach to" template is used. To determine whether it should use the "slide on" or "insert into" template, Virtual Author draws several lines that are perpendicular to the insertion vector toward the collision point. If most of the lines intersect the mobile assembly first, then the "slide on" template is used, otherwise Virtual Author uses the "insert into" template.

Templates from Groups 2, 3, and 4 are optional. Virtual Author may pick several or none from each group depending on the conditions. Virtual Author may pick one of the templates in Group 2 by calculating centers of features and parts and comparing them to the center and dimensions of the mobile part or assembly. To pick a template from this group, Virtual Author also compares the direction of motion of the mobile assembly to the vector from the center of the assembly to the center of one of the parts or features. If a declared feature or part is found near the end of the assembly that is facing toward the receiving assembly, then the "X end of Y first" template is used. Depending on the conditions, several templates may be picked from Group 3. The method used to pick one of these templates is very similar to the method described for template Group 1. Only feature names are used inside templates from Group 3. As each declared feature collides with another feature, Virtual Author records the position associated with that interaction. After the animation completes, Virtual Author records the final positions of all features that collided. As for Group 1 templates, Virtual Author determines which of the three dimensions of a feature's bounding box are closest to being parallel to the direction of motion. For each moving feature that collided with a stationary feature, Virtual Author calculates the ratio between feature travel distance and this dimension length. If the travel distance is large enough, then Virtual Author calculates the cross section of the colliding moving feature and stationary feature. The cross section is perpendicular to the bounding box dimension that is closest, in terms of the angle, to the direction of motion. The feature with the bigger cross section is assumed to be on the outside, so the "…sliding <feature A> onto <feature B>…" template is used with the names of the appropriate moving feature and stationary feature inserted.

Lastly, Virtual Author picks none or several templates from Group 4 by checking the alignment between all the features on the receiving assembly to all the features on the moving assembly. Since each feature may be composed of several planar, cylindrical, and curved surfaces, Virtual Author picks the dominant axis associated with the greatest amount of surface area in a feature. When checking for alignment, Virtual Author only compares features of the same type. If most of the surface area and hence the dominant axis is associated with planar surface(s), then the feature is of type "planar." Then only planar stationary features are compared to planar moving features. Once the system picks all the necessary templates and fills them with the names of the appropriate features, parts, and assemblies, the templates are combined into sentences.

As an example, consider one of the steps where the instructor attached an engine cover assembly to an engine case assembly. The text instruction automatically generated by the Virtual Author was, "Attach engine cover to engine case of the engine body assembly, so that engine cover bottom mates with engine case top. During this step, please make sure cooling fins is aligned with crankshaft rod." Figure 7.5 shows the attachment operation being demonstrated in the virtual environment. After performing motion filtering, described in the next section, Virtual Author was able to correctly detect that one of the moving, cylindrical features called "cooling fins" is aligned with one of the stationary, cylindrical features called "crankshaft rod." Virtual Author also correctly detected that this was an "attach" operation, because the engine cover did not travel far after initial collision with the case. Virtual Author also detected that the engine cover "mated with" the engine case. One template was picked from Group 1, Group 3, and Group 4.

We used the Virtual Author module to automatically generate text instructions for the eight steps of a rocket motor assembly and the twenty-two steps of a model airplane engine assembly. For each step, the quality and accuracy of text instructions was similar to the example above. The average time needed to generate a text instruction was 0.0043 seconds.

7.3.3 *Motion Smoothening and Feature Alignment*

Motion smoothening is an important capability of the Virtual Author. This feature allows the instructor to have the freedom to perform the virtual demonstration completely unrestricted, without being hindered by any system-enforced constraints on movement. As the instructor attaches or inserts one part into another, Virtual Author signals that a collision has occurred by making all colliding parts translucent, but the instructor may continue to move one part through another. Such freedom requires the

Virtual Author to carry out slight adjustments to the instructor's final placement of a part or subassembly due to the fact that highly precise alignment and placement may be difficult inside the virtual environment. Precise placement is difficult for a number of reasons. Although the stereo view provided by the HMD in a virtual environment greatly helps to visualize and move the objects, it still does not match the quality of depth perception in the real world. Also, the total freedom of movement and the lack of haptics feedback reduce the chance of the user knowing if there is an invalid placement due to geometries intersecting each other. Motion smoothening utilizes the extracted surfaces (patches) and alignment constraints discussed in Section 7.3.1.

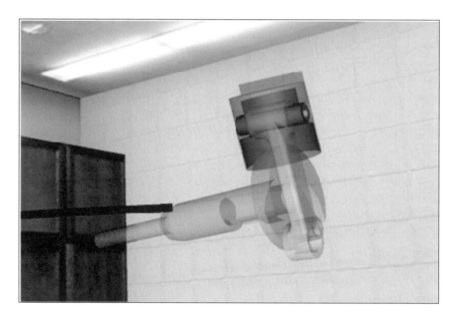

Figure 7.5: Crankshaft being manually attached to piston assembly in a virtual demonstration

The first step in motion smoothening is the logging of the motion of the held part. When the instructor picks up an object, Virtual Author stores the positions of the held part in a queue of points. The size of the queue is adjustable. Assuming the queue is of size S then the newest point is at position 0 and the oldest point is in position S – 1.

Once the user releases the part and signals to Virtual Author to perform motion smoothening, the first task that Virtual Author performs is processing of the point queue to determine the insertion vector and the insertion position. The insertion position must be ascertained, because in the Virtual Workspace, during interactive simulation, the trainee must place a part at the insertion position and then signal to the Virtual Mentor to complete the process with animation. The Virtual Mentor checks whether the position and orientation are correct and activates animation. The animation itself first gradually translates the part to the insertion position and then to the final position within another assembly. Then, the Virtual Author uses a recursive function to find the insertion point and the insertion vector. Because of space constraints, we will present a high level description of the function. The recursive function receives a queue as an argument and breaks it up into two subqueues. It then calculates the average vector for each subqueue. Next, it compares the two vectors. If the angle between the two vectors is greater than limit L (currently set to 5 degrees), then the function calls itself, passing in the left subqueue containing points 0 through queue length divided by two. If the angle is less than L, then the function declares the right end point of the right queue as the current insertion point and calls itself, passing as the argument the neighboring right subqueue of the same size (if there are any). In other words, if a significant difference between the left subqueue and the right subqueue is found, then the function keeps moving left (toward the newest points). If it does not find much difference between the left queue and the right queue, it assumes that it went too far left and that it needs to go back to the right (toward the older points) to find the insertion point.

After the insertion vector is found, Virtual Author processes a certain number of the largest planar and cylindrical patches on the stationary assembly and finds a patch with an axis that has the smallest angle with the insertion vector (i.e., nearest patch). It follows the same procedure for the moved assembly. Virtual Author then calculates a vector that is perpendicular to the nearest stationary patch axis and nearest mobile patch axis. It then rotates the mobile assembly around that vector so that the nearest mobile patch axis aligns with the nearest stationary patch axis. The system adjusts the original insertion vector established by the recursive function so that it aligns with the nearest stationary patch axis. The insertion point is also adjusted to reflect this.

The previous rotational adjustment is meant to align the moved assembly with the stationary assembly, using the insertion vector as a guide. The next rotational adjustment rotates the moved assembly around the new insertion vector in order to align closest similar features. Each patch on the stationary assembly with an axis that is not parallel to the new insertion vector is added to a list of non-parallel stationary patches, and the patch axes are projected onto the plane that is perpendicular to the insertion vector. The same is done for patches on the mobile assembly. For each stationary non-parallel patch, Virtual Author finds mobile non-parallel patches whose projected axes are within D degrees of rotation from the projected stationary patch axis, where D is adjustable. (If no mobile patches are found within D degrees, then the system continues to the next stationary patch.) Next, Virtual Author repeatedly rotates the mobile assembly around the insertion axis so that the current stationary projected patch axis aligns with a projected mobile patch axis. After each rotation, the system compares the unprojected mobile patch axis to the unprojected stationary patch axis. If they are parallel and of the same type, Virtual Author stores the number of degrees that was required for rotation to make them match. Finally, Virtual Author finds the smallest such angle and rotates the mobile assembly one last time by that amount. Rotation around the insertion axis is limited to D degrees. The reasoning is that if the instructor wanted to align such distant features, then he would have done a better job of manually aligning the mobile assembly with the stationary one.

The Virtual Author simulates this process for cylindrical mobile and stationary patches that are parallel to the new insertion vector and have about the same surface area by computing the vector from the center of the assembly to the center of the cylindrical patch, projecting that vector to the plane perpendicular to the insertion vector, and adding an abstract patch with an axis matching this vector to the list of non-parallel stationary or mobile patches. This way, the Virtual Author is capable of aligning cylindrical features that are parallel to the insertion vector by rotating the mobile assembly around the insertion vector. An example of this is the rotation of the crankshaft so that the crankshaft pin aligns with a hole in the piston rod.

The final step in the motion smoothening process is the translational adjustment. The Virtual Author shifts the mobile assembly along the plane that is perpendicular to the insertion axis and then translates along the insertion axis so that the nearest similar planar patches or cylindrical patches align. Figure 7.5 shows the screen capture of a demonstration in the virtual environment for a model airplane engine assembly. A crankshaft is being attached to the piston assembly. The manually-placed crankshaft is clearly misaligned with the piston assembly. The stored points in the queue are being displayed in this virtual demonstration in the form of cubes.

Figure 7.6 shows the adjusted placement of the crankshaft after motion smoothening. The line represents the unadjusted insertion vector and the prism represents the system resolved insertion point. In the new placement, the crankshaft is perpendicular to the piston rod and the crankshaft has been rotated around the adjusted insertion vector so that the crankshaft pin matches the piston rod hole. It should be noted that normally the piston assembly is inside the engine block, but for better illustration, the crankshaft is assembled directly onto the piston assembly in this step.

We have tested motion smoothening and feature alignment on a large collection of parts and have confirmed that the employed algorithms work accurately on a wide variety of parts and assemblies. Testing has shown that the algorithms are sufficiently fast to be used inside a virtual environment where the system must be highly responsive to user's actions. Smoothening and alignment is carried out, on average, in 0.044 seconds for assemblies, where the average assembly is composed of 6.7 parts.

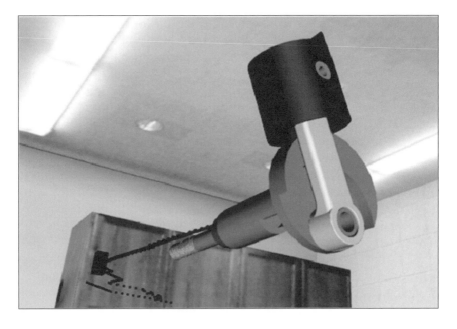

Figure 7.6: Automatically-adjusted placement of crankshaft after motion smoothening

7.4   Discussion

The ability of the Virtual Author, a component of the Virtual Training Studio, to quickly generate device assembly training instructions for the virtual environment is supported by three novel capabilities implemented within Virtual Author.

First, the Virtual Author tool is able to extract surfaces and alignment constraints needed for performing virtual assembly operations using polygonal models represented by STL files. The ability to extract this information from STL files makes our tool independent of any particular CAD system. The fact that the vast majority of CAD systems on the market can export to the STL format, makes Virtual Author, and VTS in general, highly versatile and able to accommodate engineers working with a wide variety of CAD tools.

Second, the Virtual Author performs logging and motion smoothening on the assembly demonstrations inside the virtual environment, allowing instructors to easily demonstrate how they want the assembly process taught to trainees and make sure that the relevant features of various parts in the assembly align and mate perfectly after a quick and imprecise virtual demonstration. Not enforcing non-penetration constraints makes it possible to achieve very high refresh rates on an inexpensive computer during virtual demonstrations. By using motion smoothening, the system is able to cope with minor errors during virtual demonstration that result due to lack of haptics feedback and lack of enforcement of non-penetration constraints.

Finally, the Virtual Author automatically generates (1) 3D animations of the assembly steps for the instructor to verify; (2) highly detailed text instructions by employing an instructor declared dictionary; and (3) data for 3D interactive simulations. Detailed text instructions can not only be used inside the virtual environment but also on the shop floor as a quick reference. Automatic generation of text instructions ensures that the text instructions are in complete agreement with the 3D animations.

The design and implementation of these novel capabilities has led to a huge improvement in the amount of time it takes to generate detailed, high quality multi-media training instructions for the virtual environment. Before the implementation of the Virtual Author, we needed about one week (40 hours) to manually generate training instructions for use in the Virtual Workspace. Virtual Author has reduced the time commitment for generating training instructions down to just several hours. As a specific example, the twenty-three part model airplane engine assembly tutorial used in many examples and screen captures in this book was re-generated after completion of the Virtual Author tool in just 133 minutes. Previously, it took us just over a full work week to generate the same data for the model airplane engine tutorial.

Currently, there are a number of limitations in the Virtual Author that will be addressed in the future. Tool use is currently not supported in the Virtual Workspace by trainees or in the Virtual Author by instructors.

In the future, we will design and implement algorithms that will allow instructors to import CAD models of tools into Virtual Author, define their behaviors, and incorporate them into the assembly instructions. Some of the future effort will also be invested in the improvement of the quality and robustness of generated text instructions. Current limitations often prevent the Virtual Author from using correct grammar when composing sentences. One example of this is the use of the word "is," and never "are," regardless of the plurality of the declared feature. "Cooling fins" is declared as one feature but must be treated as plural when choosing a verb.

Chapter 8

Virtual Mentor

This chapter describes a component of the Virtual Training Studio called the Virtual Mentor, which is responsible for interacting with the trainees in the virtual environment and monitoring their progress. The Virtual Mentor is a component that is embedded in the Virtual Workspace. Some of the tasks it performs are driving the interactive simulation code generated by the Virtual Author, executing user testing, logging user actions in the virtual environment, detecting errors and providing detailed messages and hints, and assisting the instructor in tailoring the generated training material to increase training effectiveness. This chapter presents some of the technical challenges and solutions, as well as the rationale behind the Virtual Mentor.

8.1 Background

Development of the Virtual Mentor came about because of the need for an intelligent agent to operate inside the Virtual Workspace. The Virtual Workspace was designed to be the basic infrastructure for running the Virtual Author-generated tutorials. It is capable of running animations, playing video clips, playing audio, and allowing the trainee to interact with objects in the virtual environment. It was also meant to give the trainee the capability to communicate with the Virtual Training Studio by manipulating virtual buttons on the virtual control panel and using wand commands by pressing buttons on the wand. Running interactive simulation, analyzing logs and making intelligent decisions when generating tests, however, takes more complicated logic. Using a separate module to accomplish these tasks makes it easier to upgrade and tailor the intelligent behavior of the system. It also makes it easier to plug the same functionality into other VTS components like the Virtual

Author, if, for example, the instructor wants to simulate the training session on the fly within the Virtual Author. The tasks of the Virtual Mentor can be divided into two categories: support for interactive simulation and adapting training material based on the performance of users.

A good amount of work has been done in this area in the past. Some have worked on techniques to detect errors made by trainees during training sessions and generate hints to provide them meaningful feedback. An example of a system that uses these techniques is the Georgia Tech Visual and Inspectable Tutor and Assistant, a tutoring system designed to teach satellite control and monitoring operations [Chu et al., 1995]. Lessons can be assigned one of many styles of tutoring ranging from demonstration via animation with little control of the lesson by the user to system monitoring of trainee progress with only occasional intervention by the system. In effect the tutor "fades" as the trainee progresses through the curriculum. Each lesson specifies performance requirements, which the student must satisfy to proceed to the next lesson. Another example of this type of system is "Steve", an animated agent who helps students learn to perform procedural, physical tasks in a virtual environment [Rickel and Johnson, 1999]. Steve can demonstrate tasks, monitor students and provide basic feedback when prompted by trainee. Steve signals mistakes with shaking of the head and saying "No." Yet another good example is a system designed by Abe et al., which teaches novices assembly and disassembly operations on mechanical parts inside a virtual environment by showing a technical illustration to trainees with lines representing assembly paths [Abe et al., 1996]. The hand motions of trainees are tracked and errors are detected. Trainees are alerted when they grasp wrong parts or move parts in the wrong direction. Monitoring errors and user actions in spatial manipulation tasks and providing highly descriptive feedback will require us to develop new types of algorithms.

Some work has also been done on intelligent adaptive tutorials. Various researchers have developed next generation tutorials that can adapt their instructions based on a user's capability and progress. Such systems, which adapt instructions to specific users, often use machine learning techniques from the artificial intelligence community. An example of this is AgentX, which uses Reinforcement Learning to cluster students into learning levels [Martin and Arroyo, 2004]. AgentX chooses subsets of all hints for a problem (instead of showing all possible hints) based on student's learning level. Students are grouped into levels based on pretests and their subsequent performance. If pretest data is not available for a student, then that student is automatically placed in level

L4, which represents students who perform in the 50th percentile of the performance distribution.

Subsequent sections will explain the techniques used by the Virtual Mentor and the rationale for those features. Section 8.2 presents all aspects of running interactive simulation. These include handling of part and assembly symmetries, detecting and reporting errors based on the symmetries, and using symmetry data to improve the quality of dynamic animations. Section 8.3 discusses the initial testing that led to the development of the Virtual Mentor and the idea of an intelligent agent. Section 8.4 explains the technical details of logging, log analysis, and generating tests tailored to trainees. Finally, Section 8.5 presents some concluding remarks and discusses the future path of the Virtual Mentor for achieving more autonomy in custom tailoring of tutorials.

8.2   Handling of Symmetries and Error Detection

8.2.1   *Use of Part Symmetries to Check for Correct Placement*

According to the case studies and the system testing conducted to date (discussed in detail in Chapter 9), interactive simulation, which involves manual assembly, turned out to be a popular system capability amongst users. As will be shown in Chapter 9, only one of thirty participants in the latest case study completed the training in the tutorials by using only animations and not using interactive simulation. An important aspect of a well-designed interactive simulation is the proper handling of symmetries. In real world mechanical assemblies very often there are parts that are highly symmetric along certain planes or axes. Such symmetries often mean that there is more than one correct insertion position and insertion orientation. The challenge of this problem is that the system is not aware of any symmetries and the only information it has access to is the single position and single orientation of each part within the overall assembly. This position and orientation were declared when the assembly was put together by the instructor in the virtual environment. The challenge for VTS is to find out what types of symmetries exist and to calculate other possible positions and orientations during interactive simulation. This allows a user to place a part that is symmetric in some way at one of the alternate insertion locations, as it could be done in real life, without the system giving an error. It also allows the user to use one of many clones of a part in the assembly process at a particular step without the system requiring the use of a particular clone. Proper implementation of symmetries speeds up the training process by not forcing the user to attempt various correct insertion locations or orientations until the user finally uses only those that were declared during the assembly sequence demonstration inside the Virtual Author-run virtual environment.

Another reason why part symmetries need to be properly handled is animations. After the instructor demonstrates the assembly process in the Virtual Author-monitored virtual environment, the Virtual Author automatically generates the initial animation code, in the form of Python script, which will later be executed by the Virtual Workspace, where users train to create dynamic animations. The initial code, which does not take symmetries into account, will not produce efficient animations for parts that have symmetries. This is because the generated code will always instruct the Virtual Workspace to animate the movement of a part to one particular position and orientation – that which was declared by the instructor during the demonstrated attachment. In many cases, it would be better to animate the movement of a part to the nearest symmetric orientation or position. This speeds up the animation and reduces risk of confusing the trainee.

The Virtual Mentor is responsible for enforcing correct attachments and insertions involving part/assembly symmetries, though the Virtual Author is used to declare and categorize the symmetries. As first mentioned in Chapter 7, when creating tutorials via the Virtual Author, the instructor specifies for each part that exhibits symmetry the main symmetry axis of the part. The main symmetry axis is the axis around which the assembly has the greatest number of allowable orientations. By allowable orientations, we mean that the assembly looks the same and can be attached to the receiving assembly with that orientation. If we use a tube as an example, the main symmetry axis would be the axis of the cylinder, because the tube can be rotated around that axis infinite number of ways and will still look the same. The instructor also specifies the number of different permissible orientations around this axis. We call this type of symmetry type A. In addition to this information, the instructor declares a second type of symmetry for each step, which we call type B. In type B symmetry, the instructor specifies one secondary symmetry axis, which is perpendicular to the main symmetry axis and also specifies a sub-type. By declaring the secondary symmetry axis, the instructor states that the assembly being attached may be flipped 180 degrees around this axis and the attachment would still be correct. In addition to declaring a secondary symmetry axis, the instructor also specifies a sub-type. The specified assembly sub-type informs the system about what types of rotations are allowed around the secondary symmetry axis and whether an alternate insertion position may be used for a particular step. The current version of the Virtual Mentor simplifies the problem by allowing only one alternate attachment location for the part being attached to an assembly and only one alternate orientation around the secondary axis. Sub-types for symmetry type B in the current version are:

- Sub-type B1: Allow primary position and primary orientation only.
- Sub-type B2: No alternate position is allowed, but alternate orientation for primary position is allowed.
- Sub-type B3: Alternate position is allowed, but with primary orientation only (no alternate orientation for primary position).
- Sub-type B4: All combinations of (alternate/primary) positions and orientations are allowed.
- Sub-type B5: Alternate position is allowed, but with alternate orientation only (no alternate orientation for primary position).

We developed a method to handle placement of parts at alternate locations that is not computationally expensive. Our current method causes the animation to always attach parts to their unique, designated locations and orientations, which were declared during the instructor's assembly sequence specification. This strategy simulates the placement of parts at their alternate locations and orientations by rotating, swapping, and repositioning parts in a way that is least noticeable to the trainee before activating the animation mechanism, which is part of the Virtual Workspace infrastructure.

One example of such swapping is how identical parts are handled. Upon loading all the parts, the Virtual Author automatically detects and marks identical parts. It does this by comparing the number of vertices and the bounding boxes of the parts. At the end of interactive simulation, right before the animation that completes the step is activated, the system swaps clones depending on which clone was originally the designated attachment part for that particular step. This strategy once again allows the Virtual Workspace animation to always attach parts to their unique, designated locations and orientations.

After the check for clones is made, the Virtual Mentor checks if the position of the released part is close enough to the ideal position(s) relative to the receiving assembly. The correct position for the attaching part depends on the sub-type of symmetry type B. For sub-type B5, for instance, there are two allowed positions – primary and alternate. The primary position is specified by the instructor explicitly via the Virtual Author. The Virtual Mentor automatically ascertains the alternate position for sub-type B5 by first drawing a vector from the primary insertion location to the final location and then doubling that vector. A marker is placed at the tip of this vector. The Virtual Mentor then checks if the released part is close to the alternate position. An example of sub-type B5 symmetry is shown in Figure 8.1, where a primer retainer is being inserted into the inner tube. One interesting aspect of sub-type B5 symmetry is that if the alternate insertion position is used on the other side of the inner tube, then the primer retainer must have the alternate orientation relative to the receiving assembly so that it is once again facing the inner tube. Alternate orientation is achieved by rotating the primer retainer around the secondary symmetry axis 180 degrees. If the trainee has placed the primer retainer at its alternate position, then the Virtual Mentor checks if the primer retainer has the alternate orientation. If that is the case, the Virtual Mentor flips the receiving assembly/part, in this case the inner tube, 180 degrees around the instructor-specified secondary axis before passing control to the Virtual Workspace animation-generating mechanism. By rotating the receiving assembly, the attaching subassembly is now at its primary insertion position and orientation, and as we already mentioned, all parts must be placed at their primary positions and orientations before animation is activated and the attaching part is inserted into the receiving part. In most cases the trainee does not notice this rotation.

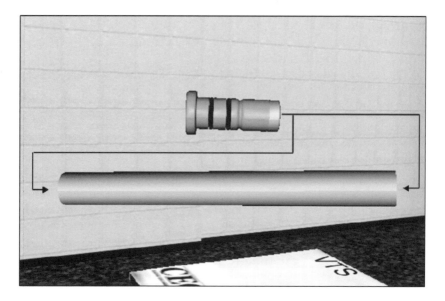

Figure 8.1: Primer retainer with two correct insertion positions

The final check that the Virtual Mentor makes is the correctness of rotation around the primary symmetry axis. If the placement is correct, the Virtual Mentor rotates the attaching part in increments based on the number of permissible orientations. For example, if this number is 3, then the increment is 120 degrees. If the number is 4, then the increment is 90 degrees. The system must rotate in these increments to make sure the user does not notice a change in rotation. By rotating in these increments, the Virtual Mentor takes advantage of the attaching part's symmetry to conceal the rotation. The reason why the attaching assembly must be rotated at all is because without such "setup rotation", the animation will be forced to rotate the part until it reaches its designated orientation within the assembly, slowing down the training in the process.

Figure 8.2 shows an example of sub-type B1 symmetry. A front plate assembly containing the needle and needle valve is being attached to the engine block. There are no alternate orientations or positions. The trainee must place the front plate assembly very close to the primary orientation and positions declared by the instructor within the Virtual Author. Otherwise, an error message is given to the trainee describing the flawed orientation or position.

Figure 8.2: An example of sub-type B1 symmetry where only the primary position and primary orientation is allowed. In effect, there is no symmetry.

Figure 8.3 shows an example of sub-type B2 symmetry. An outer tube is being attached to the rest of the rocket motor assembly. Sub-type B2 symmetry says, "No alternate position allowed, but alternate orientation for primary position is allowed." This means that the outer tube can only be attached from one side of the rocket motor assembly – the primary position declared during authoring. However, the outer tube is symmetric along the plane that is perpendicular to the outer tube's main symmetry axis. The main symmetry axis of the outer tube is the axis of the cylinder. This means that if the instructor chooses a secondary symmetry axis that is perpendicular to the main symmetry axis and flips the outer tube 180 degrees around the secondary symmetry axis, then the outer tube will look the same and can be attached to the rocket motor assembly with that orientation. This flipped orientation is called alternate orientation and for sub-type B2, it is allowed. In this scenario, the mobile part, the part being attached, also has an infinite number of symmetric orientations around the main symmetry axis. Since this orientation has to do with the main symmetry axis, it is type A symmetry. The trainee can use any orientation around the main axis during placement and the Virtual Mentor will allow that instead of generating an error.

Figure 8.3: An example of sub-type B2 symmetry where the attachable part (outer tube) can only be inserted at the primary position, but with either primary or alternate orientation (around the secondary axis). Secondary axis is perpendicular to the main axis, which is the axis of the cylinder.

Plate 9 (in the color section) shows an example of sub-type B4 symmetry. A connecting pin is being inserted into the hole of the piston assembly. The trainee is allowed to use either the primary position, which was declared during authoring, or the alternate position, which is on the other side of the piston. For both the primary position and the alternate position, the trainee is allowed to use either the primary orientation or the alternate, flipped 180 degrees, orientation. Since the pin is once again a cylinder, it has an infinite number of symmetric orientations around the main symmetry axis.

Finally, Plate 10 (in the color section) shows an example of how, taking advantage of symmetries, the system can make animations more efficient and clear. In Plate 10, a nut is being attached to the threaded crankshaft rod. Even though during the virtual demonstration, the instructor specifies one orientation, the nut has a hexagonal shape and, therefore, has six symmetric orientations around the main symmetry axis. If the trainee places the nut close enough to one of the symmetric orientations relative to the crankshaft and signals for animation to take over, then the Virtual Mentor rotates the nut in 60 degree increments as close as possible to the primary orientation. Rotating in 60 degree increments takes advantage of the symmetry of the part in order to conceal any rotation that may be occurring behind the scenes. Once the nut is rotated as close as possible to the ideal rotation without the rotation being noticed, animation is allowed to proceed. This prevents the animation from performing unnecessary rotation around the main symmetry axis prior to moving the part into its final location within the receiving assembly.

The two tutorials used in the latest case study contain twelve steps involving symmetries out of a total of nineteen steps. Three steps out of nineteen also involve the use of clones. During the case study we observed users placing symmetric assemblies and parts at both their primary and alternate locations. The Virtual Mentor demonstrated 100 percent accuracy in detecting alternate correct placements and allowing users to proceed. One such case that we observed was step three of the ejection seat rocket tutorial, in which one of the users had to place a cartridge propellant grain into a cartridge case. The propellant grain was cylindrical while the case was a tube. The user placed the cartridge propellant grain on the other side of the cartridge case, which was not the original insertion location declared in the Virtual Author. The Virtual Mentor correctly gave the user a success message and correctly animated the propellant grain going into the case from the alternate location. Please see Plate 11 (in the color section) for a screenshot of the placement of the propellant grain at its alternate location relative to the case and the Virtual Mentor's response.

8.2.2 *Error Messages*

Detailed and precise error messages are important in the quick diagnosis and resolution of a problem, such as, for example, an incorrect assembly attempt. In order to provide detailed error messages and helpful hints in the event of a mistake, the system must first determine exactly what type of error was made. The current version of the Virtual Mentor is capable of detecting five types of errors:

- Incorrect part was used for the given step in the process.
- Part was placed at an incorrect position.
- Primary axis of the part is not correctly aligned.
- Part is not correctly rotated around the primary axis of the part.
- Primary axis of part is correctly aligned by object facing in the opposite direction.

Whenever the Virtual Mentor gives the third, fourth, or fifth error to the user, it draws the primary axis through the part which the trainee attempted to assemble to another part or subassembly. This way the trainee knows exactly what axis is being referred to by the Virtual Mentor.

In the process of testing our system using volunteers, we observed that when trainees paid attention to the text error messages, they corrected their mistakes more quickly, on average, in order to complete the step. Trainees who, for whatever reason, did not pay attention to the text errors took significantly longer, on average, to correct their mistakes.

For the two tutorials used in our case studies, the Virtual Mentor reported a total of 146 errors during training. While monitoring the training of each trainee in VTS, no error detection or error classification mistakes on the part of the Virtual Mentor were observed. One of the instances of error detection and classification that we observed typified the detection and classification of an error by the Virtual Mentor. In the fourth step of the model airplane engine tutorial, a trainee had to place a cylinder head on top of the engine case. The cooling fins on the cylinder head had to be aligned parallel to the crankshaft. The user positioned the cylinder head correctly above the engine case but did not align the cooling fins with the crankshaft. After signaling to the Virtual Mentor to complete the assembly by pushing the "Complete" button, the trainee received a text error message saying, "Error: The object which needs to be inserted is not oriented correctly." Plate 12 (in the color section) shows how this error appears in the virtual environment. The trainee then watched an animation of the step and completed it correctly.

8.3   Annotation of Ambiguous Instructions

Once again, the first major task of the Virtual Mentor is providing support for interactive simulation by using information about part and assembly symmetries at each step in the assembly process to detect correct and incorrect part placements, report errors, and to prepare the part being attached for animation by performing a series of hidden rotations and translations. The second major task of the Virtual Mentor is to assist the instructor in adapting the training material based on the performance of trainees. The need for the second task came about as a result of some informal testing conducted early in the development of the VTS.

As the infrastructure of the VTS was built up to a certain level and a sample tutorial was created, we used six volunteers, consisting of graduate and undergraduate engineering students, to test the training effectiveness of the system and its user interface. At the time, the Virtual Author was not available so all the custom code needed for the tutorial was written manually in Python script by a programmer. The custom code included the text instructions, video and audio files, rules for dynamic animations, code to run interactive simulation, and variable detail visual hints to be used within interactive simulation. The six volunteers were trained inside the VTS to assemble a navy rocket that is a component of an ejection seat. The navy rocket components are shown in Plate 13 (in the color section). After the virtual environment training with CAD models of these devices, the trainees were given actual parts and asked to assemble real devices. Even though most volunteers felt very confident after VTS training and felt they could easily assemble the real devices, a good number of them made some mistakes during the assembly of the real devices. What is interesting is that the errors were pretty consistently being made at a certain set of points in the assembly process. Plate 14 (in the color section) shows one such point in the assembly process where the trainee must attach a small cap to one side of a rocket nozzle. The cap must be attached to the side of the nozzle with a relief. The animation that all volunteers saw during training showed the cap moving toward the side of the nozzle with a relief. Unfortunately, the limitations of the virtual reality display technologies used during testing made it difficult to see the relief due to a low 640 X 480 resolution. During physical testing some trainees attempted to attach the cap to the wrong side of the nozzle without the relief. Plate 15 (in the color section) shows another point in the assembly process that caused problems for several volunteers. Here the trainee must slide a rubber o-ring onto the right rectangular o-ring groove on the primer retainer. Some trainees slid the real o-ring onto the rounded groove next to it, which is not designed for o-rings. The trainees who did this did not notice the difference between rounded and rectangular grooves during virtual reality training.

After the initial testing, we added more detail to the tutorials to highlight the problem areas. The added details were in the form of additional text and audio instructions and more detailed animations. Animations were expanded in certain steps to include flashing 3D arrows that pointed out important features of the assembly. Plate 16 (in the color section) shows the first scenario where a cap must be attached to a nozzle. Figure 8.4 shows the second scenario where an o-ring must be rolled on top of a rectangular o-ring groove.

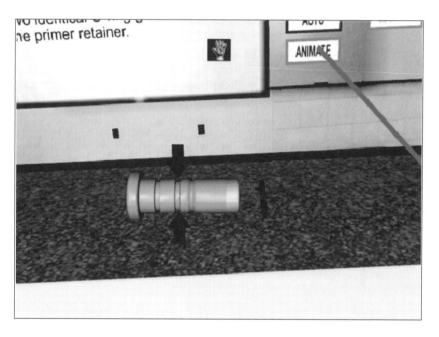

Figure 8.4: Detail in the form of flashing arrows added to the animation of rubber o-ring attachment to o-ring groove

After the changes were made, we conducted a second round of training and testing with another six volunteers. During the second round of testing the new volunteers made fewer errors. These results showed that no matter how clear the instructor tried to be when generating the training material, certain flaws in the training material could only be detected after user testing and analysis of the results. This spurred the need for development of an intelligent agent operating inside the virtual environment that is capable of not only logging all the actions of the trainees during training sessions, but also capable of generating targeted tests, analyzing the results, and later even automatically adapting the tutorials. The more such tasks the Virtual Mentor can perform automatically, the less of a burden will be placed on the instructor. The current version of the Virtual Mentor performs logging during training sessions and tests within the virtual environment, analyzes the logs, generates tests that are customized for each trainee based on that trainee's performance, and provides recommendations to the instructor. Later in this chapter, we also discuss the future path of the Virtual Mentor. We envision the Virtual Mentor not simply giving the instructor advice on what parts of the tutorials to adjust, but actually adapting the tutorials automatically with the instructor's approval.

8.4   Logging, Analysis, and Generation of Custom Tests

While trainees train to assemble a device in the Virtual Workspace and interact with the system, the Virtual Mentor logs a very wide range of events. Each event is logged with a timestamp representing the number of expired seconds since the beginning of the tutorial. Some of the events that the Virtual Mentor logs are:

- Activation of buttons on the virtual control panel
- Activation of animations
- Activation of hints
- Activation of video clips
- Browsing of steps in the assembly process by skipping to the next step or going back to a previous one
- Pick up of objects
- Release of objects
- All errors detected during interactive simulation and the type of error
- Successful completions of steps
- Use of wand functions like rotation of objects with wand buttons and trackball

In addition to events, the Virtual Mentor also periodically logs the position of the user's head and the position of the wand. This information is logged in order to analyze the range of movement of users in the virtual environment. The amount of movement can later be used to determine the efficiency of the virtual room by answering such questions as:

- Are the parts on the table spread out too much or arranged inefficiently, causing excessive wandering?

- Are the users moving and rotating objects manually by picking them up with the virtual laser pointer, or are they using the wand buttons and trackball to rotate and move objects?
- Are the users looking at parts from a different perspective by walking around them, or are they picking up and rotating them with the laser pointer?
- Should the size of the room be increased or decreased?

The logs are stored as text files in a format that can be loaded into Microsoft Excel. A new file is generated for each trainee. Figure 8.5 shows a snap shot of one such log which has been loaded into Excel.

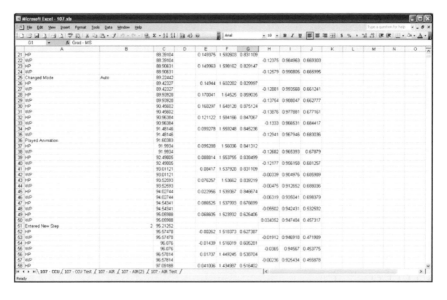

Figure 8.5: Snapshot of a tutorial log in Microsoft Excel

After the training session inside the Virtual Workspace is over, the Virtual Mentor performs some analysis on the trainee's log in order to generate the appropriate test for the trainee. The trainee receives a message from the Virtual Mentor that is displayed on the projector screen that a test is being generated. The trainee remains inside the Virtual Workspace while the Virtual Mentor analyzes the log and generates the test. After the Virtual Mentor finishes analyzing the log, it generates new random positions for all parts on the table and chooses a subset of the training session assembly steps for the trainee to perform in the Virtual Workspace. Certain features like text and audio instructions, hints, videos, and step browsing are disabled during test mode. The subset of steps on which the trainee is tested contains about 50 percent of the total number of tutorial steps. A certain number of steps is first chosen based on log data, and the rest are picked randomly.

The process of choosing test steps based on log data begins with extraction of the following information from the log: number and type of errors made, number and type of hints used, and the number of times the animation has been played. Each of these pieces of data is extracted for each step in the tutorial. Next, the Virtual Mentor gives each step in the tutorial a difficulty rating. When calculating the difficulty rating, the Virtual Mentor uses the occurrence and the weight of the extracted events. Errors have a weight of 3, hints have a weight of 2, and animations have a weight of 0 or 1. The first animation event has a weight of 0, while all subsequent animation events for a particular step have a weight of 1. The reason why multiple animation events are used to gauge step difficulty is because it was noticed during user testing and case studies that some trainees used animations as hints instead of using the hint feature in interactive simulation mode. Those trainees would switch to auto mode, play an animation and switch back to interactive simulation mode. Next, the Virtual Mentor sorts all steps in descending order based on the difficulty rating.

After the steps have been sorted, the Virtual Mentor must rearrange some steps depending on the error type of the problem steps. There is only one error type that requires this – assembly sequence error. Assembly sequence error occurs when the trainee forgets what step to perform next by trying to attach the wrong part for a particular step. In order to test for assembly sequence memory, the Virtual Mentor must present the trainee with two steps – the step where the error occurred and the step before it. The only exception to that is if the step where this type of error occurred is the first step in the tutorial, in which case only the step where this error occurred will be used. To perform the rearranging of sorted steps, the Virtual Mentor visits each step in the queue where difficulties were detected. If a problem step S contains an assembly sequence error, then the Virtual Mentor moves step S − 1 in front of step S.

After the rearrangement has been done, the Virtual Mentor takes the steps in the top fifty percentile and uses them as steps the user will be tested on. If the number of problem steps makes up less than fifty percent of the total number of tutorial steps, then the Virtual Mentor chooses some random steps as filler. This strategy ensures that all trainees are given tests of the same length to maintain consistency for future gathering of statistics.

The trainee is then put into interactive simulation mode and given the chosen test steps in the proper sequence. If the trainee performs a particular step correctly or makes three errors while in that step, the Virtual Mentor loads the next step in the queue. While the trainee is being tested, all of his actions are once again monitored and logged in a separate test log file. At the conclusion of the test, the Virtual Mentor analyzes the log file associated with the test and updates the master log associated with the used tutorial. The master log contains a sorted list of tutorial steps and errors associated with those steps. Steps at the top of the list have the highest occurrences of errors for all trainees. After updating the master log, the Virtual Mentor checks the top thirty three percentile of steps for changes in position. If a particular step in the top thirty three percentile advances to a higher position, the Virtual Mentor adds it to the list of steps to bring to the instructor's attention. At the end of the analysis, if the list of changed steps is not empty, the Virtual Mentor sends out an email to the instructor containing the list of steps of a particular tutorial which have advanced in difficulty level as well as the error types that caused this rise. The logging and testing process flow is summarized in Figure 8.6.

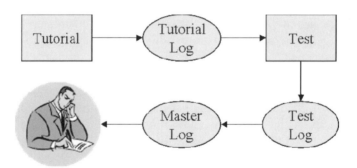

Figure 8.6: Flow of information in the log analysis process

8.5   Discussion

The Virtual Mentor is a software component embedded in the Virtual Workspace which is responsible for monitoring trainees, logging their progress, automatically generating customized tests and sending out reports to the instructor. The need for the Virtual Mentor arose as a result of informal user testing conducted to test the training effectiveness of

VTS. We realized that tests given to the trainees at the end of a tutorial can reveal confusing areas of the tutorial which may need additional detail for clarification. The current version of the Virtual Mentor merely alerts the instructor of the detected problems of the tutorial. Future versions of the Virtual Mentor will take over the task of changing the level of detail, automatically adding more detail to tutorials when problems are detected and removing detail after long periods of good trainee performance. The Virtual Author always generates the maximum level of detail when it automatically produces text instructions. Currently, the instructor is responsible for removing too much detail from text instructions and adding arrows to animations when necessary. Future versions of the Virtual Mentor will automatically control the detail level of generated text instructions, the detail level of animations, and the detail level of the hints.

Chapter 9

Assessment of the VTS and Training Performance

This chapter details the purpose, design, and results of a user study, in addition to outlining the procedures followed while conducting the study. It begins by presenting the details and methodology of the user study. It then presents user performance data to illustrate the effectiveness of the VTS. Finally, the results of the study pertaining to the three main modes of training in the virtual training studio – three-dimensional animation, interactive simulation, and video instruction – are presented. After presenting each set of results, there is a discussion of the roles and utility of each training mode on an individual basis. Next, the results of the four training features that were available to the users in the virtual training studio are presented. The four selected training features were hints, rotation mode, fast forward and rewind, and standard operating procedure (SOP). After presenting each of these results, the roles and utility of each feature are discussed individually. Next, a model that can be used to predict training time for future tutorials and an analysis of training paths selected by the users are discussed. Finally, a summary of the results from the study, recommendations for training mode and feature use, and guidelines for training, tutorial development policies, and future system policies are discussed.

9.1 Background

The Virtual Training Studio incorporates several features and training modes to aid users in learning and practicing steps in a tutorial. These features were developed and incorporated into the system without any knowledge of how they would be used or how successful they would be at aiding training. The study presented in this chapter investigates the use of each training feature and mode that was incorporated into the system [Brough, 2006]. There are several reasons for this investigation. First, in order for the system to train efficiently and address the various learning styles that users may have, one training mode would not suffice. However, too many training modes could overwhelm the users by inundating them with choices and forcing them to focus on how they are training, not on the process at hand. The overall goal is to minimize the number of training features and modes, while maximizing the flexibility of the system to accommodate all users, so training is not only complete but efficient.

There are three primary modes of training available to the users of the Virtual Training Studio: three-dimensional animation, interactive simulation, and video instruction. The data presented in this chapter will explain how the training modes and features are used and for what types of tasks they are most effective on individual steps, across user groups, and across tutorials to provide an in-depth analysis of the utility of each mode or feature.

9.2   Methodology

This study consists of 30 participants and 2 different tutorials. The 30 participants consist of 10 University of Maryland undergraduate engineering students, 10 University of Maryland full-time graduate engineering students and 10 full-time working engineers, all tested individually and without outside influence. These three demographics were selected to encompass the majority of the users of the system. In reality, 35 subjects participated in the study, but 5 subjects stopped during the first training session, because they were feeling nauseous and could not continue. This equates to about 15 percent of the subjects tested having feelings of VR sickness while using VTS. This is most likely caused by the slight latency in the system causing conflicting messages from the brain and the eyes. Each person was asked if they were prone to motion sickness while riding or reading in a vehicle. All said that sometimes they experienced motion sickness while riding in a vehicle and that reading for more than a few minutes was out of the question while traveling in a vehicle.

The structure of the study allowed it to be broken up into two parts, training session I and training session II. This was done for two reasons: (1) to make it easier on the test subjects, so they would not have to dedicate a three-hour block of time to complete the study; and (2) it provided a natural stopping point, because the subjects were asked to reflect back on their performance in training session I before beginning training session II. Both training sessions consisted of surveys, question and answer session, training in the VTS, and real life testing.

The data logging system, set to collect every 0.5 seconds, was activated for each tutorial and during the VE testing sessions. This information included modes and function being used, time, and errors.

9.2.1   *Tutorial Overview*

Before beginning the discussion of the two tutorials, it is important to mention that the steps in both tutorials have been classified into two different types, Type A and Type B. Steps classified as Type A are steps involving parts with simple geometry, multiple correct assembly orientations or positions, and/or have a close similarity to a previous step. Usually, these steps can be considered the easier of the two types. Type B steps involve parts with more complex geometry, only one correct assembly orientation or position (asymmetry) and minimal similarity to other steps in the process. An example of a Type A step is shown in Figure 9.1; the o-ring can be oriented two ways and the step has similarity to the next two steps. An example of a Type B step is shown in Figure 9.2; the environmental cap only fits on one side of the nozzle. See Table 9.1 for a summary (by tutorial) of the steps and their classifications.

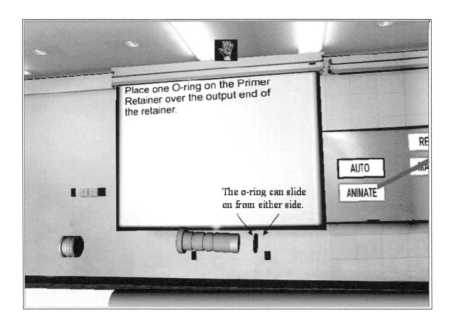

Figure 9.1: Screenshot of a Type A step – Assembling the o-ring to the primer retainer

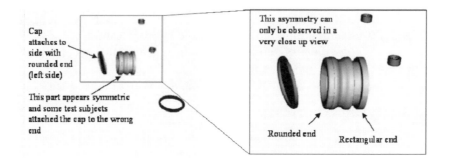

Figure 9.2: Screenshot of a Type B step – Assembling the environmental seal to the nozzle

Rocket Motor Assembly			
Step#	Description	Type A	Type B
1	Primer Retainer Cap		X
2	Nozzle Cap		X
3	Propellant Grain Installation	X	
4	Primer Retainer O-Ring (1)	X	
5	Primer Retainer O-Ring (2)	X	
6	Nozzle O-Ring	X	
7	Primer Retainer Installation		X
8	Nozzle Installation		X
9	Outer Tube Assembly	X	
Airplane Engine Assembly			
1	Piston Assembly Installation		X
2	Crankshaft Installation		X
3	Front Cover Installation		X
4	Cylinder Head Installation		X
5	Glow Plug Installation	X	
6	Muffler Installation		X
7	Inner Bushing Installation		X
8	Wood Block Installation	X	
9	Outer Bushing Installation	X	
10	Propeller Nut Installation	X	

Table 9.1: A summary of all tutorial steps including step types

9.2.2   *Rocket Tutorial*

The first tutorial created for use in this study is based on a small military rocket motor. The tutorial teaches the proper assembly of the rocket motor from beginning to end. The assembly consists of 9 steps and 10 components with varying geometric complexity. This device was selected, because most test subjects would not have experience in assembling devices similar to this, and its part count and step count were in the desired range, so that the amount of time subjects were committing to the study was manageable. Table 9.2 lists and describes the components shown in Figure 9.3 (a screen shot showing the parts on the table awaiting assembly) and Table 9.3 lists and describes the assembly steps.

Rocket Tutorial Components			
Step#	Component Name	Component Description	Quantity
1	Environmental Seal (lg)	An environmental seal to keep moisture and dirt from entering the assembled rocket	1
2	Environmental Seal (sm)	An environmental seal to keep moisture and dirt from entering the assembled rocket	1
3	Inner Tube	A steel tube which creates the pressure chamber necessary for propulsion	1
4	Nozzle	A cylindrical device used to create thrust	1
5	O-ring	A rubber ring installed on the nozzle and primer retainer that creates a seal	3
6	Outer Tube	A steel tube that is installed over the inner tube to act as a protective barrier	1
7	Primer Retainer	A cylindrical device that is used to hold the ignition source	1
8	Propellant Grain	The energetic material that powers the rocket	1

Table 9.2: List and description of rocket tutorial components

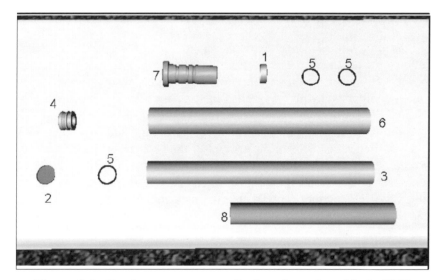

Figure 9.3: Rocket components displayed on the table in VTS

Rocket Tutorial Steps	
Step#	Step Description
1	Install the large environmental seal on the primer retainer
2	Install the small environmental seal on the nozzle
3	Insert the propellant grain inside the inner tube
4	Install the first o-ring on the primer retainer
5	Install the second o-ring on the primer retainer
6	Install the third o-ring on the nozzle
7	Insert the primer retainer into one end of the inner tube
8	Insert the nozzle in the other end of the inner tube
9	Install the outer tube over the inner tube

Table 9.3: Description of rocket tutorial assembly steps

9.2.3   *Airplane Engine Tutorial*

The second tutorial created for use in this study is based on a small, single cylinder (0.60 cubic inch displacement) model airplane engine. The assembly consists of 10 steps and 11 components. This device was selected because it is similar in difficulty to the rocket tutorial and because most test subjects would not have experience in assembling devices similar to this. Also, its part count and step count were close to the rocket tutorial. Table 9.4 lists and describes the components shown in Figure 9.4 (a screen shot showing the parts on the table awaiting assembly) and Table 9.5 lists and describes the assembly steps.

\multicolumn{4}{c}{Airplane Engine Tutorial Components}			
Step #	Component Name	Component Description	Quantity
1	Crankshaft	A machined component that translates linear motion into rotational motion	1
2	Cylinder Head	A round, finned cylinder that seals the combustion chamber	1
3	Engine Case	The outer case that all of the components assemble to	1
4	Front Cover	A structural piece that provides support for the crankshaft and seals the crankcase	1
5	Glow Plug	Ignites the air/fuel mixture	1
6	Inner Bushing	Provides support for the propeller	1
7	Muffler	Provides a directed route for the exhaust	1
8	Outer Bushing	Provides support for the propeller	1
9	Piston Assembly	Consists of the piston, the connecting rod and the wrist pin	1
10	Propeller Nut	Secures the propeller to the crankshaft	1
11	Wood Block	A stand-in for the propeller of similar thickness and size	1

Table 9.4: List and description of airplane engine tutorial components

9.2.4   *Training Session I*

The following is a step by step description of the procedures followed in the first training session, which demonstrated the assembly of the rocket motor.

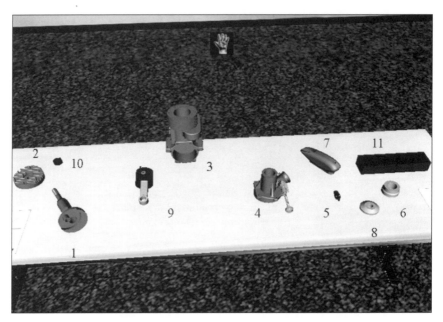

Figure 9.4: Airplane engine components displayed on the table in VTS

Airplane Engine Tutorial Steps	
Step #	Step Description
1	Insert the piston assembly into the engine case
2	Insert the crankshaft into the free end of the connecting rod
3	Install the front cover over the crankshaft
4	Install the cylinder head, aligning the fins correctly
5	Install the glow plug in the center of the cylinder head
6	Install the muffler with the exit turned away from the crankshaft
7	Install the inner bushing over the crankshaft
8	Install the wood block over the crankshaft
9	Install the outer bushing over the crankshaft
10	Tighten the propeller nut on the threaded end of the crankshaft

Table 9.5: Description of airplane engine tutorial assembly steps

1. Each participant began by reading and signing the consent form that was part of the approved Institutional Review Board package.
2. Before any discussion of the study began, the subjects were asked to complete one survey and one set of questionnaires. This was done before the study began to avoid any potential influence on the subjects' opinions and to establish a baseline. The survey presented each subject with the same scenario and the same set of seven learning modes and asked them to rank order the learning modes from 1 to 7, 1 being their most preferred method of learning and 7 being their least preferred method of learning.
3. The subjects were then asked to complete a questionnaire that gathered information about their current knowledge of virtual reality and virtual reality-based training. It also inquired about video game experience and if the subject had ever had a virtual reality experience before.
4. Each subject was then given the same introduction to the Virtual Training Studio consisting of an explanation of the purpose of the system and a description of current and potential applications of the system. The function of the individual hardware components was explained, along with a quick overview of the software being used.
5. The subject was then given a quick overview of the wand and asked to enter the virtual environment and participate in an interactive wand training session to familiarize him or her with the controls.
6. The subject was asked several questions to verify their knowledge of the wand interface. The subject was required to know all of the functions before moving on to the first tutorial.
7. A short training demonstration was given to show each subject how to use the modes and features available to them.
8. Prior to entering the virtual environment to begin the first training session, each subject was given an explanation of the goals of the study and how they would be tested after completing the training, so they could tailor their learning as they saw fit. The training session was completely free form and user-driven to allow each subject to develop their own training process without any outside assistance. The twenty-five-minute training session was broken up into two parts, so the potential for VR-related motion sickness was minimized. The first part was a fifteen-minute session and the second part lasted ten minutes. If the subject was comfortable with their knowledge of the process

after the first part, the second part was not required. Again, this decision was up to the individual knowing that it would be necessary for them to pass two tests upon completion.

9. Upon completion of the training session, each subject was asked to complete a series of questions related to their likes and dislikes about training in the virtual environment, specific information about the some of the modes and features, and whether or not they felt as though they could perform the operation in real life as a result of their training.

10. Two tests were created to verify that the users were learning in the virtual environment. The first test was a virtual environment test that consisted of three steps (steps 1, 3, and 8). The subject had to perform those steps in the virtual environment without any help. In order to successfully complete the test, the subject was required to analyze the state of assembly of the rocket and based on the parts remaining on the table, determine and correctly perform the next step without any instructions, animations, video or audio help. Once the step was completed correctly, the system automatically jumped to the next selected step, and the process continued until all three steps were completed successfully or the five-minute time limit was reached.

11. Once the VE test was complete, the subject was asked to complete a second test to verify learning. The subject was asked to assemble the real device from their memory without any outside assistance. There was no time limit on this test, and the only requirements were that the exact order of steps must be followed, and the parts must be assembled correctly.

9.2.5   *Training Session II*

The following is a step by step description of the procedures followed in the second training session, which demonstrated the assembly of a model airplane engine.

Before beginning training on the second tutorial, each subject was asked how they planned to train in this tutorial based on their performance in training session I. They were instructed that they were not required to follow their proposed training path if it was not working for them, but they would have to explain why they deviated from it in the post training questionnaire.

Prior to entering the virtual environment to begin the second training session, each subject again received an explanation of the goals of the study. Each subject was also reminded how they would be tested after completing the training, so they could tailor their learning as they saw fit. The training session was completely free form and user-driven to allow each subject to develop their own training process without any outside assistance. As before, the twenty-five-minute training session was broken up into two parts, the second part being optional.

Upon completion of the training session, each subject was asked to answer a series of questions related to their likes and dislikes about training in the virtual environment.

The same two tests to verify that the users were learning in the virtual environment were used in this tutorial. The first test, as before, was a virtual environment test consisting of steps 1, 3, and 6. Again, in order to successfully complete the test, the subject was required to analyze the state of assembly of the engine, and based on the parts remaining on the table, determine and correctly perform the next step without any instructions, animations, video, or audio help. Once the step was completed correctly, the system jumped to the next selected step and the process continued until all three steps were completed successfully or the 5 minute time limit was reached.

Once the VE test was complete, the subject was asked to complete the second test to verify learning. As before, the subject was asked to assemble the real device from his/her memory without any outside assistance. Again, there was no time limit on this test. The only requirements were that the exact order of steps must be followed and the parts must be assembled correctly.

In the first training session, the subjects were asked to complete a survey where they rank ordered learning preferences based on a predetermined scenario. Each subject was again asked to fill out this survey upon completion of the training to see if there was any change in their preferences as a result of being exposed to the Virtual Training Studio. Again, the survey presented each subject with the same scenario and the same set of seven learning modes and asked them to rank order the learning modes from 1 to 7, 1 being their most preferred method of learning and 7 being their least preferred method of learning.

Finally, each subject was asked to complete a questionnaire about their overall experience using the Virtual Training Studio to learn a new process, including their favorite and least favorite part of the training, their desire to use this system again, and whether they felt that their performance improved between the first and second tutorial.

9.3   Data Analysis: System Performance

The Virtual Training Studio was successful at training users to perform assembly steps. The system, costing less than USD 50,000, trained 30 subjects to assemble two completely different mechanical devices with an average overall success rate of 94.1 percent. Breaking this composite number down shows that on the first tutorial, the navy rocket, subjects only averaged a score of 2.67 out of 3.00 (88.9 percent) with a standard deviation of 0.55 on the virtual environment test. This score improved to 8.50 out of 9.00 (94.4 percent) with a standard deviation of 0.90 on the test where the subjects assembled the real device. On the second tutorial, the airplane engine, improvement in performance was evident. The subjects averaged a 2.87 out of 3.00 (95.6 percent) with a standard deviation of 0.35 on the VE test and an even better 9.73 out of 10 (97.3 percent) with a standard deviation of .52 on the live test. These high average scores and the decrease in the standard deviation between the groups indicate better performance on the second tutorial. More importantly, the average scores indicate a high level of learning in both training sessions and the ability to transfer the knowledge gained and apply it in a real situation. It can be concluded that the VTS is a successful training system for assembly training involving devices with up to 11 components and 10 assembly steps.

9.4   Data Analysis: Training Modes

Before beginning this part of the data analysis section, it should be noted that the use of each mode and feature will be presented by illustrating the percentage of users, by group, who used the particular feature. Because users could use one or all of these features during their training sessions and the data is being reported on an individual feature basis, the sum of the percentages for each group does not total 100 percent.

This section discusses the data associated with the three training modes available inside VTS. The first learning mode discussed is the video mode, a mode that allows the trainee to view a live video of the assembly. The second feature is 3D animation mode, a mode that allows the trainee to view a 3D animation of the assembly. The final learning mode is interactive simulation, a mode that allows the trainees to interact with the objects in the VE and perform the assembly themselves.

9.4.1   *Video-Based Instruction*

Video instruction mode is the simplest mode to use and requires the least amount of interaction with the system by the users, only requiring them to select video mode and press the "Play" button to view the video of the particular step inside the virtual environment. This mode of training provides the trainee with information not available in the other modes offered in VTS – a visualization of what the actual components look like and how the components are assembled in real life, as opposed to a computer-generated simulation of the operation. For some users, this mode adds a necessary level of detail that may help them connect the virtual environment to the real environment and allow them to better transfer the knowledge from one environment to the other.

The percentage of subjects using the video mode during training was the first piece of data analyzed. The rocket and airplane engine tutorials were first analyzed separately. There was very little difference in the use of the video instruction mode between the rocket and airplane engine tutorials. The trends between the two tutorials were almost identical, so the results were aggregated and analyzed by test subject group, because there were some interesting trends between the groups.

The results showed that the overall utilization of the video mode can be categorized as low. The usage was 29 percent for the undergraduate students, 16 percent for the graduate students and 9 percent for the full-time engineers, overall average being only 18 percent. Only 9 percent of the full-time engineers used this feature in comparison to 29 percent of the undergraduates – a fairly significant difference. The test subjects from each of the two groups were contacted to see if this difference in use could be explained. The overarching answer was that the undergraduates seemed to be more curious about the features available to them and were more willing to try them while the full-time engineers were more focused on learning what they needed to get the job done and less interested in exploring the system.

Another interesting piece of data is the distribution of the use of the video training mode by type of step. As mentioned previously, each step in the tutorial was classified as either Type A or Type B. The results of the study reveal that of the 18 percent of users, 39 percent used the video training mode on steps of Type A and the remaining 61 percent of users used the video training mode on steps of Type B. This indicates that the video training mode is not used as much on the less challenging steps and is utilized more on the Type B steps.

Analyzing video use on a time basis further illustrates the difference in use between the two step types. On average, users of the video mode on Type B steps spent 2 to 3 times as long as they did on Type A steps as shown in Figure 9.5 and with a lot more variability in the average time spent on a per step basis. This variability can be attributed to the difficulty and complexity inherent in the Type B steps and the variable amount of time each user takes to understand the process. The Type A steps are much simpler and more straightforward, so the majority of users clustered more around the average time, resulting in the lower standard deviation for those step types. The other interesting trend that appears in Figure 9.5 is the shorter time per step for the full-time engineers as compared to the other groups, especially on the Type B steps. This corresponds with the lower use rate discussed previously. Not only did the full-time engineers use this feature less, but they also used it for a shorter amount of time for the same reasons.

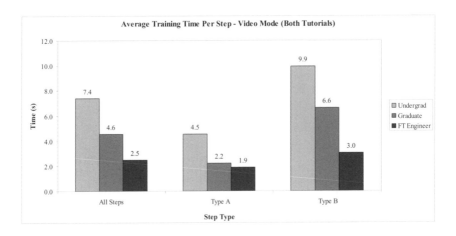

Figure 9.5: Average time spent training using the video mode on both tutorials on a per step basis – organized by step type

After mining and analyzing this data from the user logs, it can be concluded that the video mode was under utilized. On average, only 18 percent, or about 5 subjects out of 30, used this feature to train on every step of both tutorials. The use of this mode in both tutorials seems to be much more random than in the other modes. This trend could be due to the curiosity of the users trying the training method, coupled with a few subjects who used this training mode on a majority of the steps. The data shows that video training is necessary in some instances for a minority of the users, especially on steps of the Type B nature. These results prompt the question of whether or not the time required to produce helpful and detailed videos is justified by the low level of use that the mode received in this study. After reviewing the data and the responses from the undergraduates and the full-time engineers, this learning mode can be classified as a non-critical feature for successful training. Its development should only be pursued in certain cases where seeing the real part is known to be helpful. This sentiment is further acknowledged in the results of the questionnaires each subject filled out after each training session. The subjects were asked to indicate on each step whether or not the video instruction feature was helpful to them. In this questionnaire, the video training mode yielded only 20 percent utilization, which was very close to the actual level of utilization in the tutorials and correlates nicely with the data logged from each user group.

9.4.2 *3-Dimensional Animation Mode*

The second mode of instruction in VTS is the 3D animation mode. It allows the users to be slightly more involved in the training process by allowing them to choose the distance and perspective from which they view the animation of each step in the assembly by walking around in the virtual environment as the animation plays, a benefit that is not available from the video mode. It still only requires limited interaction with the parts themselves, but it lets the users progress through the tutorial at their own pace and from the point of view that conveys the most information to them. It also lets the users see the object in three dimensions, as opposed to two dimensions in video mode, even though it is not photorealistic. Despite this potential limitation of the 3D animation training mode, its utilization, on average, increased almost four-fold over video mode.

The trends between the two tutorials were almost identical, so, as before, the results were aggregated and presented by test subject group in Table 9.6. The overall utilization of the 3D animation mode can be categorized as high: 68 percent for the undergraduate students, 86 percent for the graduate students, and a slightly higher 90 percent for the full-time engineers. This mode averaged 81 percent utilization overall. There was an interesting difference between the undergraduates' use of this mode and the other two groups' use, especially the full-time engineers, which can be explained by the increased use of the video training mode by the undergraduates. It should be noted that a single subject can use this mode more than one time on a particular step. Since there is a large overlap between the information that the video mode and animation mode present, any kind of increased use of the video mode would decrease the use of 3D animation mode.

Training Mode\Subjects	Undergraduate	Graduate	Full-Time Engineer	Overall Average
Video	29	16	9	18
3D Animation	68	86	90	81
Interactive Simulation	98	88	94	94

Table 9.6: Percentage of subjects using various training modes

The results of the study also revealed that of the 81 percent of users, 47 percent used the 3D animation mode on steps of Type A, and the remaining 53 percent of users used the 3D animation mode on steps of Type B. This indicates that this mode is useful on both types of steps almost equally.

Analyzing and plotting 3D animation data illustrated that even though there was a significant difference in the use of this mode by the undergraduates, the average times spent using this mode per step was very close between groups, and there was little variability in the use of this feature within groups. Standard deviations remained relatively low given the size of the study. Use of the 3D animation training mode on the Type A and Type B steps does not vary as much as it did in the video mode, most likely due to a much higher percentage of use by the three groups and wider acceptance of the training method by the participants.

The 3D animation mode was highly utilized, because, on average, 81 percent, or about 24 subjects out of 30, used this feature to train on every step of both tutorials. There is no question as to whether it is necessary to create high quality 3D animations. It is justified by the high level of use that the mode received in this study and the consistent amount of time spent on each step using this mode. After reviewing the data, this learning mode can be classified as a critical feature for successful training and should be developed further. This belief is further acknowledged in the results of the questionnaires each subject completed after each training session. The subjects were asked to indicate on each step whether or not the 3D animation mode was helpful to them. In this questionnaire, the 3D animation mode yielded an 89 percent utilization, which was very close to the actual level of utilization in the tutorials and correlates nicely with the data logged from each user. We can conclude from this that based on the data collected from this study, 3D animation is a useful training tool inside VTS. Its overall utility is fairly steady, increasing only slightly with an increase in geometric complexity and orientation complexity.

9.4.3   *Interactive Simulation*

The last mode of instruction in VTS is the interactive simulation mode. It allows the user to be completely involved in the training process by permitting them not only to choose the distance and perspective from which they view each step in the assembly, but also to select the correct object and position and orient it so that it can be assembled. This mode of training is highly interactive and requires the user to not only know which step they are on, but how the parts actually fit together. This mode reinforces learning by doing, i.e. interaction with the parts in the virtual environment. Just as in the 3D animation mode, the users progress through the tutorial at their own pace and from the point of view that conveys the most information to them. This mode also allows the user to see the object in three dimensions, as opposed to the two dimensions of the video mode, but it does not portray the object exactly as it looks in real life due to a lack of photorealism of the parts. Despite this potential limitation of the training mode, its utilization increased almost five-fold over video mode and about 17 percent over 3D animation mode.

As for the percentage of subjects using the interactive simulation mode, the trends between the tutorials were again almost identical, so, as before, the results were aggregated and presented by the test subject group in Figure 9.6. The graph shows that the overall utilization of the interactive simulation mode can be categorized as high, with usage numbers being 98 percent for the undergraduate students, 88 percent for the graduate students, and a slightly higher 94 percent for the full-time engineers, with the overall average being 94 percent. There was only a very slight difference in utilization of the training mode between the three user groups.

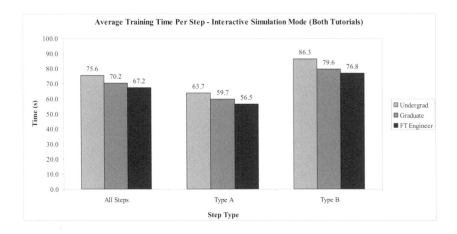

Figure 9.6: Average time spent training using the interactive simulation mode on both tutorials on a per step basis – organized by step type

According to the user study, of the 94 percent of users who used interactive simulation, 47 percent used it on steps of Type A, and the remaining 53 percent of them used it on steps of Type B. This indicates that this mode is useful on both types of steps almost equally.

Interestingly, this is the same distribution seen from the 3D animation data.

Analyzing and plotting interactive simulation use on a time basis illustrated that even though the distribution of uses of this mode on the two types of steps was fairly close, the average amount of time spent training on steps was not. The average time spent training on a Type B step (on a per step basis) increased 30-35 percent over the time spent training on a Type A step. Also, the average time spent on a step using interactive simulation increased about 3 times over the time spent on a step using 3D animation. This can be attributed to the almost unlimited freedom given to the user when training in this mode. Being given that much choice and ability to control the situation, as allowed in the interactive simulation mode, leads to much higher use times and more variability between users.

Breaking this data down further to a step by step basis allows us to see the performance on a more detailed level, and the aggregated variability can be seen on each step. Steps 3, 4, and 5 are very similar. The steps involve installing identical o-rings onto components. The data for the rocket tutorial shows the time spent on each consecutive step decreases and that learning has occurred and the process becomes easier as the number of encounters with a similar step increases. Similarly, in the airplane tutorial, steps 7 and 9 (two similar steps) show the same characteristics as steps 3, 4, and 5 in the rocket tutorial. These steps are considered similar, because the second step is a logical follow up to the first step and involves very similar position and alignment to complete. Step 7 involves installing a bushing with complex internal geometry onto the crankshaft, and step 9 involves installing a different bushing with simple geometry onto the crankshaft.

After analyzing the experimental data it is evident that the interactive simulation training mode was the most important and most widely used mode, with an overall average use of 94 percent. It is also interesting that when the data is inspected on a step by step basis, it is evident that use increases and decreases slightly on certain steps. Taking a more in depth look and realizing that each step in the tutorials does not have the same geometric complexity or similarities, a better understanding of the importance of the interactive simulation mode can be determined. The first trend that is evident in the rocket tutorial data is the decline in the number of uses of this mode in steps 6, 7, 8, and 9. Starting with steps 5 and 6 (Type A), this can be explained because it is almost identical to the operation in step 4; installing an o-ring onto one of the parts. Because these are similar operations, repetitive and performed back to back, it is easy to understand why less practice would be necessary.

In the airplane engine tutorial, the components are more geometrically complex and more sensitive to orientation during assembly than the components in the rocket tutorial. The use of the interactive simulation mode remains steady for the first 7 steps and only begins to noticeably decline on the last three steps, 8, 9, and 10 (Type A), because of their low level of geometric complexity and on steps 8 and 10, the lack of an orientation requirement. Step 9 requires one correct orientation, but is particularly obvious due to the geometry of the part and is very similar to the operation in step 7, a Type B step with complex internal geometry.

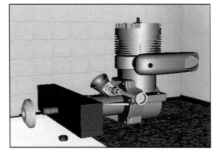

Step 7 – Inner bushing installation   Step 9 – Outer bushing installation

Figure 9.7: Illustration of similar steps in the airplane engine tutorials

After reviewing the data, interactive simulation could be classified as a critical feature for successful training and should be developed further. Based on the data collected from this study, interactive simulation is a useful training tool inside VTS. Its utility increases as the geometric complexity and orientation complexity of the particular step increases and the time spent training with it decreases as the similarity of steps increases. It is also beneficial for reinforcing more trivial steps (Type A) but requires fewer uses to convey the information to the user than the more intensive steps (Type B) in the training process.

9.5   Data Analysis – Training Features

This section discusses the data associated with the features implemented to aid the three training modes in their transfer of knowledge to the trainees. The first feature is audio delivery of the standard operating procedure, a feature that allows the user to hear the audio instruction at any time. The next feature discussed is the fast forward and rewind feature, a feature that allows the trainee to easily and quickly navigate through the tutorials. The third feature discussed is the rotation function, a unique feature that allows trainees to easily manipulate and rotate objects. The last feature discussed is the hint function, a feature that the trainee can use if he/she is unsure of how to perform the step.

9.5.1   *Audio Delivery of Standard Operating Procedures*

This section begins the presentation and analysis of the data collected on the various training features implemented in the Virtual Training Studio that aid the three training modes in their transfer of knowledge to the user with the standard operating procedure, or SOP function. This function is designed to work in conjunction with the interactive simulation mode, so the user can play the audio instruction at anytime. The function can be useful in the other training modes, but each of those methods automatically plays the audio instruction while interactive simulation does not.

The results from rocket and airplane engine tutorials were aggregated and presented by test subject group. Overall utilization of the SOP function was rather unimpressive and can be categorized as very low: 2 percent for the undergraduate students, 3 percent for the graduate students, and a slightly higher 14 percent for the full-time engineers, while averaging only 7 percent overall. There was only a slight difference in utilization of the training mode between the undergraduates and the graduate students, with a significantly higher utilization by the full-time engineers. The full-time engineers used this function more than the other two groups, because they work with SOPs every day and for some, the label "SOP" sparked an interest which motivated them to use the feature.

The standard operating procedure function had a very low level of utilization in these tutorials, with an overall average use of 7 percent. Its use was very sporadic in both tutorials, as was expected because it is only designed to be used when a participant needs to hear the instruction again and does not want to read it from the projector screen. The only training mode that does not play the audio instruction is the interactive simulation mode, so the number of times that it is potentially necessary is significantly limited. Also, by the time most users were using the interactive simulation mode to train, they had already heard the audio instruction at least one time and were using the interactive simulation mode to reinforce what the 3D animation mode taught them. Even though its use is very infrequent, the SOP function is an important feature in the Virtual Training Studio and requires very little additional development time. The SOP feature can sometimes convey information to users in a shorter amount of time than watching an animation of a step, but with less visual detail. An additional benefit is that the user can hear the exact step from the paper SOP that they will be using to assemble the device, once certified. The SOP feature's ease of implementation into the system far outweighs its low use in these tutorials. Also, looking at the answers to the questionnaire pertaining to the importance of audio instructions on each step of the tutorials, it can be seen that hearing the instructions is important to most users, with audio instructions receiving an average score of 61 percent. We can conclude that, based on the data collected from the questionnaire, the SOP function is a useful training tool inside VTS. However, from the data collected during the training sessions, it is not possible to draw any definitive conclusions about the SOP function's use relative to the geometric complexity and orientation complexity of particular steps.

9.5.2   Fast Forward and Rewind Feature

The second feature that is important to discuss is the fast forward and rewind (FFWD and RWD) function. This function is designed to work in any of the modes to allow the user to quickly jump from one step to another without viewing animations or videos or listening to audio instructions, and it is very simple to implement. This feature is useful for quickly assembling or disassembling the device and for advancing to the next step in video mode.

The rocket and airplane engine tutorials were analyzed separately. The results were then aggregated and presented by test subject group. It is clear from the graphical representation of the results that the overall utilization of the fast forward and rewind functions can be categorized as moderate, accounting for 51 percent for the undergraduate students, 55 percent for the graduate students, and 27 percent for the full-time engineers.

One trend that was noticed is that as the subjects got further into the tutorial, the number of times they used the fast forward and rewind function followed a slightly negative trend. Also, the full-time engineers used the mode less on the airplane engine tutorial than they did on the rocket tutorial. This can be attributed to their more focused approach to learning in the virtual environment, while the other two groups spent more time exploring the features of the system. Also, the undergraduates' rate of use increased from the first tutorial to the second, indicating their liking for the feature and its usefulness for their training.

Additionally, while analyzing a plot of the distribution of the subjects using the fast forward and rewind function by type of step, we noticed that of the 44 percent of users, 45 percent used the fast forward and rewind function on steps of Type A, and the remaining 55 percent of users used the fast forward and rewind function on steps of Type B. This indicates that this function is useful for both types of steps almost equally.

Based on the results, the fast forward and rewind function was moderately utilized. On average, 44 percent, or about 13 subjects out of 30, used this feature to train on every step of both tutorials. This is a rather high level of use for a feature that does not convey as much information to the user compared to the other functions and modes available. However, the feature does allow the trainee to quickly navigate through the tutorial without listening to audio instructions, aligning parts, or watching 3D animations or videos. One trend that was evident was the decrease in use of the function as the user progressed through the tutorial. This trend could be related to the decrease in available parts as the tutorial progressed and the reduced uncertainty in the next step. There seems to be no dependence on geometric complexity, orientation complexity, or repetition of steps as in the previous training modes.

This data is important to further developing the infrastructure of the VTS, because it dictated how a process was broken down into steps. Implementing this feature causes the developer to consider the granularity of the steps, so the information can be conveyed to the user at the appropriate level of detail. The results of this study confirmed that the steps were broken down to the appropriate level. Before seeing this data, it was unclear if breaking the steps down further would increase the effectiveness of the tutorial. After seeing the data, the level of detail turned out to be appropriate. The users of this feature were looking to quickly move forward or backward through the tutorial, without inspecting the process closely.

The fast forward and rewind feature is a useful training tool inside VTS. Its overall use is fairly steady regardless of geometric complexity and orientation complexity of the particular step. After reviewing the data, this learning function can be classified as a non-critical feature for successful training and more of a convenience feature to quickly navigate through the tutorial. However, it is recommended that this feature be kept because of its ability to speed up training time. Its current state of development is sufficient to serve the desired function.

9.5.3   *Rotation Feature*

The rotation function is designed to work primarily in the interactive simulation mode but can also be useful in the 3D animation mode to manipulate and inspect various parts during animation. The feature allows trainees to rotate held parts by rotating a trackball on the wand. It was developed because the system utilizes a wand-based interface to keep the system cost down, as opposed to the more expensive glove-based or haptics systems other researchers may be using. Our wand design initially had a very cumbersome rotation function that made it hard to visualize the amount of rotation necessary to align the part. After receiving feedback from several users, the design was changed to its current configuration – the configuration that was used in this study. It was necessary to test this new implementation for further refinement and improvement and to determine its value in the infrastructure. This feature is particularly helpful for orienting and aligning objects that would normally require multiple hand/wand rotations to correctly align for assembly or inspection.

Table 9.7 presents the results by test subject group for both tutorials. It shows that the overall utilization of the rotation function can be categorized as moderate, accounting for 66 percent usage for the undergraduate students, 56 percent for the graduate students and 45 percent for the full-time engineers. The average utilization was 56 percent.

	Undergrad	Graduate	Full-Time Engineer	Overall Average
Percentage Using SOP Function	2	3	14	7
Percentage Using FFWD/RWD	51	55	27	44
Percentage Using Rotation Feature	66	56	45	56
Percentage Using Hint Feature	22	8	14	15

Table 9.7: Percentage of subjects using various features

The overall trends are more random and sporadic on this mode when analyzed on a step-by-step basis. The full-time engineers used the feature the least and the undergraduates, the most. This phenomenon can be attributed to the same theory given for the previous features - the (more experienced) full-time engineers were more concerned with executing the training while the undergraduates were interested in exploring the features of the system and finding the ones that worked for them.

The results also showed that of the 56 percent of users who used this feature, 44 percent used the rotation function on steps of Type A and the remaining 56 percent of users used the rotation function on steps of Type B. This indicates that this feature is useful on both types of steps almost equally. Interestingly, this is almost the same distribution seen on many of the modes and functions.

The rotation function was moderately utilized, because on average, 56 percent, or about 17 subjects out of 30, used this feature to train on every step of both tutorials. This is a rather high level of use, considering the method of rotation was not completely intuitive and there were other more physical ways of rotating objects in the virtual environment. The biggest trend that was evident in looking at the data was the increase in the use of the rotation function as geometric complexity and orientation complexity increased (Type B steps). In the airplane engine tutorial, there were multiple Type B steps that were both geometrically complex and had very particular orientations that were required in order to successfully assemble the device. This is evident in the data because the first 7 steps, 6 of which are Type B, had a much higher rate of use of the rotation function than the last 3 steps (all Type A). As stated before, the last 3 steps in the airplane engine tutorial are trivial in nature compared to the earlier steps and the objects can be easily manipulated by just moving around the room and rotating the wrist. Steps such as aligning the crankshaft pin to the hole in the connecting rod in the airplane engine tutorial are not trivial and require fine alignment in order to perform the operation successfully. The same trends are evident in the rocket tutorial; the more complex the steps are, the higher the rate of use of the rotation function. This is particularly evident in step 2 (Type B) of the rocket tutorial, where a small cap must be placed on the correct side of the nozzle, the side with a very small relief machined in it that allows the cap to sit securely. Here, there is a spike in the number of uses of the rotation feature due to the precise rotation and alignment needed in order to successfully complete the step.

Based on the results of the study, the rotation function is a useful tool in the Virtual Training Studio that aids users on steps with orientation complexity or geometric complexity in aligning the parts correctly during the assembly process. On less complex steps, the importance of the rotation function comes down to user preference and familiarity with the controls. After reviewing the data, this function can be classified as a critical feature for successful training and is recommended for further development to improve the rotation method and interface. Because the use of the wand requires a tutorial to teach the rotation method, a more predictable and common method could be implemented to further improve the efficiency of the wand.

9.5.4 Hint Function

The last feature that is discussed here is the hint function. This function is designed to work in the interactive simulation mode to aid the trainee in performing the current step by first flashing the part that is supposed to be picked up and then animating a ghost of the mobile part to its insertion location. It is a useful function if the trainee is stuck on a step or continues to make mistakes on a step and is unsure of the error being made. Without it, the user has to switch modes and either use the video mode or the 3D animation mode. These alternatives slow down the user.

The results for the rocket and airplane engine tutorials were combined and organized by test subject group. The overall utilization of the hint function can be categorized as low, with the utilization level of 22 percent for the undergraduate students, 8 percent for the graduate students and a slightly higher 14 percent for the full-time engineers, averaging only 15 percent utilization overall.

Another interesting plot is the one depicting use, grouped into three distinct ranges: low (0 to 3 uses per step), moderate (4 to 7 uses per step), and high (8 + uses per step). The frequency of the hints used increased from the first tutorial to the second. This can mostly be attributed to the fact that the second tutorial was more geometrically complex and had more difficult steps than the rocket tutorial, so users needed more assistance on the second tutorial.

Breaking this data down on a step-by-step basis by user group for both the rocket and the engine tutorials shows the steps where the hint function was used the most. Table 9.8 presents the data for the rocket tutorial and the airplane engine tutorial. These figures show that there are some fluctuations in the use of the hint function on various steps in the two tutorials, due primarily to the complexity of the steps. Also worth noting is that the hint use was aggregated, because individual group hint use was low, and the trends were not as evident.

Tutorial/Steps	1	2	3	4	5	6	7	8	9	10
Rocket Motor	7	9	7	5	0	4	20	10	2	-
Airplane Engine	6	14	11	12	13	10	6	0	2	0

Table 9.8: Number of hints used

An interesting trend was found in the analysis of the distribution of the subjects using the hint function by type of step. According to the results, of the 15 percent of users who used the hint function, 28 percent used the hint function on steps of Type A and the remaining 72 percent of users used the hint function on steps of Type B. This indicates that, based on this data, the hint function was more useful on the Type B steps than the Type A steps. This was the expected distribution, because the hints are designed to help on the most difficult steps, typically Type B steps.

After mining this data from the user logs, it can be concluded that the hint function had a low level of utilization in both tutorials, with an average use of 15 percent, or about 5 subjects out of 30, using this feature to train on every step of both tutorials. A high level of use was not expected because the function is designed to be used intermittently, i.e., when subjects are unsure of the next step. As the subject learns the process, his reliance on the hint function should decrease; however, the more complex the steps and the geometry of the parts (Type B steps), the higher the rate of use of the hint function will be. Steps 1, 2, 7, and 8 in the rocket tutorial are all Type B steps and have the highest usage of hints. The same is true for steps 1-7 in the airplane engine tutorial, with all but one being classified as a Type B step. It is possible that step 5 falls into this group because it is a Type A step in a long series of Type B steps and this is not the only time that this trend has appeared in the data. Another reason for the low utilization of the hint function is that it is only available during the interactive simulation mode, because it is the only fully interactive mode where subjects are required to pick up objects and perform the steps themselves, which limits the availability of the function and its overall use.

We can conclude from this study that the hint function is a useful tool in the Virtual Training Studio that aids users on steps with orientation complexity or geometric complexity in aligning the parts correctly during the assembly process. On less complex steps, the importance of the hint function comes down to the user's memory. After reviewing the data, this learning function can be classified as a non-critical feature for successful training, because the same information can be conveyed by using the 3D animation mode; however, it is suggested that it be kept in its current state, because it has been shown to be very useful for certain users and does not require further development to remain successful.

9.6   Learning Paths

Analyzing the use data on a larger scale resulted in some interesting trends. The thirty users could be categorized into five primary learning categories: 3D-IS, 3D/IS, 3D, IS, and Combination. The first category is called 3D-IS, where the user completes all of the steps in a tutorial first in 3D animation and then switches to interactive simulation. This may occur only one time or several times in a row, depending on the particular user's preference. The next learning category is called 3D/IS, where the user completes the steps in the tutorial by first watching the step in 3D animation and then performing the step in interactive simulation before moving on to the next step. The user may perform this multiple times, but the data shows that users take longer using this training path and usually do not have time to perform it multiple times. The next learning category is called 3D, where the user only watches the 3D animations to learn the assembly process. This method is much less interactive than the others but allows the user to view the animations multiple times because the cycle time is low. The next category is called IS, where the user only uses interactive simulation to learn the assembly process. This method is highly interactive and is good for those who do not want to deal with the time delay associated with watching the 3D animations and would rather use the hint function to help them learn the process. The final category is called Combination and is for the users who used a combination of the 3D-IS and the 3D/IS categories. Some users started out with one method and decided to try a different method at some point during the training.

Figure 9.8 plots the use of each of the learning categories by the 30 participants in this study. The 3D-IS training method was the most widely used method overall, followed by the 3D/IS method, the IS method, the Combination method, and lastly, the 3D method. There are some probable reasons for these trends. The 3D-IS mode (38 percent) may have been the most popular method because it allowed the users to watch the entire process by viewing the step by step 3D animation and then move on to interactively assembling the device themselves and repeating the process as necessary. This process turned out to be very efficient and allowed the user to move quickly through the tutorials. The next most popular mode was the 3D/IS mode (32 percent), which on paper would seem to be the best choice, but in reality, turned out to be rather time-consuming, due to constant switching between modes. Most users could only complete one to two training cycles when using this mode.

Figure 9.8: Training paths followed by subjects in the study

The next most popular mode, IS (17 percent), was more geared toward people who immediately felt comfortable using the system and could train by performing the steps themselves instead of watching an animation of the steps. Most users could complete several training cycles when using this mode. The Combination mode (10 percent) captured the few people who did not follow one of the other modes completely through a training cycle and those users who decided that one method was not working for them and switched during the training session. The lowest used method, 3D (3 percent), provided minimal interactivity with the system and did not reinforce what the user had been shown while training. This method allowed multiple cycles through the tutorial, but its low interactivity did not provide enough practice for most users.

The participants' learning paths were analyzed for each tutorial. There is one interesting shift in the data between the first tutorial, the rocket, and the second tutorial, the airplane engine. The largest percentage of users (40 percent) used the 3D/IS mode in the first tutorial. That percentage dropped significantly in the second tutorial to only 23 percent. This shift is most likely due to the users learning that the 3D/IS mode is less efficient than the other modes. This inefficiency occurs because the user must toggle between modes and use the rewind function on every step so that the user can repeat the step in interactive simulation mode. Most users who used this method took the majority of the first 15 minutes of training to complete it one time, while users using the other methods could train multiple times in the same 15-minute time span. The

15-minute training limit was enforced to reduce chance of motion sickness in virtual reality. The other noticeable shifts are the increase in the use of the IS mode, netting a 7 percent increase, and the increase of users who decided to combine modes in the second tutorial. The rise in Combination use (6 percent) could also be due to the users realizing the inefficiencies of the 3D/IS mode and switching to the 3D-IS mode part of the way into the tutorial. Correspondingly, the 3D-IS mode increased 3 percent as well.

All of the learning categories discussed in this chapter can be considered successful ways to learn in the VTS, depending on user preference and the speed at which the user likes to train. There were no preconceived ideas of how the participants would train using the modes available to them in VTS. The results are interesting and show that the users preferred to be more linear in their training by sticking to one mode and then changing to another mode after each cycle through the steps. As the users became more experienced with the system, they showed less interest in toggling between modes. The increase in use of the IS mode shows that the users headed straight for the mode that allowed them to learn the steps on their own and helped them only when help was requested.

9.7   Survey Results

A survey was conducted as part of this study to determine user preferences of various learning methods. The survey consisted of 7 methods of learning a mechanical process, including drawings, an instruction manual, virtual environment, video, 3D animation, classroom instruction, and one-on-one training. Prior to being introduced to the VTS, each user was asked to rank order each learning method from 1 to 7, 1 being their most preferred method of training and 7 being their least preferred method of training. Then, after each user finished the second training session, they were asked to fill out the survey again to see if their preferences had changed. The results of both surveys are displayed in Table 9.9.

Looking at the results, it can be seen that there was little change for most of the categories; however, the individual interactive virtual environment training method improved one point from a rank of 3 to a rank of 2, displacing 3D animation with sound and text instruction from its number 2 spot and sending it to number 3. This data indicates that the implementation of VTS worked as designed and was successful, because the subjects' perceived preference improved to number 2, just behind one-on-one training with an expert. The remaining preferences of the users remained unchanged, further indicating a valid survey and consistency in the users' preferences. This finding indicates that there is interest in training in the virtual environment, and after using the VTS, this method of training is more desired than most of the other methods, except for one-on-one training, the learning style this system was modeled after.

Before and After Training		Overall Rank		
	Learning Methods	Rank Before	Rank After	Change
A	Drawings – 3-D exploded view and assembly views	7	7	0
B	Instruction Manual with 3-D renderings and text instructions	5	5	0
C	Individual interactive virtual environment-based training	3	2	1
D	Video of the process with audio instructions	4	4	0
E	3-D animation with sound and text instructions – not interactive	2	3	-1
F	Classroom instruction with peers	6	6	0
G	1 on 1 training with an expert	1	1	0

Table 9.9: Training preference survey results

9.8   Estimating Training Time

As the data was collected for this study, a predictive model was developed. The model predicts the overall time to train for a new user. The basis for the model is the time data collected for each user during their training session on both the rocket tutorial and the airplane engine tutorial. With this data, a model based on the average time it takes a user to perform a Type A step or a Type B step was created. The purpose of this model is to make designing future training sessions more efficient and improve scheduling of users. The time to train is a function of the average time spent training on a Type A step, the number of Type A steps, the average time spent training on a Type B step, and the number of Type B steps.

The basis for the time predictive model is shown below, where X equals the predicted time to train, Y equals the average time per step for a type A or B step, and Z equals the number of steps of type A or B.

$$X = \sum_{i=A}^{B} Y_i Z_i$$

Predicted time to train = F(Type A time, # Type A steps, Type B time, # Type B steps)

Type A Time = 90.4 seconds (per step)
Type B Time = 116.5 seconds (per step)
Type A Variance = 2613
Type B Variance = 3839

The model predicts the time by summing the product of the number of Type A steps and the Type A Time with the product of the number of Type B steps and the Type B time. See the example training situation below:

Type A Steps = 3
Type B Steps = 6

Predicted Training Time = (3X90.4) + (6X116.5) = 970.2 seconds

Although the model is simple in design, it can come in very handy when an approximate training time is necessary. In order to verify the model, it was used to predict the training time for users of the two tutorials that are a part of this study. Using the model to predict the training time for the rocket tutorial, with five Type A steps and four Type B steps, it yielded a time of 917.7 seconds. The predicted time to train is below the average of 970 seconds calculated from the data collected. Next, the model was used to predict the training time for the airplane tutorial. The model yielded very similar results, but instead of predicting low, it predicted high. The airplane tutorial has four Type A steps and six Type B steps and when entered into the model, it yielded a training time of 1060.3 seconds, slightly above the average of 1008 seconds. Looking at the results and determining the percent error, the model is only off by about +/- 5 percent. The results of this model are rather impressive given the relatively small amount of information that went into its development.

The model can be further refined to include the effects of similar steps on the total predicted time to train. Preliminary results indicate that a reduction factor of anywhere between 15 percent and 50 percent can be applied to a step if it is very similar to a previous step. The data indicated that on these types of steps there was a reduction in the amount of time it took to complete the next similar step. When two Type A steps are similar, a reduction of 15 percent can be applied to the time to complete the second step. When a Type B step is the first step and a Type A step is similar, the reduction in time can be much greater – up to 50 percent.

The model has been shown to be useful in predicting training times on tutorials. This model was based on tutorials with 9-10 steps and may be extrapolated but with additional uncertainty in the predicted value. Also, if the complexity of the process increases or decreases significantly, the model will most likely yield a result with higher uncertainty.

9.9   Future Tutorial Development Analysis

The data reported in this chapter is significant to the future development of tutorials. The results of the study yielded some expected results and some unexpected results. Three scenarios will be analyzed in this section. The first scenario is when a new tutorial must be developed on a limited budget. In this situation, the developer only wants to use the features that are absolutely necessary, are the least difficult to implement, and have the highest level of usage. The second scenario that will be addressed is when the trainees will have a limited amount of time to get trained. In this situation, the developer is interested in using the most preferred methods that require the least amount of training time. The third and final scenario is one where only a limited number of subjects are being trained and the developer wants to be sure that the tutorials are tailored to those trainees, keeping in mind both time-to-train and development cost.

Table 9.10 shows a breakdown of the three scenarios and the modes and features that have been selected for each. The first scenario is one where the developer has a limited training budget and needs the bare minimum modes and features in the system. The solution was to create a tutorial only using interactive simulation (because it was the most widely used), hints (because they provide the instruction and demonstration to the trainees), and the SOP feature so the trainee can hear the audio instructions. This combination saves money by not implementing the other modes and features and maximizes usability because the highest ranking mode was selected to be the only training mode.

The next scenario describes a situation where there is limited training time, and the developer needs to train many people quickly and efficiently. The solution to this was to build a system utilizing all of the features and modes. This allows the user to learn using any of the methods that have been developed and provides a completely customizable package that will allow each trainee to learn as quickly as possible. This combination costs more money to develop, but provides a wide variety learning paths to accommodate most users.

Scenario	Modes			Features			
	3-D Animation	Interactive Simulation	Video	Hint	Rotation Function	FFWD & REW	SOP
Limited Budget		X		X			X
Limited Training	X	X	X	X	X	X	X
Limited Subjects	X	X			X	X	

Table 9.10: Training requirements addressing various scenarios

The final scenario describes a situation where only a few subjects need to be trained and the developer wants to have some variety but really is interested in the core features that interest most users. The solution to this scenario was to implement the highest ranking training modes and features. 3D animation, interactive simulation, rotation mode, and fast forward and rewind were selected to be the features implemented. These features are the most popular and provide a broad set of learning paths that users can take to develop their skills. This system will cost less than the system designed for limited training time, but it will offer more flexibility than the system developed for the limited training budget. This design will yield the most utility for the least amount of money.

Analysis of these training scenarios shows that the VTS is a dynamic system that can be adapted depending on the developer's and user's needs.

9.10 Main Findings

The use of the features and modes discussed in this chapter is very important to future system development. Quantitatively being able to rate and understand the use of the various features developed sheds light on where and when they should be used in future tutorials. Some features are highly dependent on the complexity (or type) of the step, others are user-preference dependent, and still others are useful in almost all situations. This information has allowed us to evaluate various future training scenarios and provide recommendations that will help streamline the training process. More detailed studies are necessary to more thoroughly investigate the preliminary findings presented in this chapter, but some unique generalizations are very evident from the data presented, such as the importance of the 3D animation mode and the interactive simulation mode to the overall learning process. Also unique and important in this study was the ability to pull in some qualitative data from the test subjects to back up the quantitative data presented to further prove the preliminary findings in this study. Below is a list of the main findings from the study.

1. A low cost (under USD 50,000) virtual environment training system can successfully be used for teaching assembly operations.
2. Users show different preferences for learning modes based on the task at hand and individual learning styles (i.e., differently people chose to train differently on the same task).
3. All three learning modes were used and worked satisfactorily during user studies, and users were able to successfully learn using these modes.
4. Learning by doing in the interactive simulation mode was the most popular learning method, with 94 percent of trainees using it on every step in both tutorials. Learning by watching in the 3D animation mode was the second most popular learning method, with 81 percent of trainees using it on every step in both tutorials. This method was also preferred over the video training mode, which only yielded 18 percent usage.
5. The most preferred training path was going through the entire tutorial in 3D animation mode and then going through the entire tutorial in interactive simulation mode. This training path also yielded the most perfect scores.
6. Users were able to seamlessly switch back and forth between learning modes and utilize multiple learning modes on the same task. The novel features that have been implemented to support learning modes and switching back and forth between them have satisfactory computational performance for assembly tasks requiring 11 parts and 10 assembly steps.
7. Five out of 35 participants experienced symptoms of motion sickness and could not continue training in the virtual environment.

8. Subjects who are not prone to VR-induced motion sickness are able to learn an 11-step assembly sequence in less than 17 minutes. This length of training did not have any adverse effect on the subjects.

9. The wand-based interface is an effective user interface for tasks where process learning is required as opposed to motor skill development. This interface is significantly less expensive than the glove-based and/or haptics type of interface.

10. The average training time for a Type A step was 89 seconds, while the average training time for a Type B step was 116 seconds, a 30 percent increase.

11. Training using the Virtual Training Studio was successful; the average test score was 94 percent.

12. Survey results showed that users' preferences for training in an interactive virtual environment improved from a rank of 3 to a rank of 2 after training in the Virtual Training Studio.

Chapter 10

Emerging Technologies

This chapter presents a summary of the limitations of the existing virtual environment-based training applications. It also describes on-going work that is geared towards overcoming these limitations and significantly impacting the future virtual environment-based training applications.

10.1   Stereo Displays without Glasses

Stereo displays in the market today use some type of eye glasses to provide the user with depth perception. These glasses basically help in providing slightly different images for each eye and hence create the depth perception. Wearing glasses reduces realism and is uncomfortable for many users. Stereo displays without glasses have been the holy grail of the VR display research community. Currently, work is in progress along two different technical directions to come up with stereo displays that eliminate the need for the users to wear glasses. The first direction is to develop a display unit such that each pixel presents slightly different images to the left and right eyes by utilizing differences in visibility of its three dimensional surface. The differences perceived by two eyes help in generating the depth perception for the user. The second technology that is in the works is the development of 3D holograms using a series of spinning disks. Spinning disks get illuminated by specialized lights at specific points and create a 3D hologram. The availability of stereo displays without glasses is expected to help in increasing the use of VR technology in many new training areas. It might be particularly helpful in reducing the instances of motion sickness.

10.2   Improved User Interfaces

User interfaces that are currently available inside virtual environments are often cumbersome and not convenient to use. The video game industry is coming up with many new user interface concepts. As these video game interfaces become popular, they will also significantly help the virtual environment-based training applications. In the past, gesture-based interfaces have been tried in training applications. However, these interfaces did not gain popularity due to the difficulty in reliably identifying gestures as a result of limitations in sensing technology and pattern recognition algorithms. Recent advances in both of these areas are expected to significantly improve performance and easy-of-use for gesture-based interfaces. Recent advances in the voice recognition area are also making voice-based interfaces an attractive alternative. We believe that a combination of new user-interface hardware, gesture-based interfaces, and voice-based interfaces will truly revolutionize the user experience in the virtual environments and make it attractive to many new types of users who did not like the virtual environment user interfaces in the past.

10.3   Ease of Creating 3D Models

Many training scenarios involve defining complex workspaces with many different objects. Creating such workspaces requires a significant amount of effort in terms of modeling 3D objects and applying appropriate textures to them. This in turn increases the training costs significantly and thus limits the use of VE-based training. The availability of low cost and high speed 3D scanners is providing users an alternative way of defining the objects in the workspace. Currently, the spatial range of the commercially available 3D scanners is limited. Moreover, significant human intervention is needed in cleaning up the acquired data to create 3D models. However, recent advances in 3D scanners are expected to significantly speed up the process of creating high quality 3D virtual objects. This development in turn will make virtual environment-based training attractive to many new application areas.

10.4   Mixed Reality

The current generation of virtual environments exclusively makes use of virtual objects. In many training tasks, it might be possible to better train users by incorporating use of both physical parts and virtual objects. Recent advances in fast 3D scanning and RF identification technology are creating unique opportunities where physical parts and their virtual counterparts can be used together in a training session. For example, low cost rapid prototyping processes can be used to create physical parts. During the beginning of the training session, these physical parts are positioned on the workspace. The computer can recognize each of the parts using either 3D scanning technology or RF identification and can create virtual representations of these parts. The user is simultaneously able to interact with two workspaces. The first workspace consists of the physical parts. The second workspace is virtual workspace and consists of virtual parts. The computer can show the user annotation in the virtual workspace. However, the user can practice the assembly step with the physical parts. This type of scenario allows mixing physical reality and virtual reality in the same training session and combines the best features of both of these mediums. The computer can also use the projector to highlight the physical parts in the real workspace if the user forgets to pick the right part. The key to the deployment of mixed reality systems is making sure that the virtual world and the physical world remain synchronized at all times. As mentioned earlier, recent advances in fast 3D scanning and RF identification technology are creating foundations for this capability.

10.5   Models for Virtual Humans

Many training tasks require collaborative work between multiple human operators. In such situations, it becomes very important to have detailed models of virtual humans in the virtual world to make sure that users can visualize how the presence of other humans will influence their own tasks. Currently, most virtual environment-based training applications do not incorporate detailed models of humans in the workspace. Entertainment and computer games industries have made significant progress in developing realistic-looking human models. However, these models were mainly developed for generating realistic images on the screen for non-interactive applications. Currently, work is in progress that is further advancing the human body modeling by incorporating realistic degrees of freedom and mechanics. However, a realistic human model has many degrees of freedom and getting it to produce the desired behavior poses many user interface challenges. Significant additional work is needed to ensure that these sophisticated models can be easily instructed to produce the desired behavior. We believe that the availability of high fidelity and easy-to-use human models will significantly expand the realm of applications where VE-based training can be used.

The use of detailed mechanics-based human models in VR applications will also ensure that the operations performed by humans are ergonomically sound. This helps in two major ways. First, it increases productivity of the operator. Second, it reduces chances of accident and, therefore, reduces costs. In order to create ergonomically sound operations, we will need a system that can compute required forces and human movements during assembly operations. These required forces and human movements can be analyzed for their ergonomic correctness. If any operation poses threats to operator safety, it should be modified to meet the specified ergonomic requirements.

10.6   Context Dependent Simplifications

Most of the current virtual environment-based training applications including the Virtual Training Studio (VTS) system do not support real-time interaction with compliant parts, such as sheet or plastic parts. Supporting real-time interaction with compliant parts will require us to include finite element-based simulation capability. Our prior experience indicates that CAD model simplification was a crucial factor in achieving interactive performance from the collision detection and rendering point of view when dealing with rigid body parts. Hence, we believe that CAD model simplification will also be crucial to achieving interactive speeds during finite element-based simulation.

A fundamental characteristic of virtual assembly operations is the presence of multiple simulation scenarios. In other words, a given component may have to be analyzed under different sets of conditions during the assembly process. An important fact is that a significant feature in the first scenario may be insignificant in the second scenario, and vice-versa, leading to the notion of numerous simplification contexts associated with each component. The first challenge then is the definition and representation of simplification contexts, and their extraction from the training scenario. The next challenge is to systematically and quickly identify the significant and insignificant features for each simplification context. A typical mechanical component may contain hundreds of features, and multiple simplification contexts. Hence, the combinatorial complexity associated with the simplification process can be overwhelming. Due to the presence of multiple simplification contexts, it is not desirable to maintain numerous simplified models since their uploading during interactive virtual assembly can be challenging. We are currently working on identifying the main characteristics of the virtual assembly process that affect the simulation time and results and using these characteristics to generate various simplification contexts. Then, through a fundamental understanding of the interplay between simplification, computational speed, and accuracy, we are also developing a framework for optimizing the simplification for virtual assembly.

10.7   Capturing Cognitive Activities during Complex Training Tasks

The current virtual environment-based training applications only support training for physical activities. Many complex training tasks also involve cognitive activities. For example, troubleshooting is an integral part of the service and maintenance procedures. Some of the assembly and disassembly steps during service and maintenance tasks require significant cognitive activities in addition to usual physical activities. Based on our preliminary research, these cognitive activities include (1) planning to ensure that the task is performed in the minimum amount of time, (2) planning to avoid certain assembly states to eliminate the possibility of accidental damage to the nearby components, and (3) determining the spatial constraints for selecting and using the proper tools. We are currently working toward ensuring that these cognitive activities are captured as a part of the training instructions so that the trainees can become aware of these activities and also learn the appropriate problem solving strategies to carry out these cognitive activities. As a part of our on-going effort, we are planning to ask the instructors to think aloud as they demonstrate the assembly and disassembly operations during the instruction generation phase. Statements recorded during think-aloud sessions will be used to capture and classify the cognitive activities. We envision integrating the voice-to-text technology in the proposed system to do this classification automatically. The ability to capture cognitive activities and include them in the training instructions will significantly expand the scope of the virtual environment-based training applications.

10.8   Incorporating Annotations in 3D Animations

Three-dimensional animations are becoming a popular medium in training applications. However, sometimes, purely graphical instructions are unable to show the subtle asymmetry or small features due to the limitations of the spatial resolution in 3D animations. We are currently investigating the limitations of purely visual cues in 3D animations and the automatic creation of text instructions to compensate for or alert the user to those limitations. An example of the limitations in visual cues is when there are parts or part features in the environment which look similar. For example, a part may have a very slightly rounded end with a relief and a rectangular end on the other side. The system must detect that this is something that the human eye may not easily detect in the low resolution virtual environment. The system must then bring the user's attention to the subtle differences with additional text instructions. This requires that we determine and implement geometric comparison of parts, geometric comparison of features, and recognition of certain features that are difficult to register in the virtual environment. We believe that 3D animations with the right level of embedded textual annotations will improve the instruction quality significantly. The recent advances in the automated instruction generation area are preparing the foundations for creating such instructions automatically.

10.9   Automatically Adjusting the Level of Detail in Instructions

Currently, environment-based training systems offer a fixed level of detail in the training instructions. As a result of testing our current system we discovered the need to provide multiple levels of detail for the steps of training instructions. Having highly detailed instructions for every single step seems to slow down the training and obscure the details that are important. We realized that the system has to automatically make the decision about what level of detail to use based on user errors. Hence, we plan to experiment with the idea of automatic instruction optimization for maximum training effectiveness. This feature of the system would serve a dual purpose. First, it would tailor instructions for each trainee based on their individual performance. Second, it would automatically detect and clarify the potentially confusing areas of the instructions based on performance of many trainees.

The system for generating adaptive instructions should keep track of errors made in various steps by a particular trainee. At the end of the training session, the system could replay steps in which the trainee was having difficulties. This would be a series of quizzes. Those steps would be replayed with a twist, however. The positions, orientations, and even scale may change in the replayed "quiz" version of the original step. The purpose of the step replay is to reinforce in the trainee's memory the correct actions in areas where the trainee had difficulties and made prior mistakes. In addition to the basic ideas mentioned so far, we plan to investigate more advanced forms of custom tailoring instructions to individuals, such as altering the animations or breaking down a confusing step into smaller steps, and inserting additional text when necessary.

The system for generating adaptive instructions should analyze multiple logs in the database associated with a particular training instruction set and should attempt to fix steps where multiple people made mistakes. When trainees reach the end of the instructions, the system would give the trainees a test of the entire process. The results of the test would then be placed in the database and later analyzed by the system to detect problem areas where many people made mistakes. The system could then try to clarify problem areas by changing the level of detail for the confusing steps. The instructions for these steps could be made more detailed with the addition of visual aids, such as arrows, and the insertion of more detailed text/audio instructions.

The availability of adaptive instructions capability will significantly help to make sure that the virtual environment-based training instructions will be useful for people with different backgrounds and learning preferences. This will in turn improve the overall training process. Given the large amount of work currently under way in VE, future training using tools such as VTS will play a significant and important role in workforce development.

References

[1]   N. Abe, J.Y. Zhang, K. Tanaka, and H. Taki. A training system using virtual machines for teaching assembling/disassembling operations to novices. In Proceedings of *IEEE International Conference on Systems Man and Cybernetics*, pp. 2096-2101, 1996.

[2]   E. Aimeur, G. Brassard, H. Dufort, and S. Gambs. CLARISSE: A machine learning tool to initialize student models. In Proceedings of *the 6th International Conference on Intelligent Tutoring Systems*, 2002.

[3]   T.S. Andre, W.R. Bennett, A.R. Castillo, D.P. McClain, M.D. Purtee, B.M Wenzel, and M. Graci. Generalized operations simulation environment for aircraft maintenance training. RTO HFM Symposium on Advanced Technologies for Military Training, RTO-MP-HFM-101, Genoa, Italy, 13-15 October 2003.

[4]   J.R. Anderson. *Rules of the Mind*. Erlbaum, 1990.

[5]   R. Arangarasan and R. Gadh. Geometric modeling and collaborative design in a multi modal multi-sensory virtual environment. In Proceedings of *Computers and Information in Engineering Conference*, Baltimore, MD, September 2000.

[6]   E.G. Ashby and W.T. Maddox. Human category learning. *Annual Review of Psychology*, 56: 149-178, 2005.

[7]   E. Bachelder. Helicopter aircrew training using fused reality. In *Virtual Media for Military Applications* (pp. 27-1 – 27-14).

Meeting Proceedings RTO-MP-HFM-136, Paper 27, Neuilly-sur-Seine, France: RTO, 2006. Available from: http://www.rto.nato.int/abstracts.asp.

[8]   A. Banerjee and J Cecil. A virtual reality based decision support framework for manufacturing simulation. In Proceedings of *Computers and Information in Engineering Conference*, Chicago, IL, September 2003.

[9]   P. Banerjee and D. Zetu. *Virtual Manufacturing*. John Wiley and Sons, New York, NY, 2001.

[10]   J.E. Beck and B. P. Woolf. High-level student modeling with machine learning. *Lecture Notes in Computer Science*, 1839: 584-593, 2000.

[11]   J.E. Beck, B. P. Woolf, and C. R. Beal. ADVISOR: A machine learning architecture for intelligent tutor construction. In Proceedings of the *17th National Conference on Artificial Intelligence*, 2000.

[12]   W.F. Bischof. Visual learning: an overview. *Swiss Journal of Psychology*, 63 (3): 151-164, September 2004.

[13]   D. Bodemer, R. Ploetzner, I. Feuerlein, and H. Spada. The active integration of information during learning with dynamic and interactive visualizations. *Learning and Instruction*, 14 (3): 325-341, June 2004.

[14]   A.C. Boud, D.J. Haniff, C. Baber, and S.J. Steiner. Virtual reality and augmented reality as a training tool for assembly tasks. In Proceedings of *IEEE International Conference on Information Visualization*, pp. 32-36, 1999.

[15]   A.C. Boud, C. Baber, and S.J. Steiner. Virtual reality: A tool for assembly. *Presence: Teleoperators and Virtual Environments*, 9(5), pp. 486-496, 2000.

[16]   J.E. Brough. Assessment of Training Modes and Features in the Virtual Training Studio. Master's Thesis, University of Maryland, College Park, MD, 2006.

[17]   J.E. Brough, M. Schwartz, S.K. Gupta, D.K. Anand, C.F. Clark, R. Pettersen, and C. Yeager. Virtual Training Studio: A Step Towards Virtual Environment Assisted Training. *IEEE Virtual Manufacturing Workshop*, Alexandria, VA, March 2006.

[18]   J.E. Brough, M. Schwartz, S.K. Gupta, D.K. Anand, R. Kavetsky, and R. Pettersen. Towards development of a virtual environment-based training system for mechanical assembly operations. *Virtual Reality*, 11(4):189-206, 2007.

[19]   G.C. Burdea and P. Coiffet. *Virtual Reality Technology*. Hoboken, New Jersey: John Wiley and Sons, 2003.

[20]   K.E. Bystrom and W. Barfield. Collaborative task performance for learning using a virtual environment, *Presence*, Volume 8, Number 4, 1999.

[21]   C. Camachon. Learning to use visual information. *Ecological Psychology* 16(2): 115-128, 2004.

[22]   E. Chen and B. Marcus. Force feedback for surgical simulation. In Proceedings of the *IEEE*, 86 (3): 524-530, March 1998.

[23]   R.W. Chu, C.M. Mitchell, and P.M. Jones. Using the operator function model and OFMspert as the basis for an intelligent tutoring system: towards a tutor/aid paradigm for operators of supervisory control systems, *IEEE Transactions on Systems Man and Cybernetics*, 25(7):1054-1075, July 1995.

[24]   M.M. Chun and Y.H. Jiang. Implicit, long-term spatial contextual memory. *Journal of Experimental Psychology-Learning Memory and Cognition*, 29 (2): 224-234, March 2003.

[25]   M. Dickinson and A.S. Morris. Co-ordinate determination and performance analysis for robot manipulators and guided vehicles, In *IEE Proceedings*, 135(2), pp. 95 – 98, 1988.

[26]   V.G. Duffy, F.F. Wu, and P.P.W. Ng. Development of an Internet virtual layout system for improving workplace safety. *Computers in Industry*, 50 (2): 207-230, February 2003.

[27]   N. Endo and Y. Takeda. Selective learning of spatial configuration and object identity in visual search. *Perception and Psychophysics*, 66 (2): 293-302, February 2004.

[28]   E. Foxlin, M. Harrington, and Y. Altshuler. Miniature 6-DOF inertial system for tracking HMDs, *SPIE vol. 3362, Helmet and Head-Mounted Displays III*, AeroSense 98, Orlando, FL, 1998.

[29]   L. Gamberini, P. Cottone, A. Spagnolli, D. Varotto, and G. Mantovani. Responding to a fire emergency in a virtual environment: different patterns of action for different situations. *Ergonomics*, 46 (8): 842-858, June 20, 2003.

[30]   A. Gertner, C. Conati, and K. VanLehn. Procedural help in Andes: Generating hints using a Bayesian network student model. In Proceedings of the *15th National Conference on Artificial Intelligence*. Madison, WI, 1998.

[31]   S. Gottschalk, M.C. Lin, and D. Manocha. OBBTree: A hierarchical structure for rapid interference detection. In Proceedings of *International Conference on Computer Graphics and Interactive Techniques*, p. 171-180, 1996.

[32]   T.D. Green and J.H. Flowers. Comparison of implicit and explicit learning processes in a probabilistic task. *Perceptual And Motor Skills*, 97 (1): 299-314, August 2003.

[33]   R. Gupta, D. Whitney, and D. Zeltzer. Prototyping and design for assembly analysis using multimodal virtual environments. *Computer-Aided Design*, 29(8), pp. 585-597, 1997.

[34]   S.K. Gupta, C. J. Paredis, R. Sinha, and P. F. Brown. Intelligent assembly modeling and simulation. *Assembly Automation*, 21(3):215-235, 2001.

[35]   C.J. Hamblin. *Transfer of Training from Virtual Reality Environments*. PhD Dissertation, Wichita State University, 2005.

[36]   Hatanaka et al. Development of semi-spherical screen VR system for exploring urban environment. *ICAT*, 1998.

[37]   S.P. He, Z. Qin and X.P. He. Artificial intelligence applications in the design of STE virtual reality operation training system. In

International Conference on Machine Learning and Cybernetics, 4, pp 2324-2328, 2003.

[38]   N. Heffernan et al. Workshop on dialog-based intelligent tutoring systems: State of the art and new research directions. *Intelligent Tutoring Systems, Lecture Notes in Computer Science*, 3220: 914-914, 2004.

[39]   F.S. Hill Jr. *Computer Graphics Using Open GL*. Prentice Hall, Upper Saddle River, NJ, 2001.

[40]   D. Holl, B. Leplow, R. Schonfeld, and M. Mehdorn. Is it possible to learn and transfer spatial information from virtual to real worlds? Spatial Cognition III *Lecture Notes in Artificial Intelligence*, 2685: 143-156, 2003.

[41]   P. Hsieh, H. Halff, and C. Redfield. Four easy pieces: Developing systems for knowledge-based generative instruction. *International. Journal. of Artificial Intelligence in Education*, 1999.

[42]   S.J. Hsieh and P. Y. Hsieh. Integrated virtual learning system for programmable logic controller. *Journal of Engineering Education*, 93 (2): 169-178, April 2004.

[43]   S. Hsi, M. Linn, and J. Bell. The role of spatial reasoning in engineering and the design of spatial instruction. *ASEE Journal of Engineering Education*, 86, 2, 151-158, 1997.

[44]   M. Hodges. Virtual reality in training. In *Computer Graphics World*, Vol 21. No 8, 1998.

[45]   J.R. Hogue, R.W. Allen, S. Markham, A. Harmsen, J. MacDonald, and C. Schmucker. Parachute mission planning, training and rehearsal using a deployable virtual reality simulator. 17th AIAA Aerodynamic Decelerator Systems Technology Conference and Seminar, AIAA 2003-2156, Monterey, CA, 19-22 May 2003.

[46]   H.C. Huang, S.H. Nain, Y.P. Hung, and T. Cheng. Disparity-based view morphing - A new technique for image-based rendering. In Proceedings of the *ACM Symposium on Virtual*

Reality Software and Technology, Taipei, Taiwan, pp 9-16, 1998.

[47]   Intersense company website (available at http://www.intersense.com), viewed on July 27, 2006.

[48]   S. Jayaram, U. Jayaram, Y. Wang, H. Tirumali, K. Lyons, K., and P. Hart. VADE: A virtual assembly design environment. *Computer Graphics and Applications*, 19(6), pp. 44–50,1999.

[49]   U. Jayaram, H. Tirumali, and S. Jayaram, A tool/part/human interaction model for assembly in virtual environments. In Proceedings of *Computers and Information in Engineering Conference*, Baltimore, MD, September 2000.

[50]   U. Jayaram, S. Jayaram, C. DeChenne, and Y. Jun Kim. Case studies using immersive virtual assembly in industry. In Proceedings of *Computers and Information in Engineering Conference*, Salt Lake City, UT, September – October 2004.

[51]   P. Johansson and A. Ynnerman. Immersive visual interfaces-assessing usability by the effects of learning/results from and empirical study. *Journal of Computing and Information Science in Engineering*, Vol 4, pp. 124-131, 2004.

[52]   T. Jong and W.R Van Joolingen. Scientific discovery learning with computer simulations of conceptual domains. *Review of Educational Research*, 68 (2): 179-201, 1998.

[53]   S. Kalyuga, P. Chandler, and J. Sweller. When redundant on-screen text in multimedia technical instruction can interfere with learning. *Human Factors*, 46 (3): 567-581, Fall 2004.

[54]   J. Kawahara. Contextual cueing in 3D layouts defined by binocular disparity. *Visual Cognition*, 10 (7): 837-852, October 2003.

[55]   M.M. Keehner, F. Tendick, M.V. Meng, H.P. Anwar, M. Hegarty, M.L. Stoller, and Q.Y. Duh. Spatial ability, experience, and skill in laparoscopic surgery. *American Journal of Surgery*, 188 (1): 71-75, July 2004.

[56]   C. Kim and J. Vance. Using VPS (Voxmap Pointshell) as the basis for interaction in a virtual assembly environment. In Proceedings of *Computers and Information in Engineering Conference*, Chicago, IL, September 2003.

[57]   R.L. Klatzky, Y. Lippa, J.M. Loomis, and R.G. Golledge. Learning directions of objects specified by vision, spatial audition, or auditory spatial language. *Learning & Memory*, 9 (6): 364-367, Nov-Dec 2002.

[58]   N. I. Badler and J.M. Allbeck. Advanced Visual and Instruction Systems for Maintenance Support (AVIS-MS), AFRL-HE-WP-TR-2007-0018, 20070509258, Air Force Research Laboratory Human Effectiveness Directorate Warfighter Readiness Research Division Logistics Readiness Branch, Wirght-Patterson AFB, OH, December 2006.

[59]   B.W. Knerr and D.R. Lampton. An Assessment of the Virtual-Integrated MOUT Training System (V-IMTS), Technical Report 1163, 20050930 047, United States Army Research Institute for the Behavioral and Social Sciences, June 2005.

[60]   K.R. Koedinger, V. Aleven, N. Heffernan, B. McLaren, and M. Hockenberry. Opening the door to non-programmers: authoring intelligent tutor behavior by demonstration. *Lecture Notes in Computer Science*, 3220, 162-174, 2004.

[61]   A.Y. Lee. Exploring the relationship between distributed training, integrated learning environments, and immersive training environments, Air Force Research Laboratory Human Effectiveness Directorate Warfighter Readiness Research Division, AFRL-HE-AZ-TR-2007-0001, January 2007.

[62]   K. Lee. *Principles of CAD/CAM/CAE Systems*, Addison Wesley Longman, Reading, Massachusetts, 1999.

[63]   M. Lin and S. Gottschalk. Collision detection between geometric models: a survey. In Proceedings of *IMA Conference on Mathematics of Surfaces*, 1998.

[64]   J.F. Lu, Z.G. Pan, et al. Virtual learning environment for medical education based on VRML and VTK. *Computers & Graphics*, 29 (2): 283-288 APR 2005.

[65]   M. Lutz and D. Ascher. *Learning Python*, O'Reilly and Associates, Sebastopol, CA, 1999.

[66]   P.G. Maillot. *Using quaternions for coding 3D transformations. Graphic Gems I*, p. 498. Academic Press Inc., 1990.

[67]   K. Mania and A. Chalmers. The effects of levels of immersion on memory and presence in virtual environments: A reality centered approach. *Cyberpsychology & Behavior*, 4 (2): 247-264, April 2001.

[68]   K. Mania, T. Troscianko, R. Hawkes, and A. Chalmers. Fidelity metrics for virtual environment simulations based on spatial memory awareness states. *Presence-Teleoperators And Virtual Environments*, 12 (3): 296-310, June 2003.

[69]   K.N. Martin and I. Arroyo. AgentX: Using reinforcement learning to improve the effectiveness of intelligent tutoring systems. *Lecture Notes in Computer Science*, 3220: 564-572, 2004.

[70]   D. Maxwell, R. King, and A. Butler. Design synthesis in a virtual environment. In Proceedings of *Computers and Information in Engineering Conference*, Pittsburg, PA, September 2001.

[71]   R.E. Mayer. *Multimedia Learning*. Cambridge University Press 2001.

[72]   A. Mikchevitch, J.C. Leon, and A. Gouskov. Numerical modeling of flexible components for assembly path planning using a virtual reality environment. In Proceedings of *Computers and Information in Engineering Conference*, Chicago, IL, September 2003.

[73]   T.A. Mikropoulos. Brain activity on navigation in virtual environments. *Journal of Educational Computing Research*, 24 (1): 1-12, 2001.

[74]   D. Morris, C. Sewell, N. Blevins, F. Barbagli, and K. Salisbury. A collaborative virtual environment for the simulation of temporal bone surgery. Medical Image Computing And

Computer-Assisted Intervention, *Lecture Notes in Computer Science,* 3217: 319-327, Part 2, 2004.

[75] M.E. Mortenson. *Geometric Transformations,* Industrial Press, New York, New York, 1995.

[76] M.E. Mortenson. *Geometric Modeling,* John Wiley and Sons, New York, 1997.

[77] A. Munro and D.M. Towne. Productivity tools for simulation-centered training development. *Educational Technology Research and Development,* 40 (4): 65-80, 1992.

[78] T. Murray, B. Woolf, and D. Marshall. Lessons learned from authoring for inquiry learning: A tale of authoring tool evolution. *Lecture Notes in Computer Science,* 3220: 197-206, 2004.

[79] S. Nichols, S. Haldane, and J. Wilson. Measurement of presence and its consequences in virtual environments. *International Journal of Human-Computer Studies,* 52, pp. 471-491.

[80] J. Nomura and K. Sawada. Development of spherical screen VR system for human media design and exploration of urban environment. The 3rd *VRSJAC,* No. 67. Science & Technology in Japan, pp. 9-15.

[81] K.L. Norman. Spatial visualization: A gateway to computer-based technology. *Journal of Special Education Technology,* 12, 195-205, 1994.

[82] NVIS company website (available at http://www.nvisinc.com), viewed on July 27, 2006.

[83] S.K. Ong and A.Y.C. Nee. *Virtual and Augmented Reality Applications in Manufacturing,* Springer-Verlag London Limited, 2004.

[84] A. Paiva and I. Machado. Vincent: An autonomous pedagogical agent for on-the-job training. *Lecture Notes in Computer Science,* 1452: 584-593, 1998.

[85] N. Pathomaree and S. Charoenseang. Augmented reality for skill transfer in assembly tasks. In Proceedings of *IEEE International*

Workshop on Robot and Human Interactive Communication, pp. 500-504, 2005.

[86]   C.A. Pelz, N. Brickman, C.Y. Liang, J.R. Hogue, and B.L. Aponso. Tactical insertion mission planning and rehearsal using virtual reality simulation. AIAA Atmospheric Flight Mechanics Conference and Exhibit, AIAA 2003-5610, Austin, TX, 11-14 August 2003.

[87]   R.S. Perez, W. Gray, and T. Reynolds. Virtual reality and simulators: Implications for web-based education and training. In *Web-Based Learning: Theory, Research, and Practice* (edited by H.F. O'Neil and R.S. Perez), Lawrence Erlbaum Associates, 2006.

[88]   X. Peng, X. Chi, J.A. Ochoa, and M.C. Leu. Bone surgery simulation with virtual reality. In Proceedings of *Computers and Information in Engineering Conference*, Chicago, IL, September 2003.

[89]   M.D. Piburn, S.J. Reynolds, C. McAuliffe, D.E. Leedy, J.P. Birk, and J.K. Johnson. The role of visualization in learning from computer-based images. *International Journal of Science Education*, 27 (5): 513-527, Apr 2005.

[90]   Python User's Manual (available at http://www.python.org), viewed on July 27, 2006.

[91]   J. Rickel and W. L. Johnson. Animated agents for procedural training in virtual reality: perception, cognition and motor control. *Applied Artificial Intelligence*, 13 (4-5): 343-382, June-August 1999.

[92]   J. M. Ritchie, R.G. Dewar, and J. Simmons. The generation and practical use of plans for manual assembly using immersive virtual reality. *Journal of Engineering Manufacture*, 213(5): 461-474, 1999.

[93]   D.M. Romano and P. Brna. Presence and reflection in training: Support for learning to improve quality decision-making skills under time limitations. *Cyberpsychology & Behavior*, 4 (2): 265-277, April 2001.

[94]   F.D. Rose, E.A. Attree, B.M. Brooks, D.M. Parslow, and P.R. Penn. Training in virtual environments: transfer to real world tasks and equivalence to real task training. *Ergonomics*, 43(4), pp. 494-511, 2000.

[95]   K.J. Stroud, D.L. Harm, and D.M. Klaus. Preflight virtual reality training as a countermeasure for space motion sickness and disorientation. *Aviation Space and Environmental Medicine*, 76 (4): 352-356, April 2005.

[96]   M. Schwartz, S.K. Gupta, D.K. Anand, J.E. Brough, and R. Kavetsky. Using virtual demonstrations for creating multi-media training instructions. In Proceedings of *CAD Conference*, Hawaii, June 2007.

[97]   M. Schwartz, S.K. Gupta, D.K. Anand, and R. Kavetsky. Virtual mentor: A step towards proactive user monitoring and assistance during virtual environment-based training. *Performance Metrics for Intelligent Systems (PerMIS) Workshop*, Gaithersburg, MD, August 2007.

[98]   N. Shibano, P.V. Hareesh, H. Hoshino, R. Kawamura, A. Yamamoto, M. Kashiwagi, and K. Sawada. CyberDome: PC clustered hemi spherical immersive projection display. *ICAT*, Tokyo, Japan, December 3-5, 2003.

[99]   M.J. Singer, J.P. Kring, and R.M. Hamilton. Instructional Features for Training in Virtual Environments. Technical Report 1184, 20060929048, United States Army Research Institute for the Behavioral and Social Sciences, July 2006.

[100]   J. Sweller. *Instructional Design in Technical Areas*. Acer Press, 1999.

[101]   H.K. Tabbers, R.L. Martens, and J.J.G. van Merrieboer. Multimedia instructions and cognitive load theory: Effects of modality and cueing. *British Journal of Educational Psychology*, 74: 71-81 Part 1, March 2004.

[102]   E.K.Tam, C. Maurel, P. Desbiens, R.J. Marceau, A.S. Malowany, and L. Granger. A low-cost PC-oriented virtual environment for operator training. *IEEE Transactions on Power Systems*, 13 (3): 829-835, August 1998.

[103] F. Taylor, S. Jayaram, and U. Jayaram. Functionality to facilitate assembly of heavy machines in a virtual environment. In Proceedings of *Computers and Information in Engineering Conference*, Baltimore, MD, September 2000.

[104] F. Tendick, M. Downes, T. Goktekin, M.C. Cavusoglu, D. Feygin, X.L. Wu, R. Eyal, M. Hegarty, and L.W. Way. A virtual environment testbed for training laparoscopic surgical skills. *Presence-Teleoperators and Virtual Environments*, 9 (3): 236-255, June 2000.

[105] J. Tracy, A. Flanders, S. Madi, J. Laskas, E. Stoddard, A. Pyrros, P. Natale, and N. DelVecchio. Regional brain activation associated with different performance patterns during learning of a complex motor skill. *Cerebral Cortex*, 13 (9): 904-910, September 2003.

[106] Z. Tuncali. Machining in a Virtual Environment. Master's Thesis, University of Maryland, College Park, MD, 2003.

[107] B. Tversky. Spatial schemas in depictions. In M. Gattis (Ed.), *Spatial Schemas and Abstract Thought* (pp. 79-112). Cambridge, MA: The MIT Press. 2001.

[108] R.B. Valimont, D.A. Vincenzi, S.N. Gangadharan, and A.E. Majoros. The effectiveness of augmented reality as a facilitator of information acquisition. In Proceedings of *Digital Avionics Systems Conference*, 2, 7C5-1-7C5-9, 2002.

[109] G. van den Bergen. Efficient collision detection of complex deformable models using AABB trees. *Journal of Graphics Tools*, ,2(4), p. 1-13, April 1997.

[110] D. Waller. Individual differences in spatial learning from computer-simulated environments. *Journal of Experimental Psychology-Applied*, 6 (4): 307-321, December 2000.

[111] D. Waller. The WALKABOUT: Using virtual environments to asses large- scale spatial abilities. *Computers in Human Behavior*, 21, pp. 243-253, 2005.

[112] H. Wan, S. Gao, Q. Peng, G. Dai, F. Zhang. MIVAS: A multi-modal immersive virtual assembly system. In Proceedings of

Computers and Information in Engineering Conference, Salt Lake City, UT, September – October 2004.

[113]   J. Wann and M. MonWilliams. What does virtual reality need? Human factors issues in the design of three-dimensional computer environments. *International Journal of Human-Computer Studies*, 44 (6): 829-847, June 1996.

[114]   G.J. Wiet, D. Stredney, D. Sessanna, J.A. Bryan, D.B. Welling, and P. Schmalbrock. Virtual temporal bone dissection: An interactive surgical simulator. *Otolaryngology-Head and Neck Surgery*, 127 (1): 79-83, July 2002.

[115]   P.N. Wilson and P. Peruch. The influence of interactivity and attention on spatial learning in a desk-top virtual environment. *Current Psychology of Cognition*, 21 (6):601-633, December 2002.

[116]   R.A. Wisher, D.H. Macpherson, L.J. Abramson, D.M. Thornton, and J.J. Dees. The Virtual Sand Table: Intelligent Tutoring for Field Artillery Training. Research Report 1768, US Army Research Institute for the Behavioral and Social Sciences, Alexandria, VA, March 2001.

[117]   B.P. Woolf. Intelligent multimedia tutoring systems. *Communications of the ACM*, 39 (4): 30-31 APR 1996.

[118]   WorldViz. Precision Position Tracker PPT Operating Instructions. WorldViz LLC. December 2004.

[119]   WorldViz company website (available at http://www.worldviz.com), viewed on July 27, 2006.

[120]   N. Ye, P. Banerjee, A. Banerjee, and F. Dech. A comparative study of assembly planning in traditional and virtual environments. *IEEE Transactions on Systems, Man, and Cybernetics*, 29(4), pp. 546-555, November 1999.

[121]   M.L. Yuan, S.K. Ong, and A.Y.C. Nee. Assembly guidance in augmented reality environments using a virtual interactive tool. *Innovation in Manufacturing Systems and Technology*, 2005.

[122] J.M. Zacks, B. Tversky, and G. Iyer. Perceiving, remembering, and communicating structure in events. *Journal of Experimental Psychology: General*, 130(1), 29-58, 2001.